A TEAM, A STUNNING GOLD MEDAL AND NEWFOUND DREAMS FOR AMERICAN GIRLS

A MIRACLE OF THEIR OWN

KEITH GAVE | TIM RAPPLEYE

FOREWORD BY HILARY KNIGHT, OLYMPIC GOLD MEDALIST

A MIRACLE
OF THEIR OWN

Cover design: Tara Carlin
Interior design: Allan Nygren

ISBN: 978-1-952421-26-6

First Edition

Printed and published in the United States of America.

Visit our website at: www.keithgave.com.
Contact the authors at: keith@keithgave.com; tim.rappleye@gmail.com

This book is available in quantity at special discounts for your group or organization. For further information, contact media@keithgave.com

For our daughters

Contents

Foreword

I remember staying over at a friend's house for the 1998 gold-medal game. My Mom told my friend's parents to make sure we were up at a certain time because the game was so important. I was super young—10 years old—but I remember afterwards jumping up and down on the couch and screaming after we won. To have women's hockey in the Olympics in 1998, and have the U.S. team win it, was huge for so many of us looking for heroes who looked like us. A lot of girls from my generation just wanted to go to the NHL. That was all we saw on TV. There were no women's hockey role models. It's one of those things: If she sees it, she can be it.

The relationships I had with that 1998 group are organic. You look up to those who have come before you and paved a brighter future for you. I had the opportunity of playing with both Angela Ruggiero and Jenny Potter in the 2010 Olympic Winter Games – so I got to know them as both teammates and sports icons. I got to know them through the rigors of a season and the Games in Vancouver. Angela took me under her wing as soon as I joined the national team in 2006. She was an important mentor to me. I'll never forget being in the trenches with her in 2010, and her giving advice and telling stories about how cool it was to be part of that '98 team. She and Jenny were so competitive, really wanting to win every time we stepped on the ice. It set the tone, voiced or not, of how to conduct oneself and what it meant to be part of Team USA.

It wasn't good enough to just make the Olympic team. Ruggiero and Potter hold their group in high regard because they know what a winning team can accomplish both on and off the ice. This mindset is part of their legacy, something that has stuck with me, and one that I hope lives on with my imprints on our current team.

We ended up falling short in 2010 and then again in 2014. Those two Olympic cycles were grueling, but to finally bring home the gold in 2018 after a 20-year drought, that was pretty incredible. Angela was there representing the IOC, handing out medals. I actually chirped her during the ceremony. She always told me she was going to be the one to put a gold medal around my neck, but the other IOC official handed me mine. "C'mon Ang, you couldn't just switch the order?" Kidding aside, to win the gold in 2018, and have Angela on the ice with us was a full-circle moment.

The 2017 player strike, followed by winning the World Championship, is the most meaningful thing I've ever been a part of; it's right up there with winning Olympic gold. It's one thing to suit up and win a big hockey game—that's great for sure—but to be the spark for change, and have the entire country stand up and say, "We're with you guys, we're with the women," that's what Disney movies are made of, right? And it wouldn't have happened without Cammi Granato, what she tried to do in 2000. It's not lost on anyone that her work and her efforts, the price she had to pay, helped us succeed years later.

We always want Cammi to be a part of whatever we are doing on our national teams.

When she came and spoke to our team out West, it shaped the belief that we were destined for gold. She saw it within our group, this legend in our presence. She spoke to its existence, and from that point forward the belief that we had a golden future was secured. No matter what type of adversity this team encountered, we would get the job done.

Cammi's energy is contagious. It's hard to put into words. It's her care and her kindness, she just connects the right way. To even have a touch point: a text, a group chat, or even a phone call from her is just so special. I went to her hockey camp when I was younger. It's one of those things where she's your idol, and you're terrified, but you so badly want to meet and talk to her. Being who she is as a player, and a human being, makes her so impactful.

My first time on the national team was in 2006-07, right after she was let go by USA Hockey. Her Number 21 was available, which was an interesting scenario considering what Cammi means to the sport of hockey – you would think USA Hockey would let her number breathe for a few years, if not retire it. But there was a silver lining when I picked up her number, an opportunity for a young kid to continue the legacy that she built – I couldn't think of a greater honor. I've always felt a special bond, wearing the number of my idol.

When I broke her scoring record last season, it was one of those things where you can pass someone in numbers, but in my view she will always be Number 1. It's a special honor, but it doesn't feel like I broke anything, it doesn't feel real. I'm sure if anyone came close to Wayne Gretzky's records, they'd feel the same way. There's only one Wayne Gretzky, there's only one Cammi Granato.

Like Cammi, I understand the value of sport. I love hockey, and I want to share that love with everybody. As female athletes, we know our moments are limited, and we definitely don't get paid what we're worth. But we didn't sign up to play the sport we all fell in love with for multi-million dollar contracts. We're laying groundwork now to set up the next generation. I look at myself and others as pieces of the puzzle, moving the sport forward. The Winter Olympics provide us with a unique opportunity to gain more traction and

visibility, but it really shouldn't be every four years. It should be every single night, similar to the guys. It's a daily undertaking to try and move the needle forward, especially on the women's side in any sport.

It's hard to imagine where we would be if not for that original gold-medal team in 1998. It was a watershed moment for the growth of our sport. It opened a lot of doors, doors that team kicked wide open, doors we were lucky enough to skate through.

Hilary Knight
March 2022

Introduction

NAGANO, Japan – They stood in line, exhausted and sweaty – no, no that's not quite right. These were women, and women perspire. They were holding hands along the line, clearly relieved but somehow looking as nervous as they had been about three hours earlier, before the puck dropped on the most important game of their lives.

All eyes were fixed on a tray being carried in their direction from across the ice in the Big Hat Arena, where a standing-room-only crowd of more than 10,000 fans remained to witness history. The tray was laden with precious metal. Precious medals, to be more precise.

As it came to a halt at the start of the line, Lisa Brown-Miller, the oldest and smallest player on Team USA, was unable to contain herself, doubling over with emotion, her arms around her waist. At the same time, one of the two officials who accompanied the cart reached down, grabbed a ribbon and whispered a few words of congratulations to the American team captain.

Then, Cammi Granato leaned forward from the waist, back straight, eyes cast down with her hands at her thighs, executing the perfect keirei – a traditional Japanese bow meant to show respect, humility and politeness – and accepted the first Olympic Gold Medal ever awarded to a female hockey player.

And the sport, at least for girls and young women around the world, was forever changed. Now they could believe in miracles, too.

PART ONE

GENESIS

Of Pucks
and Ponytails

"When you're a girl playing among boys, you just want to play. I authentically wanted to play hockey. Luckily, I had the support of my family, but it wasn't easy. There were tough times. Looking back on it as an adult, you see it through different eyes. A lot of it wasn't okay."

—Cammi Granato

There may be no crying in baseball – believe that if it makes you feel better – but in ice hockey emotions run deep. So once the heart has been taken hostage by the sport and the opportunity to play it is threatened, then well, we do whatever is necessary to change that.

If that means shedding a few tears, which many of the sports pioneering women will confess to, then so be it. Expect no apologies.

To be sure, there were tears when Santa apparently delivered the wrong package beneath the tree at Christmastime at a Cape Cod, Massachusetts home. Colleen Coyne was seven at the time, an age, she says, "when you don't have the wherewithal to just be grateful." After unwrapping a pair of glistening white figure skates, she began to cry.

"No, not these," she told her parents. "I want to play hockey!"

There were tears when Cammi Granato, then about 11, heard the cruel facts of life from her mother. You're a girl, her mom said, and hockey was a boy thing. Growing up in suburban Chicago, Cammi had dreamed of playing hockey for the Blackhawks in the National Hockey League one day. Her mother's words crushed her, and she wept. "Hey, I loved hockey just as much as the boys did," she recalled.

There were tears when 16-year-old Sarah Tueting was tending goal for her New Trier High School team in the Illinois state hockey finals against cross-town rival Loyola, when three boys in the United Center stands unfurled a huge white sheet with a cruel painted message: "Sarah Tueting has a big 5-hole." In hockey parlance, the 5-hole is known as the space between a goaltender's pillowy shin pads sometimes exploited by sharpshooters. But instead of crying, there was only pure, unmitigated rage. "Assholes," she murmured behind her mask, vowing, "You and your little Loy Boys will not score tonight." A few hours later, she stood at center ice surrounded by teammates, their fingers raised in the air celebrating a state championship. Yes, there were tears that night. Tears of unadulterated joy.

And years later, in the mountains of northern Japan, Coyne, Granato and Tueting stood on the center podium with their teammates – Chris Bailey, Laurie Baker, Alana Blahoski, Lisa Brown-Miller, Karen Bye, Sara DeCosta, Tricia Dunn, Katie King, Shelley Looney, Sue Merz, A.J. Mleczko, Tara Mounsey, Vicki Movsessian, Angela Ruggiero, Jenny Schmidgall, Gretchen Ulion and Sandra Whyte – as a tsunami of tears fell while they sang America's National Anthem. Against enormous odds – every one of these 20 women able to recount myriad tales of challenges and adversity in the game they loved – they were the newly minted gold-medal champions in the first-ever Olympic women's ice hockey tournament.

Oh, and at that moment at Big Hat Arena in Nagano in 1998, there were plenty of tears on the silver-medal podium, too, because the heavily favored Canadians failed to deliver the gold amid soaring expectations after years of dominating Team USA on the world stage.

And just like that, ice hockey was no longer just a boys' game. Now young girls across America had their own miracle to sustain them.

Eighteen years earlier, the game was a niche sport, a distant fourth after North American heavyweights like the National Football League, Major League Baseball and the National Basketball Association. Professional hockey spent most of the 20th century supported by small pockets of passionate fans in a handful of cities located from the East Coast across America's rust belt: Boston and New York, Detroit and Chicago among the NHL's "Original Six" with Montreal and Toronto. From 1967-79, the league grew to 21 teams with varying degrees of success.

America's perception of the game forever changed at the Winter Games in Lake Placid, New York, in 1980, when an eclectic group of mostly college kids upset one of the greatest hockey teams ever assembled, the mighty Soviet National Team, 4-3. This is widely considered to be the greatest sporting event of the twentieth century. Lest anyone forget, the Americans went on to defeat Finland for the gold medal.

But the headline was beating the Soviets, America's archenemy at the height of the Cold War – at a time when things were going badly for the good guys. The economy was in shambles, gas lines were on every corner, Iran was holding 52 American diplomats hostage for 444 days, and the Soviets were flexing their power by invading Afghanistan just a few months before Opening Ceremonies in Lake Placid.

And a hockey team – a bunch of no-name skaters with a puck and a dream – did something that transcended sports. The closing seconds of that game, broadcast on ABC by Al Michaels and analyst Ken Dryden, are as striking and emotional today as the day they were spoken, on February 22, 1980.

"Five seconds left in the game…," said Michaels, his voice beginning to swell.

Filling a space left by a small pause, Dryden nailed it: "It's over!"

And then that unforgettable line from Michaels: "Do you believe in miracles?"

"Yes!" he added, and an entire nation starving for just a scrap of anything that would make us feel better about ourselves said it with him.

Yes indeed.

While Michaels' Miracle call to this day remains one of the most iconic in broadcasting history, we shouldn't overlook Dryden's two-word interjection, ironic as it turned out to be.

At that moment, as captain Mike Eruzione celebrated with his teammates and flag-draped goaltender Jim Craig was searching the crowd for his father, it really wasn't over. For a generation of American boys and their families it was really the beginning.

They included Mike Modano and Doug Weight, both nine at the time and growing up in suburban Detroit, and Jeremy Roenick, 10, Bill Guerin, nine, and Keith Tkachuk, eight, all Massachusetts-born and raised. They were all elite athletes by that age who could have gone in other directions, like baseball or football. All chose hockey. And all, by the way, formed the nucleus of the Team USA men's team in Nagano – the first Olympic Games that featured NHL stars.

But that Miracle team in 1980 also inspired many young girls, who at that time couldn't dream of playing professional hockey, or even compete in the Olympics. Still, they wanted to play for the pure joy and love of the game.

"We weren't a hockey family like the Granatos, but yes, 1980 was absolutely on the radar at the time," said Colleen Coyne. "I had a brother (Brian) who was 11, and we played a lot of street hockey – always taking turns being Jim Craig or Mark Johnson or Mike Eruzione."

She was eight by then, a year after her little Christmas-morning tantrum over the figure skates, and just starting to play organized hockey. Cammi Granato was a month shy of turning 10, the fifth of six kids in what many consider to be America's first family when it comes to hockey.

With no ponds and little available indoor ice around their Downers Grove, Illinois home, the Granato kids turned their basement into a makeshift hockey arena. Ball hockey or tape-ball hockey, full-on, mini-stick, two-on-two, usually Cammi and Tony, seven years older, against Donnie and Rob. As the youngest and smallest in the group, Cammi was the most prone to getting hurt. But she never backed down, always came back for more. There was only one rule for those games: Don't tell Mom.

On occasion, Cammi – christened Catherine – would relent and join her sister, Christina, to play with their Barbie doll collection. Now obviously Barbie started out as a teenage fashion icon. She enjoyed all the designer clothes. Later, her stylish hair became a trend. Eventually, Barbie got more involved in activities such as swimming, gymnastics, and horse riding. To Christina's dismay, Cammi made sure Barbie experienced another sport.

"We'd have all these dolls out, and pretty soon I'd be playing hockey with them," Cammi confessed. That's how much she revered the game.

And she was hardly alone.

Little girls fall in love with hockey for the same reasons little boys do: for the sheer joy of propelling themselves around a sheet of smooth, frozen water on a pair of thin steel blades. Faster and faster, forward and backward, stopping and starting, falling down and getting back up and doing it all over again, only now with a stick in the hands to control a one-by-four inch rubber disk. Heads up always. Myriad skills choreographed meticulously, and when they all work in harmony? Nirvana.

And then there's the equipment. Not just skates and sticks and pucks, but big puffy gloves to protect little fingers, pads for the shins, the elbows, the hips and the shoulders to create little gladiators. Finally, the helmets to protect developing young brains, and cages in front to keep those smiles intact and those teeth – those beautiful white Chiclets – in their place for years of needed service.

For some, like six-year-old Sarah Tueting playing Mite A for the Winnetka Warriors, the love of equipment found another gear. Her team of all boys – which would remain that way for another 12 years – didn't have a regular goaltender, so the job rotated with communal equipment. When her time came, she fell immediately and deeply in love with every aspect of the position – and mostly of her *self* as a goalie.

From the start, she was good at stopping the puck, mostly because she hated to be scored on whether it was in games or playing with her brother on a 10-by-15-foot "rink" marked by red paint on the basement floor. She begged her parents to let her become a goalie; they wanted her to skate out. For a time, she did both, enjoying one, loving the other. Toward the end of that season, her father surprised her with a set of goalie pads, hand-me-downs from the goalie on her brother's team.

"I pull them to my chest and inhale their lived-in smell," Tueting writes in an open letter to her children published on her website. "The pads are dark brown canvas on the outside, light brown canvas on the inside, with three brown leather straps adorned with silver metal buckles that chime together when I walk. . . Though I'm not wearing skates or any other equipment, I flop face down on the floor while my Dad buckles the new pads onto my legs. When I stand up, I am a goalie."

She rarely took them off. She wore them to play hockey in the backyard with tennis balls and in the basement taking shots from her brother off the cement floor.

"I wear them to the dinner table. I wear them to bed until my parents forbid my new sleep attire. Instead, my goalie pads lay beside me like a trusted loyal dog as I go to sleep. When Halloween rolls around, I dress in my new goalie pads and tromp from house to house. 'Look how cute. She's dressed as a goalie,' the adults would say as they held out a bowl of candy. 'I *am* a goalie,'" Sarah Tueting would respond. And that was that.

In Canada, where hockey is as much a religion as it is sport, most young-sters get an early indoctrination to the game whether or not they asked for it, thanks as much to parental influence as to long frigid winters that sustain those ubiquitous backyard rinks.

In the United States, the sport has a passionate regional following, par-ticularly in the Northeast and across the Snow Belt to the Dakotas. Most girls find hockey the way many boys do: by hanging around the rinks while friends or older siblings played the game. Not so for Lisa Brown-Miller, who grew up in lake country just north of Detroit in the 1970s. She was the second oldest of four children, with an older sister and a younger brother and sister.

"We weren't really a hockey family, but there was a neighbor down the street, Chris Byberg. We were six years old, and he was a goalie," she recalled four decades later. "He had all this cool equipment, the molded face mask, neat gloves and big leg pads! I'd go down to his house on Green Lake and we'd take turns putting on the goalie gear and shooting at one another in his family's living room. Tennis balls were bouncing off every-thing, from the huge picture window overlooking the lake, to family pic-tures, to the TV and lamps. I really can't imagine how his mother put up with that, but I'd really like to be able to thank her today because it was really pivotal for me, allowing me to discover my love for the game and pursue the chance to play it."

Soon after she announced to her parents that she wanted to play hockey, her father, Bob Brown, took her to the local Sears store. There she found a little pair of shoulder pads and everything else she needed. Then it was up to Lakeland Arena, where she started playing hockey.

"All boys. No girls," Brown-Miller recalled. "People would question why I was there, but all I can say is that I instantly fell in love with the sport. It really became a passion. My parents believed it would be a passing phase, but obviously it wasn't."

For Lisa Brown-Miller, hockey was a way to channel an abundance of energy, to burn off some steam, as she describes it. If she wasn't at the rink playing, she would gather with friends at the lake, chopping holes to make sure the ice was thick enough, and skate there. Other times, it was in the basement, firing pucks or tennis balls or rolled up socks at her brother, Darren. By the time she was 11 or so, she had developed wicked shooting skills. Occasionally, she'd ding her brother.

"I'd have to block the stairway sometimes when he wanted to go tell Mom," she said. "But hey, he eventually did become a goalie."

Falmouth was a sleepy beach community on Cape Cod in the late 1970s when Colleen Coyne started hanging around the rink because her brother, Brian, three years older, was playing organized hockey.

"Any siblings in families that have someone playing hockey will spend time at the rink," she said. "You become accustomed to it. I remember watching my brother practice and thinking, 'I want to try that.'"

She was eight when she started playing as a Mite. "I loved it from the beginning. I can't remember not loving it," she said. "All my memories are about how much fun it was. Even learning to skate, there's something about that challenge."

Coyne was one of three girls playing in a boys' league. She and Nicole Lyonnais and Beth Beagen also played Little League baseball in the summers. "We had this little tiny group of girls, and it was just nice to have others that we could point to in order to defend the fact that we were playing."

But they weren't the first of their gender to skate with the boys. "There were other girls in my town who had played hockey, two older girls, Meagan Patrick and Stephanie Kelly. Meagan was 3-4 years older than I was, and Stephanie was a couple years older than her. Steph went on to play at Northeastern. Meagan played at Colby."

Coyne gravitated toward defense primarily because of her first coach, Kye Dewan, the star defenseman on the local varsity hockey team. "So much positive reinforcement," she said. "He was my new hero. He wore Number 2, so I wore Number 2."

She didn't play on an all-girls team until she went to prep school, Tabor Academy, which had just started a girls hockey program. That's about the time, as a 15-year-old, that she started playing for the Cape Cod Aces in a women's senior league. The competition with the Aces was in stark contrast to Tabor, where many of the players were just getting started in the sport.

"I was one of the most experienced, but what's interesting about that is that I never felt like it held me back in any way," she said. "I was on the ice every day. Instead of one practice a week, or maybe two with the boys, I was on the ice five or six days a week, so I had all that opportunity to get better at practices." And she made good use of the ice time.

"I'm crazy competitive, and I didn't want to lose – even if I had to go solo sometimes," Coyne confessed. "But I did get a lot of enjoyment out of helping my teammates with less experience score goals. Once I had the puck, everybody on the other team was chasing me, so there were four teammates wide open. To be honest, I remember some of those goals better than I remember mine. And it probably made me a better playmaker."

While there are far more opportunities today for girls to play with and against other girls even at younger ages, Coyne notices a difference from when she competed with boys.

"All these girls-only teams – I do think we're getting to the point where girls at a younger age are getting better. It's exciting to watch," she said. "But girls aren't naturally aggressive at a certain age."

In the fall of 2021, Coyne's daughter, Riley, was beginning her first season on an all-girls team, and Colleen was curious about the intensity of competition.

"I think it's important to let our daughters know that they can be aggressive," Coyne said. "Like I told Riley: 'This is hockey. When you get *off* the ice, you can be as sweet as you want.'"

Some adolescent girls are just natural tomboys – and proud of it – like Chie Chie Sakuma and Shelley Looney, who wound up competing against one another in the 1998 Winter Games. Chie Chie simply wanted to do everything her brother, Teppei, did. So when their father, Hajime Sakuma, a Japanese-American businessman in Houston, signed his son up to try hockey, well, four-year-old Chie Chie started playing then, too.

"When I was eight-ish, my parents made me go to Japanese school on Saturdays, and I hated it," she said. "It was awful. One Saturday it was picture day, and my parents forced me to wear a dress. After they came to pick me up, we went to pick up my brother at hockey, and one of his teammates said, 'Hey look, your little brother is wearing a dress!' That's how much of a tomboy I was."

Chie Chie continued playing hockey with boys until she went to Brown University, which had a struggling women's hockey team.

"The only reason I even knew Brown had a women's program was through a teammate of mine in rec hockey," she said. "His father went to Brown and he made a call to Digit Murphy, the coach, and he said, 'My son plays with this girl, and you should see her play.' Honestly, that's the only reason I even thought of playing hockey in college. Until then, I thought I wanted to be in the marching band at someplace like the University of Texas."

After four years at Brown and a stint working in Japan to establish residency, Chie Chie wound up on the Japanese National Team as an alternate captain and stay-at-home defenseman in that inaugural Olympic women's tournament. Today, she is Chie Chie Yard, Vice President of Events for the National Hockey League.

Looney followed her brother to the sport as well. Her parents had no background in the sport, but some of their friends had their sons in hockey, so they started their son, who was four at the time. Shelley tagged along to watch the boys skate, but halfway through the season her brother said he'd rather stay home and watch cartoons than play hockey. He was the rare kid who didn't care much for all that equipment.

Looney, six at the time, saw her opening.

"Mom, can I take his spot?" she asked.

"Well, let me ask the coach," Mom said. "I don't know if girls can play."

"Absolutely, she can play," said the coach, Rick Slack. "There are no rules against it."

Slack took the girl under his wing, and for her first seven years playing hockey he was behind the bench as her coach.

But in those energetic formative years, hockey was just one of many physical endeavors that kept her occupied.

"I tried everything, gymnastics, then soccer, basketball, volleyball, softball. I tried running cross-country. And my parents were like, 'You're already in hockey. You can't play them all. Just pick a couple.'"

And in retrospect, it was her mother's willingness to let her play hockey even though she thought it was a dead-end sport for her daughter, that Looney most appreciates.

"She would never say, 'No playing hockey,'" Looney said. "When I was younger she would try to get me to try other sports. 'Hockey is a guy's sport and you're never going to go anywhere in that,' she would say. So she put me in speed skates. I went around the rink two or three times, did a great job, but when I came off I said, 'Mom, it's so boring. I'm just skating around in a circle. Where's the action?'"

Looney found some action on the football field in junior high. She was in the eighth grade when she learned of a seventh-grade girl trying out for the football team. When she announced she wanted to try out, too, her mother put her foot down.

"You're already playing one boys' sport you're never going to go anywhere with," she said. "No, you're not playing football."

Her daughter cried. But these days they joke about it.

"You never know, Mom," Shelley often reminds her. "I could have been in the NFL."

She's only half joking. Anybody who has seen Looney in any competition in any sport wouldn't dare to question her toughness. In one memorable game in Kitchener, Ontario, between the USA and Canada, Looney was helping to kill a five-on-three Canadian power play when she stopped a point shot with her face. It fractured her cheek in three spots.

Girls can play hockey too, eh?

Yes, they can. Nine-year-old A.J. Mleczko had an idyllic hockey childhood, enjoying virtually unlimited ice time at the toney New Canaan Winter Club, nestled in the suburban Connecticut woods. She played house-league with the Mites, and enjoyed plenty of pick-up hockey on the adjacent pond. It was during her transition to Squirt hockey that she found herself at a hockey crossroads.

Athletically superior to most of her nine-year old peers—regardless of gender—A.J. shined at the Squirt travel tryouts held the weekend after Thanksgiving. There was one serious issue, however: No girl had ever played travel hockey for the Club. The decision on whether or not she could get on hockey's fast track came down to the 53-year-old, very traditional coach, John Emmons. The evening the team was to be announced, A.J. and her parents waited in their living room for the phone to ring. When it finally jangled, Bambi Mleczko picked up while her husband Tom and A.J. looked on rather anxiously.

"I remember when he made the call," A.J. recalled "My mom was on the phone, nodding, and looking at me, and I'm like, 'Oh man, I didn't…'"

A.J. feared the unimaginable.

On the other end of the line, Emmons spoke slowly and cautiously. He was taking every conceivable precaution before taking a leap he never expected to make.

"Are you prepared to have your daughter play on an all-boys travel team?" Emmons asked. "There would be no other girls playing."

"And they said 'Yes!'" A.J. said, her voice brimming with excitement and relief nearly 40 years later.

If the name John Emmons sounds familiar, it's because coach Emmons' son, John, Jr., was a seven-year pro with 85 NHL games to his credit. He was A.J.'s teammate in her first year in travel.

"There was zero controversy," the younger Emmons said. "She was one of the guys, helped the team, she was great." He said he appreciated that his father made the right call back in 1984, when such a decision wasn't exactly easy. "Dad is kind of old-school. But he thought it was a good opportunity to teach us something: She's a female, you respect her, and she's part of the team."

Later, when A.J. graduated to Peewee and then Bantam, her father Tom coached her. That's when she faced a new challenge, full-checking hockey. And because she was a girl she played with a target on her back.

"They would run me," said Mleczko, now A.J. in the game programs. "But everyone knew I was a girl because I had a braid hanging down my back. Everybody would try and run me, but I could see it coming. Usually I could anticipate it, a lot of times I could side-step it. Not always. I certainly took a beating a bunch of times.

"A lot of the parents, particularly the moms, would always want my dad to pull me off the ice when it got particularly rough. But my dad always kept me out there. He knew I was strong enough to handle it, a strong enough skater. And he was my father; he wouldn't put me in danger. He just knew I could handle it."

For both genders, puberty presents myriad challenges. For some girls in hockey, it can be a sword with two sharp edges. Karyn Bye experienced that while honing her skills at Hunt Arena in River Falls, Wisconsin. She remembers being 12 or 13 when she looked around the ice and saw the unmitigated proof that girls tended to hit puberty ahead of boys.

"There was a time there, I would say first or second year of Peewees, when I was the tallest one on the ice, and I was the fastest one on the ice," she said. "When we did sprints, I won every time. I remember thinking, 'Hey, this is good stuff. I'm going to ride this for a while.' I could beat all the boys."

Karyn (pronounced KAH-rin, thank you very much) was four when her father took her and her brother, Chris, two years older, to the local rink. He laced up her skates and took her by the hand for those first wobbly strides. Then he let go.

"And I just took off," she said. "I loved it."

Chuck Bye built a rink in the back yard, and every day Karyn would get home from preschool, lace up her own skates, grab a stick and a puck and glide around the ice waiting for her brother to get home. By the time

Chris was nine, he had been playing youth hockey for a couple of years, and one evening he was sick and unable to go to practice. So father approached daughter with an idea.

"Hey Karyn, let's dress you up in Chris's equipment and send you to practice," he said. "We'll try and fool the other guys thinking that you're Chris."

Karyn, of course, thought that was a fabulous idea. So she stood patiently in her bedroom while her father dressed her in all the gear, the shin pads, socks, garter belt, elbow pads, shoulder pads and helmet. He put her in the car, and when they got to the rink he told her not to say anything – just go out and skate around.

It didn't take long for the boys to realize it wasn't Chris buried beneath all that equipment. But it didn't matter. She could skate with those boys, and she loved it. After that practice, Chuck Bye signed his daughter up, and from then on, through Mites, Squirts, Peewees, Bantams, and all the way through high school, she was the only girl on her team.

Clear sailing – at least until puberty caught up with the boys, and they became bigger, stronger, faster, and more aggressive. By high school, Karyn Bye felt the need to camouflage her gender as best she could. She'd always had short hair, so that wasn't an issue. But in game programs she became K.L. Bye.

That wasn't uncommon for girls competing on high school boys' teams in that era. She recalled how Stephanie O'Sullivan put her name in a program as Stephen, and Kelly O'Leary played under the name Kevin. Allison Mleczko was fine when she wore figure skates for three years. In hockey, she became A.J., hoping to avoid some of the opposing bullies.

Cammi Granato, too, had to stickhandle around some ominous moments – with the support and guidance of the man she calls the most influential and courageous coach she ever played for, Gregory Lopatka.

Granato had appeared on his radar when he took a team from Northern Illinois to Kitchener, Ontario, for a friendly tournament. On arrival, they learned that Canada didn't permit girls to compete with boys. So Cammi became Carl for the weekend.

A year later, when Lopatka was holding tryouts for his program, perennially one of the best in the state, he found enough talent for three elite teams of 13- and 14-year-olds. On his top club, there were just two 13-year-olds. Granato was one of them.

"Oh, I got instant complaints," Lopatka told ESPN interviewer Emily Kaplan for a piece that ran in January 2021. "Why did you pick that girl over my son? Well, I hate to say this, but Cammi is better than your son."

Granato could feel it when she walked into an arena, the whispers, the negative attention, the passive-aggressive harassment, like flicking off of the lights in the ladies room where she dressed for the games – away from the boys in the locker room.

"Once I got on the ice, all that went away," she told Kaplan. "Frankly, I knew I belonged. I knew when I got on the ice I could show everybody."

Which she did, and in the process turned some of her greatest detractors into her most ardent supporters. She also became a target for opposing coaches who didn't appreciate how she showed up their teams. After one such game, in a bar over perhaps a few too many pops, a coach vowed that the next time the teams faced off Granato was going to wind up with a broken collarbone.

Right before the next encounter, Lopatka met with Granato and her parents to explain what was being said. Granato insisted on playing. Lopatka moved her to center with two of his biggest and most talented wingers, both of whom went on to play college hockey.

"Keep your head up and stay in the middle," the coach told her. "You've got nothing to worry about."

And she didn't. In fact, she scored a goal in a lopsided win, and in the handshake line she looked the opposing coach in the eye and, completely out of character, rolled her shoulder mockingly, as if to say, "Yep, everything is OK here. No broken bones."

Lopatka knew all the boys on his team had her back, but there was one boy, he noticed, who had a bit of a crush on her. "He was a big bruiser," the coach said, "and he took a lot of penalties if anybody even brushed up against her."

But it was during a tournament in Edina, Minnesota – serious hockey country where an Illinois team had never won – that Granato faced the most combustible moment. Just before the game Lopatka overheard an opposing coach tell his team, "I want you to hit No. 21. She's a girl. The first chance you get, go for it."

Lopatka entered his team's locker room, looked around and caught the eye of Bobby Granato, Cammi's cousin, who was at least 3-4 inches taller and 50 pounds heavier than Cammi.

"Bobby, you're wearing No. 21 today. You two switch jerseys," he said, looking at Cammi. They did, and the rest is sweet history.

"Just a really cool way of turning something potentially bad into something really great," Cammi said. "As much as Bobby wasn't a very pretty girl, it worked."

Lopatka said he was often asked if he was worried that playing such physical hockey would eventually take a toll on the only girl on his team. "Not at all," he'd reply, "because her brothers had been beating her up since she was three years old."

Finally, a word about locker-room etiquette, which again wasn't a problem until puberty reared its acne'd mug.

Granato tired of the harassment with the lights in the ladies room and eventually made her encampment in a tiny closet, ducking beneath brooms to strap on her gear. "I actually loved it," she said. "I felt much more comfortable in there, and it was right across from the team locker room.'

Bye transitioned from the locker room with the boys to restrooms when puberty intervened. "I can't tell you how many bathrooms I was in putting my stuff on," she said. "But typically, once you get your shorts and T-shirt on, the boys would get in their shorts and T-shirts, and I could be in the locker room. After that, you're all covered up."

Then again, boys will be boys, eh?

That's pretty much what Sarah Tueting told herself as she was changing her undergarments in a bathroom stall when she heard two teammates enter the locker room, whispering loudly to one another.

"You're right, you can totally see down her shirt when she's tying her skates," one boy said. "I knew they were small, but I didn't know they were *that* small. Sarah literally has no tits. They're like two chocolate chips on a cookie platter."

She stayed in the bathroom, fighting off omnipresent adolescent insecurity until "Boomer and Billy" dropped off their bags and left the room to watch the game before their own.

"On the ice, my teammates are my loyal defenders," Tueting wrote on her blog. "Off the ice, they are a chaotic mix of budding confidence, insecurity, hormones and bravado. After sharing a locker room with twenty fourteen- and fifteen-year-old boys, nothing surprises me. But I start holding my shirt in my teeth when I tie my skates. And I don't really date until my twenties.

"And hey Boomer and Billy, my girls are now 34C, no longer deemed chocolate chips by adolescent boys, but instead admired by grown men as 'beautiful breasts,' 'a perfect rack' and 'great cans.'"

In addition to all her other extraordinary talents, Sarah Tueting had perfected the art of trash-talking as well.

Upon These Shoulders

"A really strong woman accepts the war she went through and is ennobled by her scars."

—Carly Simon, singer-songwriter

Hey Peabody! Get out here!"

Coach Tony Marmo, the unvarnished Godfather of the girls hockey traveling circus known as the Massport Jets, was barking mad. He had heard a lot about this skinny peewee from the rink manager, and wanted to see if this prospect had legs.

"I was shy as shy could be," said Lee Johnson, then a pond-hockey prodigy from Peabody, Massachusetts who recalls hiding in the back of the line. She was surrounded by two dozen rough-and-tumble East Boston girls from the other side of the puberty line. Minutes earlier, little Lee was lacing up her skates on the benches outside the lockers, pressed into a female sports genre that might as well have been from Mars. To this provincial tomboy who'd never ventured beyond Boston's insular North Shore, this was another galaxy.

"I'm sitting with all these girls from East Boston, and the language!" Johnson shakes her head at the memory from way back in 1970. "Oh my God, these girls are crazy, the things they were saying. Here I am, 12 years old, scared to death."

The stocky old coach with electric hair and cowbell nose bit down on his whistle until it shrieked. He raised his stick and pointed its blade toward the child crouching in the back.

"Hey, you back there!"

"Uh, me?"

"Peabody, you from Peabody! Get up here. This is the best of the best. I want to see what you got."

Five players, the top unit from the undefeated Massport Jets, gave the kid a smirk, and prepared to race her in hockey's equivalent of a suicide drill: blue line-back, red line-back, far blue-line back, and end boards and back. The movie *Miracle* taught the world a name for this torture: "Herbies." Tony Marmo was feeding this lamb to the lionesses.

Meanwhile, in the back corner of the rink, two middle-aged men appeared to be handling money. Pro-shop manager Woody Woodworth and rink boss Tom Doyle had found some action, and they were laying down bets that the pipsqueak was gonna beat these women's hockey badasses in this cruel sprint. The rink was taking on a carnival-like atmosphere, the spotlight shining directly onto the tongue-tied girl in the Blackhawks jersey.

Woodworth was not throwing away his money; he knew super jocks. His daughter Lori and son Richie had both played sports with Johnson their entire lives, and everyone in Peabody knew Johnson had the goods. Two generations later there are still Facebook debates as to who was the best athlete in Swampscott history, pro skier Richie Woodworth or two-sport legend Lee Johnson, who moved up to Swampscott in junior high. Smart money still takes Johnson.

Woodworth and Doyle had both seen the determined little girl most weekend mornings, walking across a quarter mile of frozen cornfields—in her figure skates!—to participate in daily pond hockey clashes. The hockey skates she laced up that morning in Peabody were her first pair without picks on the toes. But equipment was secondary—this kid was nails. She and the Woodworth kids flipped sports every season: breaking windows playing baseball in the summer, street hockey in the fall, pickup puck on Brown's Pond in the winter, hoops in the spring. Now she was poised to race five players, all bigger and stronger. Marmo's whistle screeched once again. Johnson jumped off the line. The broads from Eastie had never witnessed such speed. The kid raced out to a lead that just kept getting fatter.

"I beat 'em all by half the rink," Johnson said with a good-natured chuckle, all fact, no brag. Woody and Doyle laughed all the way to the bank, pockets bulging with cash. This was a scene straight out of the Robert Redford film *The Natural*. Or for those who prefer non-fiction, it's a true-to-life story like the barnstorming tales of Babe Ruth penned by authors Jane Leavy and Leigh Montville. Thus began Lee Johnson's own unique story, women's hockey's answer to Roy Hobbs.

Young Lee was immediately adopted by the Massport Jets, and soon emerged as their scoring ace. In no time she was the leader of a band of sisters who were living out their own version of *A League of Their Own*, thanks to the combination of political power and the personal will of Boston Housing Inspector and girl-dad Tony Marmo. He was a close friend and political comrade of Massachusetts Governor Frank Sargent. As a result, the Massport Jets had luxuries today's hockey girls can only dream about: primo ice time in their home rink in East Boston, a state-of-the-art bus at their disposal, and a teenage prince of a coach. Future president of the Massachusetts Senate, Bobby "Babyface" Travaglino became Marmo's associate head coach at age 18. How this all came about—a true-life version of Tom Hanks and Geena Davis with a 10-year run—is a classic Boston tale: geography, opportunity, and raw political power.

Logan International Airport fills up most of East Boston, a spit of land extending into Boston Harbor. When Logan inevitably expanded in the late 1960s, the Massachusetts Port Authority was particularly unpopular in Eastie. Marmo, whose stubbornness months earlier had triggered his ouster from the East Boston Youth Hockey Association, saw a golden opening.

Port Authority executive director and former Massachusetts Governor Ed King was taking political hits for all the land being sacrificed to Logan. So when his old pal Marmo approached him about starting a women's hockey league in East Boston, King was all in. "He saw an opportunity for some public relations points," said Travaglino. "By joining in on this unique opportunity, in the heart of the district that was severely impacted by the Logan operations, [King could] finally get some points, rather than criticism."

The Metropolitan District Commission (MDC), the city group responsible for public rinks sprouting up like mushrooms in Boston during the Bobby Orr era, was under the umbrella of the Port Authority. So months after being axed by the local boys hockey association, Marmo was swinging a much bigger stick. A father of two dynamic daughters, he loved nothing more than scoring prime-time ice at Porrazzo Rink in Eastie for his new league of women, at the expense of the boys league that had just canned him.

The subsequent house league was so popular that Marmo doubled down in the 1971-72 season. In the midst of the Boston Bruins Stanley Cup mania, he created the American Girls Hockey Association. His next step was to get the word out. Knowing his own limitations as a public speaker, he enlisted the charismatic teenager Bobby Travaglino, the son of his former hockey pal. The two leveraged their way onto a Bruins telecast, and put out an APB for any girl who wanted to play hockey in their new circuit.

"It was like doing a commercial for women's hockey," said Travaglino. "Anybody that watched the Bruins now realized that if they had a daughter, she could play ice hockey in a fine-tuned operation."

That intermission segment, playing before New England's rabid hockey nation, ignited interest like an exploding mushroom-cloud. "The response was immediate, more than ever expected, unlimited numbers coming to the East Boston rinks," said Travaglino. "Down south on Cape Cod, north to Essex, they just kept coming." There was even a girl whose parents commuted from Delaware to latch onto this Title IX comet.

Marmo now had a league to create, so he took his troupe on the road as hockey missionaries. When they weren't playing the best Bantam boys teams in the Bay Area, they were performing exhibitions throughout the state: "Swampscott, Saugus, Brockton, Framingham, any place that called him, he [Marmo] would get in the car, go to their rinks and meet with the people that wanted to establish organizations," said Travaglino. "He would give them the template, make himself available in any way, shape, or form to assist in getting them off the ground. Tony knew how to play the phone game. If he picked up the phone, things happened."

It was at one of those recruiting missions that Johnson was discovered, and playing on the Massport Jets "A" team was the perfect vehicle for young Lee's rapid ascent to stardom. "We used to play boys teams, men's teams, the Hull Bantams," said Johnson.

On one memorable trip, she and her mates, outfitted in the red, white and blue, crossed the Canadian border in their furnished Port Authority bus to play the champions of North American hockey, the Agincourt Lions of Scarborough, Ontario.

No one challenged the supremacy of Agincourt when it came to girls hockey, let alone a group of Americans, considered second-class hockey citizens back in the 1970s. In a shocking upset, known only through Homeric history, Johnson carried the Jets to a stunning upset over the previously unbeatable Lions. Agincourt quickly rescheduled a visit down to the States, where it evened the score with the Yanks. But the damage was done. One myth had been shattered, another created.

In 1975, the Jets were involved in another major championship. A team from Romulus, Michigan organized the first girls hockey national championship of the United States. The hosts presumed they would glide to an easy victory. "They claimed to be the first women's team," said Johnson. "They were cocky. We annihilated them." That conquest earned the Jets a spot in the International Hockey Hall of Fame in Kingston, Ontario.

There is a photo album of the Massport girls that has resurfaced from those championships, candid snaps of the players and coaches outside their Michigan hotel. The color images contrast starkly with the stereotype of the Jets being a bunch of cursing brawlers from East Boston, the impression left on Johnson when she was a shy pre-teen. These were not a gang of broads who swore, drank and loved a good stick fight. To the contrary, the national champs displayed style, looks and the smiling disposition befitting the new queens of the sport. The majority were college bound, and most have remained lifelong friends.

The two coaches were also prominent in the album. Bobby Travaglino, soon to carry the moniker "Babyface Trav" in the Massachusetts Senate, looks like a young Paul Sorvino, the dapper gangster from the film "Goodfellas." Boss Tony Marmo exudes restrained power in the tan, collared outer shirt framing his 5-foot-11, 205 pound boxer's body. His nose appears to have absorbed a punch or two, his head a riot of wavy ringlets.

Marmo, despite being uncultured and heavy-handed, wanted to petition the International Olympic Committee (IOC), the blue-blooded lords of amateur sport, for a shot at the Olympics. He knew his girls were world-class, and was convinced that Johnson and company deserved to perform on a global stage. The season his Jets won the inaugural National Championship, Marmo shot for the moon, writing and then delivering a house call to the IOC at its annual congress. His dapper young sidekick was unavailable for the overseas adventure, but Marmo soldiered on.

"He petitioned the Olympic Committee," said Travaglino, his voice rising in incredulity. "Tony went to Denmark in '76, [stood] before the Committee to petition for the introduction and acceptance of female hockey. They denied him, but I'm telling you, it's a true story. He was so far ahead of his time, it's amazing."

There is a copy of the initial correspondence between the IOC's president Lord Killanin and Marmo. In a letter dated November 11, 1974, Killanin informs Marmo of a possible misunderstanding stemming from the initial cable. There is confusion between ice hockey and field (grass) hockey. Rather than lose anything else in translation, the middle-aged political streetfighter hopped a flight to Europe to continue his mission in person. In this case, the brawler never landed a punch, and his dream of sending the pride of Eastie to the Olympics was tabled, but never forgotten.

Johnson herself had more realistic plans in which to parlay her Massport hockey success. Her combination of speed, strength, and a wicked slapshot made her an ideal candidate for colleges looking to build women's varsity teams. This was shortly after the birth of the new Title IX federal mandates. Johnson's slapshot was something not seen in women's hockey until the arrival of Karyn Bye at University of New Hampshire (UNH) 20 years later. "Realistically, she could shoot like the best boys in Bantams," said Massport teammate Rita Roberto. Johnson was ready to take her arsenal to the next level.

"I realized after a while that a lot of the colleges playing us invited us up for recruiting," said Johnson. "We went up to McGill [in Montreal] but I was 15 or younger, so at that point no Canadian colleges recruited me. Going up to Ithaca, Cornell recruited me. Mind you, I was shy. I remember walking around this big, huge campus and I was overwhelmed. 'Yeah, I don't know, this isn't for me.' And it was an eight-hour drive, so it's kind of far from home. Around the same time, Colby recruited me. I went up there and loved the place."

Colby College in Waterville, Maine had a prominent men's program, but women's hockey only became a varsity sport in 1973. When Lee arrived on campus in the fall of 1975, the team was coached by a couple of volunteers from the men's JV Squad. Colby had never seen a woman as athletic as Lee Johnson. A photo of her from those years reveals a woman with short brown hair and a smile radiating confidence, a left shot with a wooden Christian Brothers stick, and the number six on her sleeve. A newspaper story listed her at 5-foot-8, 138 pounds.

College hockey was Johnson's opportunity to thrive. After leaving Massport, she immediately transitioned from left wing to defense, where she could play the majority of the game and dominate all four corners of the rink. She was a regular in the weight room, adding heat to her slapshot. She was now a premier athlete, something along the lines of Babe Didrikson, dominating three college sports: field hockey in the fall, ice hockey in the winter, and softball in the spring. On the ice she simply overpowered the competition.

Unlike Didrikson, however, Johnson was the consummate team player. "There's no 'I' in team" remains her signature refrain. During each book interview she insisted on mentioning former teammates like Massport captain Rita Roberta, scoring star Patty Jones, and Colby teammate Carol Doherty. Doherty is a Massport alum, also from Peabody, who combined with Johnson to form a devastating one-two scoring punch for the Colby Mules. But there was never a doubt as to who the prodigy was.

During the spring of her junior year, Massport was invited to the second U.S. Women's Nationals, this time in Buffalo. Johnson sought and gained permission from Colby to re-join Massport for one last chance at winning a U.S. Championship. In her swan song for the Jets, she led her mates to their second national title. It was a rousing final act for the queen and her court. Massport shut down its program a season later, the end of a dynastic decade.

There are no stat sheets from her days at Colby, but Johnson recalls having never lost a game until her senior year, when the Mules fell to UNH. That was the beginning of New Hampshire's reign of terror under coach Russ McCurdy, who parlayed a dozen full scholarships into an epic 72-0-1 run in Durham. As the 1980s began, UNH, Northeastern and Providence all began handing out athletic scholarships to female hockey players. New stars emerged, like Cindy Curley (Providence), Kelly Dyer (Northeastern) and Cindy MacKay (UNH). Official championships were won, stats were recorded, and the black-and-white legend of Lee Johnson slowly faded. There is one national accolade, however, that Johnson will hold forever: She was the first women's hockey player to be immortalized by *Sports Illustrated* in its weekly feature, "Faces in the Crowd."

Additional sources speak to Johnson's greatness during her epic college hockey career. Newspaper accounts reveal that Johnson averaged three goals among her six points per game during her senior year at Colby, a rate comparable to that of the great Hobey Baker at Princeton. When it comes to college hockey scoring prowess, not even Bill Cleary's 1955 NCAA record of 4.24 points per game matches the production of Hobey and Lee. If there were a podium for the deadliest scorers in college hockey history, Baker and Johnson share the golden top step; Harvard legend Cleary is relegated to bronze.

Newspapers also report that Johnson recorded four-goal performances against Middlebury, Dartmouth and Brown, and a three-goal hat trick against Cornell, her former college suitor. Johnson's skating legs, steeled by 10,000 Gladwellian hours on the frozen ponds of Peabody and Lynn, made her impossible to defend. "I was a strong skater, I could maneuver around almost anybody," said Johnson matter-of-factly. "If you're on the move, and someone is standing still, they don't have a chance." The Linda Rondstadt hit of the era, "Blue Bayou," became her trademark. Blew. By. You.

As Johnson entered her senior year, the Colby administration finally hired a women's head coach, promoting Bob Ewell from his men's JV coaching post. Ewell later established himself as one of the most devoted coaches in women's hockey, coaching Princeton's varsity after a successful run at Colby. Ewell is the ideal source to separate hyperbole from reality when it comes to Johnson. He still sounds like P.T. Barnum when discussing his former superstar.

"Bobby Orr was probably the closest," said Ewell, when asked to name a player comparable to Johnson. "Orr was obviously the best player on the ice at all times, and so was Lee, who just dominated the game.

"She was famous for her shot. She just had a cannon. I can't tell you how many times the puck would go out to the point, and instead of rushing toward the puck, everyone would get out of the way, it was Moses and the parting of the Red Sea. It was terrifying to be in front of that shot."

Ewell said that had Johnson joined the program as a freshman, she could have made the varsity at Colby, the *men's* varsity. No one, certainly not an established coach like Ewell, has ever suggested that any other woman could play men's college hockey, not even Olympic stalwarts like Tara Mounsey, Karyn Bye or Cammi Granato.

As Johnson's college career wrapped up in February 1979, there was no place for her to continue, no professional leagues, no national teams, and despite the efforts of Massport's Tony Marmo, no Olympic Games. Johnson's final contest in organized hockey was played at Cornell's Lynah Rink in Ithaca. After disposing of the Big Red for the final time, Johnson and her mates headed off the ice. But before they could get to the locker room, they were intercepted by the team in red.

This was not to be an aggressive confrontation, however; it was one born of admiration. The Cornell program, losers in the Johnson recruiting sweepstakes four years prior, had created a plaque to honor the untitled "Queen of Hockey." The entire Cornell team presented it to Johnson in an impromptu ceremony. The engraved words complemented their act of sportsmanship:

To Lee Johnson,
For your contribution to women's hockey
as an outstanding player.
From the Cornell women's hockey team, 1979

"It was like a going-away ceremony," said Johnson, who was tongue-tied by the attention. "It was a big plaque. I was embarrassed. I didn't know what to say."

"It was a wonderful gesture," said Ewell, who was on the scene. "In those days, if there was a big hockey crowd, people were there to see Lee Johnson. Women's hockey wasn't a big world, but people knew who she was, they would come to see her."

Sixty-five years earlier, Hobey Baker played his final game for the Princeton Tigers up in Ottawa, Ontario. His opponents honored the legendary Baker with a comparable post-game tribute, a dinner and a laurel crowning him, "King of Hockey." This was exactly what took place up in Ithaca, an opponent paying the ultimate respect to the sport's reigning deity.

Like her historical counterpart Hobey Baker, Johnson was born too early to participate in the Olympic Games, and the world never got to know her greatness. The first tangible step in the women's hockey Olympic movement came in the spring of 1990, when Canada hosted the first IIHF sanctioned World Championships. Johnson, 32 years old at the time, was vaguely aware of the event, but hockey was no longer on her radar.

"I was playing travel softball then, big time. I kind of got away from hockey," said Johnson, who was playing championship-caliber softball for both men and women. "One of our girls tried out for that [USA hockey] team, Patty Jones, a really, really good player, and didn't make it. We were kind of older. Some of these girls were 18 or 19. I was in my 30s, you kind of lose a step. I love softball. I was with a team from Eastern Massachusetts that went to the nationals 13 years in a row in the '80s and '90s." Johnson was no spare part on those softball clubs that threatened for national championships annually--she played shortstop and batted cleanup.

If given adequate training time, it's hard to imagine Johnson not being a major contributor to Team USA's entry into the inaugural IIHF World Championships in 1990. She and Cindy Curley of Providence would have made a deadly tandem, one that might have threatened Canada for the original women's gold. That is all tavern speculation today, like trying to imagine Satchel Paige pitching in the majors during his prime. Sadly for American hockey, the generations simply did not mesh, and the great Lee Johnson never got to represent her country in an international tournament, never had her Mike Eruzione golden moment.

February 18, 1998 was a typical morning for Lee Johnson and her husband Bill Cameron. They were up at 7 a.m., juggling three children under the age of four, surrounded by the smell of fresh coffee. Ten-month-old Tyler was whining for his breakfast while big sister Kimberly, three, was busy pouring cereal for younger brother Jake, two. Lee stood at the edge of their open kitchen, watching the large screen TV in the living room. The CBS Morning Show was gushing about the newly crowned women's hockey gold medalists. Bill knew about Lee's history as a star player.

"Why don't you try out for [the next] Team USA?"

"Yeah right," said the 40-year-old Johnson. "I'll make it, travel all over the world, and you might see me once or twice a year. Good luck with the kids!" They both shared a laugh, and went back to their multi-tasking.

Although Johnson never wore a Team USA jersey, she managed to share the ice with the heroine of the 1998 gold-medal game. Sandra Whyte, the woman with a goal and two primary assists in USA's 3-1 victory over Canada, had a brief connection with the Massport Jets franchise. As a seven-year-old, Whyte was allowed to skate at one of Massport's recruiting exhibitions in the 1977-78 season, a scene reminiscent of Johnson's tryout seven years prior. Whyte was much younger and smaller than Johnson when she debuted for Massport, but both youngsters wowed the arena with their derring-do on steel blades. Unlike Johnson, Whyte never competed for Massport. But three decades after her tryout as a youngster, Whyte found herself at a Massport alumni game in 2006.

The original core of Massport players is a proud bunch, eager to tell anyone willing to listen that they were the pioneers of elite women's hockey in America. Former goalie Joyce Inserra is a tireless promoter of the Massport story, banging the drum for every media outlet about Massport's rightful place in the pantheon of women's sports. Inserra is particularly busy during Olympic years, as was the case in 2006.

Inserra was coaching the Medford High School girls at the time, and set up a game between her varsity and the elder legends. The Jets old-timers were nearly three times as old as the high school pups. Inserra spread the word, and a standing room crowd showed up at LoConte Memorial Rink in Medford for the big Saturday night tilt. Whyte's presence—and her gold medal—was a major draw. One of the Whyte family neighbors in Saugus was Sue Campbell, a stalwart from the Jets' halcyon days. She was the connector between the Jets and Whyte. Campbell attended Sandra's tryout back in 1977, escorted the Whyte family to a Massport banquet on the eve of the Nagano games, and finally leveraged Sandra into a blue Massport Old Timers jersey in Medford. Whyte was 35 at the time.

Meanwhile, Lee Johnson had a skate problem. She hadn't worn her old CCM Super Tacks in decades, and a thorough search of her basement unearthed only a single skate. "The inside was really bad and dried out." So Johnson sucked it up and sank $300 into a new pair of skates ("My feet were killing me!") just in time for two practices before the exhibition game with Medford. The aging Jets, most of them in their late 40s or early 50s, were clearly underdogs. "They thought they were going to cream us," said Johnson.

The teens must not have realized the kind of veteran star-power the Jets had on their roster, or the ringer they had stashed on their bench. Although memories from that game are foggy, the gold-medal heroine and the living legend made beautiful music together with stick and puck.

No box score exists from that game. A published report in the Swampscott on-line periodical *Wicked Local* four years later quoted Johnson as saying the final score was 20-0 in favor of Massport; Inserra guessed that her old Massport squad tallied a dozen. Regardless of the score, it was a delightful romp for the aging legends. After the game Whyte posed with the giddy old-timers, using her gold medal as a centerpiece.

For fans of sports history, there was something magical about Whyte and Johnson playing together: the undisputed heroine of the inaugural women's hockey Olympics gold-medal game combining on scoring plays with a bona fide legend. The equivalent of Hobey Baker teaming up with Mike Eruzione, it is a fantastical sports dream. Yet in this case, Johnson and Whyte actually shared the ice. In the post-game photo, storybook heroine Lee Johnson is pictured holding the greatest prize in all of sports—an Olympic gold medal.

The Courting
of Ben Smith

*"To know the road ahead, ask someone who is coming
back."*

—Ancient Chinese Proverb

In the mid-1990s, USA Hockey's cup had runneth over. The national
governing body for hockey was hosting a World Junior Championship in
1995-96, co-hosting the inaugural World Cup of Hockey in the fall of '96,
as well as preparing for an historic 1998 Olympics. These Winter Games
would make hockey history on two fronts: the first Olympics involving
NHL players, and the first to include women's hockey as a medal sport.

Fortunately, USA Hockey had just rehired former public relations
director Dave Ogrean as its executive director. A dynamic personality with
a voracious appetite for work, Ogrean also had a television background
from his time at ESPN. Even with all the major hockey initiatives orbiting
his work life, he would not rest until women's hockey was on solid footing.
That began with the right coaching hire.

"We had a pretty long runway of preparation, but no blueprint on
how to do this," said Ogrean, who had the ideal colleague at his side for
the mission, Art Berglund, a USA Hockey veteran in charge of the international programs. Berglund was the former running mate of legendary
Wisconsin coach "Badger" Bob Johnson. They had been to countless

World Championships and other international events in which the U.S. men always struggled to medal. Berglund knew that based on the fact that Canada and the United States had met in the final of all three prior women's World Championships, the Americans would likely be in Nagano's gold-medal game, and that quickened his pulse.

"I remember having conversations with Art, and we agreed that for something as pressure-packed as the Olympic stage, any list of coaching candidates was really, really short," said Ogrean. And no one on that list was a woman.

"I want to hire somebody who, when we're down 2-1 in the third period of the gold medal game, isn't going to have their knees knocking," said Ogrean, recalling his discussions with Berglund, conversations that would be controversial today. "I don't think there's anybody coaching women's hockey that fits the bill. Let's look wider." Ogrean clarified his mindset at the time. "Looking wider meant there's a good chance we're going to be hiring a male."

Easier said than done. Back in 1994, the list of elite college coaches willing to leave the fraternity for a job coaching women was virtually nil. Women's hockey in the NCAA was a Title IX niche sport, drawing about the same amount of fans as club hockey. It was played by Ivy League schools, little Colby College, and three Eastern university pioneers: UNH, Providence and Northeastern. Ogrean and Berglund would have to maximize their powers of persuasion to bring in a brand-name men's coach, but they also had the additional challenge of finding someone with the sensitivity to coach women.

"You couldn't take somebody that walked around with a brickbat, like Dave Peterson or Lou Vairo," said wordsmith Ogrean. "You needed somebody with a different kind of touch."

This is where Art Berglund's unmatched experience in the world of international hockey paid off. "I think we ought to talk to Ben [Smith]," said Berglund, who knew Smith well from his time assisting Peterson at the 1988 Calgary Winter Games, as well as several World Junior assignments. "He's liberal, he's sophisticated, he's a Harvard guy, and he's brought up a daughter."

Bullseye. But the challenge was enormous: convincing a Division I men's hockey coach to abandon his post for the untested waters of women's hockey. And thus began the 16-month courtship between USA Hockey and Ben Smith.

At the start of the 1994-95 season, Smith was riding high at Northeastern University. In three short years, he had taken the Huskies—traditional doormats of Hockey East—to the 1994 NCAA tournament. In the Big Dance they had given eventual national champion Lake Superior State all it could handle. Smith was a former star player at Harvard, born and raised within the aura of Boston Garden. Being one of four Beanpot Tournament coaches was about as close to Shangri-La as a Boston hockey product like Smith could possibly imagine.

"I had a wonderful job at a great university, a great program," were the sentiments of Smith at the time. Nevertheless, the USA Hockey tag team of Ogrean and Berglund took their first stab at Smith in February of 1995, using a tactic that Berglund had mastered: fine dining on USA Hockey's dime.

It was a snowy Sunday night in downtown Boston, the eve of the 1995 Beanpot Championship. There was no challenge to getting reservations in and around Copley Square. Northeastern had been relegated to the consolation game after losing its semifinal the previous Monday, so Smith was content to be entertained deep into the night. The two executives from Colorado Springs floated the idea of merely selecting and coaching one team for one tournament to Smith, a trial balloon to lure this prominent figure from Boston's college hockey establishment.

"They asked me if I would try putting a team together, to get a feel for where the women's program was at the time," Smith said of that initial gathering. He did not realize that he now had one foot in the Ogrean/ Berglund trap.

"It was like a test-drive," said Ogrean.

"So in a moment of weakness, maybe after too many Bud Lights, I said yes," said Smith. "I would go to Lake Placid in August and then go over to Finland for a four-game series."

Smith then thanked the duo for their hospitality and disappeared into the driving snow. His focus was back on the Northeastern men's program. The next night Smith's Huskies were blown out in the Beanpot consolation game. Northeastern struggled to maintain home ice for the Hockey East playoffs three weeks later, a series it lost, failing in its bid to return to the national tournament.

An avid sportsman, Smith truly enjoys his off-seasons away from the rink. But his summer of '95 was cut short. "All of a sudden August rolls around, I'm thinking, 'Holy shit, I've got to go to Lake Placid!'" Smith recalled. "I've got to put the boat away, put the clubs away, and put Northeastern hockey on the back burner."

Smith drove the five hours up the Northway into the Adirondack Mountains to assess women's hockey for the first time. He and assistants Tim Gerrish and Julie Andeberhan had to whittle down 38 candidates into a 21-woman platoon to travel overseas. Smith found himself in the position of determining the fates of respected athletes, an unpleasant chore that would repeat itself throughout his tenure.

"I guess we ruffled a few feathers right at the start because I let some veteran players go," said Smith, including former Providence College superstar

Cindy Curley, a 31-year-old whose knees were significantly older. "Monumental health problems, but her heart and her head wanted to continue," said Smith. "I think she could see the Olympic Flame three years out." A flame that flickered and died under the new coach's critical eye.

Smith revealed a professional habit that he maintained throughout his career: picking teams without the hindrance of sentiment. One of his cuts that August could have damaged USA Hockey's gold medal hopes in Nagano. National team stalwart and Dartmouth College star Gretchen Ulion did not impress Smith, and he let her go, despite a terrific body of work over her career, one Smith was not familiar with. The Curley decision was more carefully considered, and ultimately an easier call. The original Wonder Woman of USA Hockey had lost her superpowers. "I could see she was laboring, unable to keep up with the kids." At the time, Curley was the best woman to have ever donned the USA hockey sweater. Her scoring totals at the 1990 World Championship, amassing 23 points in 11 games, is a USA Hockey record that may never be broken. But that was five years earlier, and Smith was busy looking forward.

The future arrived in the form of fresh-faced 15-year-old Angela Ruggiero, a girl stronger than any woman at the tryout camp. A Southern California native, the inexperienced Ruggiero wasn't even going to bring a passport to Lake Placid, a prerequisite for making the travel team. In yet another case of a hockey mom saving the day, Karen Ruggiero chose to pay the additional costs to have Angela's passport expedited. "I told her not to pay the extra money because, I'm not making the team anyway," Ruggerio wrote in her autobiography. She got her passport the day before departing for camp. "Thank God my mom had faith in me."

Three years shy of high school graduation, Ruggiero was now on a hockey fast track, which she occupied for nearly two decades. She and the rest of Team USA enjoyed success on Smith's maiden voyage, sweeping the dangerous Finns on their own soil. If this were a test drive for coaching women's hockey, Smith did not waste time haggling and kicking tires. "I was duly impressed with their skill level, their work ethic, and their team-first play," said Smith. "There was a lot of excitement, to win four straight. I don't think they'd done that before."

USA Hockey's ultimate company man wrote up a thorough report for his clients, and in his mind, said goodbye to women's hockey. "I wished them well," said Smith. "I told them, 'Hey, if you're ever in an airport or a rink and see me, say hi.'" Smith was going back to Northeastern to begin his critical fifth season. "Those early meetings didn't mean much to me because I wasn't planning on doing it [coaching the women]. I was just being courteous."

But Berglund, America's international hockey czar, wasn't going to let Smith go without tugging the line and setting the hook. "He kept telling me how great the Olympics were going to be, what a big deal it was to put women's hockey on the map," said Smith. Berglund had a pet phrase, and he beat it like a drum. "Gold medals change lives, gold medals change lives!" barked Berglund. "C'mon, you've got to get on board."

Smith didn't alter his plans, dutifully reporting back to his Northeastern office adjacent to venerable Matthews Arena. His Huskies were prepping to open their new season on October 21, taking on powerhouse North Dakota. After practice on the eve of the Saturday night opener, Smith weaved through the city's infamous traffic to get to Boston University's Walter Brown Arena to do some scouting. It was a gala event for BU hockey: not only was the team playing a marquee game against North Dakota, it was a banner-raising night. The Terriers were celebrating their fourth national championship from the previous spring.

October 20, 1995 is a date Dave Ogrean will never forget. Decades later he still texts Ben Smith on that anniversary in an act of solemn remembrance. On that date, Ogrean scheduled a full day of meetings in a conference room at Boston's Sheraton Prudential Center, bringing in USA Hockey staffers Berglund and Brian Petrovek to map out the route to Nagano for the Team USA women.

"We're in a windowless meeting room with whiteboard and markers," recalled Ogrean. "The very first meeting to organize the whole two-and-a-half year journey: begin to lay out the road, what we need to do, what are the elements, etc."

The three men hunkered down in earnest for nearly 10 hours, grinding details until the clock struck six. They intended to meet their prospective coach Ben Smith across town at the BU game. The trio crammed into a taxi, and limped along through Boston's infamous rush-hour traffic. Once they cleared Kenmore Square and finally got to Walter Brown Arena, they headed straight to the concession stands for hot dogs and coffee, the pregame ceremony minutes away. They noticed that Smith had still not arrived when they settled in to watch the NCAA champions being honored. Smith can still vividly recall his tardy arrival to 300 Babcock Street that night.

"So I walk into the upper level there, the entry way as you come into Walter Brown," recalled Smith, "and it was quieter than a cathedral. The silence was just..." Smith trails off, remembering how eerie it was for the normally raucous arena to be muted. He caught up with his USA Hockey crew in the last row of the east grandstand. In hushed tones, Berglund filled in Smith about the origin of a hockey tragedy that still haunts Boston's hockey nation. BU freshman Travis Roy had fallen awkwardly, striking his head against the dasher, a mere 11 seconds into the game. He lay motionless, his father Lee Roy kneeling next to him at ice level. The rest of the Roy family was in the row of seats directly in front of the USA Hockey contingent.

"They kind of nudged me to tell me this is Mrs. Roy in front," said

Smith, somber during his recollection. "I had tried to recruit Travis, had met the kid. I knew his dad from playing at UVM, and there we were. Lee was already down on the ice, at the far end, down by the Zamboni."

Whatever hopes Ogrean and Berglund had of getting a "yes" out of Smith this sorrowful night dissolved in a cloud of hockey heartbreak. The TV coverage from this game kept returning to the shot of Travis Roy's mom Brenda clutching her hands at chest level, trying to maintain a brave front before her daughter.

This was a night for thoughts and prayers, not closing deals with prospective coaches. Besides, even under ideal circumstances, Smith wasn't budging. He had his own team to coach, driven to get his Huskies back to the national tournament. "I was obviously most concerned with Northeastern Hockey, I was just being courteous to friends like Dave, Art and Petro."

Smith returned to his coaching chores at NU, and they appeared to be just that—a chore. His tenure with the Huskies had reached its pinnacle with their run to the 1994 NCAA's, and were in a two-year decline since. Smith's final season on Huntington Ave was his least successful: 10 wins overall; seventh place in Hockey East; stoned again in the Beanpot semis. To appease his USA Hockey pals, Smith asked Northeastern's administration if he could take a year's sabbatical to coach the women's Olympic team.

Request denied. Smith's suitors zeroed in.

After NU's quiet exit from the 1996 Hockey East post-season, USA Hockey offered Smith a week in British Columbia to scout Team USA women in the Pacific Rim Championships, part of the runup to Nagano. "Sure, I'll go," said Smith, who in his mind was more interested in recruiting a goalie prospect in that region for NU than jumping on the women's hockey bandwagon.

But the ledger sheet balance was starting to tilt toward USA Hockey. The NU athletic department had no travel money to help Smith land his goalie, while USA Hockey was happy to foot the bill for flights and hotels in Vancouver. Ben's former boss and great friend, Tim Taylor of Yale, had been granted a sabbatical to coach in the 1994 Winter Games, but no such love for Smith from NU. And speaking of love, as Smith scouted Team USA from the rear corner of Richmond's Minoru Arena, his future wife Julie Sasner was on the bench for the Americans, a fellow Harvard alum who coached alongside Smith the year before in Finland. Whether he knew it or not, Smith was ripening to be picked.

Dave Ogrean is an old soul of a sports executive, reminiscent of the 20th century public relations masters of Notre Dame, star makers who helped Paul Hornung win the Heisman Trophy despite playing for a losing team. These were guys who could influence elections, get friends promoted, and do it all while leaving the participants grinning in complicity.

It was in the far reaches of Minoru Arena during the 1996 Pacific Rim Championships where Ogrean performed his masterful art of persuasion, one that certainly would have earned the admiration from the PR kings of yesteryear.

To follow Ogrean's Pacific Northwest caper, it helps to be familiar with 1991 film *Doc Hollywood*, starring Michael J. Fox. For those who need a refresher, protagonist Fox plays a big- city physician named Ben, en route to fame and fortune in Los Angeles. The cocky doc's car breaks down, and Fox finds himself shanghaied in rural Georgia. The fictional Ben, as well as coach Ben of 1996, are both coveted, both teetering on the edge of falling in love, yet reluctant to change their primary course. Ogrean cherishes this tale, and its re-telling, 25 years later.

"The mayor of this town, at this big carnival at night, says to Michael J. Fox, whose name was Ben, 'Listen, do you hear that?' And there's music in the background, and there's wind in the trees. And the mayor's going, 'Be a doctor here, Ben. Be a doctor here!'

"Well anyway, we're at the Pacific Rim tournament, and Ben was scouting, not coaching. Coincidentally, his now wife Julie, she was there coaching. I was with him up in the corner of the arena, and I had been putting the press on him hard. He and I were all alone, and I said, 'Ben, do you hear that? Do you hear that?'

"And he looks around and says, 'Hear what? What?'

"Coach the team Ben, coach the team!'"

Ogrean always gets a deserving laugh when spinning this yarn, and although Smith claims not to recall this lore specifically, he does acknowledge that the Ogrean/Berglund full-court press was closing in on him in that spring of 1996.

"I hadn't made a commitment to anybody about being the national coach. This was April of '96, and I was still being badgered by Dave and Art."

Former BU coach Jack Parker is one of Smith's best friends, not only a Beanpot rival, but a colleague from the nine years Smith spent as his assistant coach in the 1980s. Parker knew well what kind of calculations Smith was conducting in this high-stakes poker game. The wild card was the appeal of representing his country.

"He was an assistant coach of an Olympic team already, and I don't think there was any question of the attraction of getting on stage again," Parker said about his sailing mate from Gloucester. "It doesn't matter if it's men, women, the track team or the ski team. You're coaching an Olympic team representing the United States of America. That was such a big attraction to him."

There was an additional factor weighing the scales toward Nagano—precious metal. "It was going to be a two-team tournament, it's *still* a two-team tournament," said Parker in 2021. "The chances of beating Canada and winning a gold medal, that's a pretty good carrot."

Smith was building a strong hand, but he was not ready to go all-in just yet. He needed to mitigate what he felt was substantial risk. Ogrean recalled Smith protesting until the bitter end.

"I'm afraid if I do this and it doesn't work, I'm going to have a hard time getting back into high-level men's hockey."

The dogged duo from USA Hockey didn't miss a beat. "I don't think that is true at all," said Ogrean and Berglund in chorus. "You're just going to be adding to an already-established resume, and it's international hockey for crying out loud."

They proceeded to lay out their cards, fattening the pot with an extra year's salary. Smith recalled the offer from Ogrean.

"We'll hire you full-time starting in June of 1996, right through the Olympics, a two-year deal."

Smith countered, "That's awfully nice Dave, but I want a third year. I want one year after the Olympics because—what am I getting myself into here? I feel like I'm taking a step into the abyss, and I don't know where my foot's going to land when this thing's over."

Although he couldn't land his trophy, Ogrean had hooked his fish. All he needed now was a formal OK from the exchequers in Colorado Springs.

Smith, the son of a Massachusetts Senator by the same name, proved to be as shrewd a negotiator as his old man. He demanded one final detail before agreeing to abandon men's Division I hockey – he insisted on naming his own equipment manager. Smith wanted veteran Bob Webster, the guy he ran with for two seasons in and around the Calgary Winter Games. No Webbie, no Smith.

"He's the guy!" Smith exclaimed at the mention of Webster's name. "I met him with the '88 men's team, did many international events with him. I would NOT have taken the assignment without him being part of the staff. That was one of my few demands." It may not have sounded important, but Webster was an invisible presence that could take a sad song and make it better. He became the congenial master of every rink he entered: able to get a last-second ice resurfacing; secure the primo NHL locker room for his squad, even while behind enemy lines; and most importantly for the morale of the coaching staff, procure cold beer at any rink on earth. Smith knew that even if the ship was going down, the descent would be a hell of a lot smoother with Webster at his side.

Ogrean returned to the USA Hockey offices, got all the fiscal gatekeepers to sign off on Smith's demands, and returned to Boston a couple weeks later. He had put nearly 16 months into this courtship, and wasn't going home without his prize. This dance was now getting time-sensitive; the contract Smith needed to sign commenced on June 1, barely a week away. They agreed to meet one last time at Smith's favorite venue that didn't contain a sheet of ice—Fenway Park.

"David came East in late May," said Smith, locking onto a memory that was already a quarter-century old. "We went to a Red Sox game, a day game, it was broiling hot." The afternoon sun pounded down on both men, prompting them to quench their thirst with draft beer, not a great formula for rational thoughts and action. It was in that state, while watching his beloved Old Towne Team, that Ben Smith took his extraordinary leap of faith. "That's when I finally cracked," said Smith about that sweltering afternoon in the shadow of the Green Monster.

Ogrean's year-and-a-half-long quest had earned him the prize that he, Art Berglund and their governing body dearly coveted, with only days to spare. Ben Smith was now under contract, the guy who wouldn't quake under the hot lights of a nationally televised gold-medal game. In their minds, he was the best coaching candidate imaginable, a clear edge over Canada's eventual rookie bench boss Shannon Miller.

And what of Smith? The man was abandoning one of four Beanpot head-coaching positions in the Hub of Hockey, leaving Northeastern for the uncertainty of the women's game. Had he really "cracked"?

Parker, the man who knows Smith better than anyone else, thinks otherwise. "I wasn't that surprised that he left for USA Hockey," said Parker.

"If he left for a women's college team, I would have been *really* surprised. But he was leaving to coach the Olympics. That was in his blood."

So on June 1, 1996, Ben Smith was finally under contract to skipper an Olympic ship, ready to sail through uncharted waters all the way to the Orient. He would face uncertainty, a series of brutal cuts, and a showdown with the greatest women's hockey team in history to achieve his mission. When it was all said and done, he would return from the Far East with the greatest treasure in sports – pure gold.

Game On!

"I would blow the whistle, thank them, and then wish them well."

—Ben Smith from his revolving-door tryouts

In August of 1996, Smith returned to Lake Placid for a women's national team camp, but under much different circumstances. He was now under contract to build a gold-medal contender 18 months down the road. As always, goaltending was the most important position on the ice, and he wanted bodies to compete with national team incumbent Erin Whitten. Smith, who had spent a season at Dartmouth eight years earlier, wanted more intel on its rising junior Sarah Tueting.

There was a problem. Despite finishing the season with a 50-save masterpiece against UNH in the East Coast Athletic Conference (ECAC) semifinals, Tueting was disillusioned with hockey. Former national team coach Karen Kay was not a fan of Tueting's, and the young renaissance woman was eager to engage in other pursuits, like playing the cello, running, and soccer. Smith did his due diligence, speaking to Dartmouth women's coach George Crowe about his enigmatic star. Satisfied with his former colleague's assessment, he rang up Tueting at her home in the Chicago suburbs.

"When Ben called I didn't know anything about him," said Tueting. Smith was his typical blunt self. "You know, your evaluations at camp weren't good, but I've talked to the coaches in the league and everybody says we should take a look at you, so I'm inviting you to camp."

Tueting was not exactly flattered. "Oh. That'squite the invitation."

A powerful intellect, Tueting carefully assessed her options. Her bulky leg pads were collecting dust in the basement and seemed entirely foreign. But her instincts about this tactless coach with the chowder accent informed her that Smith would be fair, if not delicate. So she hoisted 40 pounds of goalie gear over her shoulder and headed east toward the Adirondack Mountains.

Crowe's July phone call with Smith extended beyond the subject of goaltending. He wanted to get in a plug for another former player who was about to abandon the sport. "You know, Ben, I don't want to tell you your business," Crowe said, "but you might want to see this kid Ulion at her best. I don't know what happened at your camp [in 1995], but over her four years at Dartmouth, she was as good or better than most of these kids in the Ivy League."

Smith never forgot that call. "George knew his onions," said Smith, well aware of Crowe's four Ivy League women's titles during his tenure at Dartmouth. "Turns out he was right."

Tueting and Ulion joined 40 other prospects who arrived in upstate New York in August of 1996, all of them buzzing about the impending Olympic journey. There were no strangers in this group, rivals and teammates from college hockey's 10 Division I schools along with a handful of teens waiting to matriculate. From the point of view of those who hadn't yet graduated, a successful camp created a challenging dilemma: should they return to college for a full season before the Olympic year, or should they spend a year of uncertainty, training with the national team with no housing, and little support?

A.J. Mleczko had not once veered off the success track that brought her to Harvard. She fully expected to return to Cambridge for her senior year before hopefully getting a crack at the Olympic team, Crimson diploma in hand. But Smith and his staff had seen a flaw in her game: they weren't sure the crafty but lean Mleczko had the strength to make the squad.

"The message I got was that my skills and hockey IQ, all that stuff was fine; I was just weak," said Mleczko. "There was a suggestion that I should take the year off and train, but Coach Smith wasn't guaranteeing me a spot on the team. I didn't know what to do. This was two weeks before I was supposed to move into my dorm at Harvard. People just didn't do this."

David Quinn, Smith's former assistant from Northeastern, was up in Lake Placid helping out at Smith's first official camp. As a guy who missed out on the 1988 and 1992 Winter Games due to a medical condition, Quinn gave Mleczko some hard-earned perspective.

"You don't want to have any regrets," he said. "If you're destined to be sitting on the couch in February 1998, watching Team USA playing in the Olympics, you want to make sure you did everything you could, left no stone unturned. If you don't take this year off, you'll always wonder what could have been."

Quinn's words struck a nerve, prompting a remarkable about-face from Mleczko. Surrounded by dozens of like-minded athletes prepared to do anything to get on this inaugural Olympic train, Mleczko chose a course unimaginable to her two weeks prior—she postponed her Harvard graduation by two years. With no safety net, but a burning desire to scale Mt. Olympus, Mleczko took a step into the unknown. Tueting, who rekindled her love for the game at the Olympic Arena, followed suit. "I vividly remember calling my parents from the payphone at the Olympic Training Center," said Tueting, who stashed her dreams of concert recitals and long runs in the White Mountains for two years of blocking pucks. "I'm not going to go back to school in two weeks. I'm going to play hockey instead."

Ulion, having been cut exactly one year prior in the same setting, had to ignore her wounded pride to make a decision. She bravely confronted the man who crushed her dreams the year before. "I should be starting my career. Where do I stand in all of this?" asked Ulion with urgency. Smith refused to sugarcoat his message.

"I can't make any guarantees, but I see you as having a lot of potential," said Smith. "I'd hate to see you not try to do this." Reflecting on that pivotal conversation, Ulion sensed an evolution. "I think that relationship started to grow right then and there. I started to trust him."

After returning to Boston from Lake Placid, Smith made a beeline to his old coaching haunts at BU. Just across from Walter Brown Arena lies an unassuming four-story office building, 285 Babcock Street. Smith pounded up two flights and greeted the weight trainer of the Terriers, Mike Boyle. A vital asset of BU Athletics for more than a decade, Boyle just learned that his pal "Smitty" had scored the women's Olympic job when Smith popped his head into Boyle's strength emporium. Smith wasted no time making the big ask. "Hey, I'm going to try and get a bunch of these women to move out here. Can they train here?"

Boyle's operation had grown in stature and reputation since Smith left BU in 1990; NHL players had begun joining the BU undergrads in the trek up to the third floor. "We had had a lot of our BU guys by that stage, we had a lot of pro guys," said Boyle, who remembers being intrigued by the women's Olympic mission. "Can you find some way?" Smith asked.

"I didn't think about it for five seconds," said Boyle. "I just said, 'Yes. Absolutely, let's figure it out.'"

When September arrived, Smith found himself outside the familiar trappings of men's college hockey for the first time in memory. He was now coaching women, a team whose roster was in constant flux, its games scheduled in untested venues across the globe, with no rink to host big games.

A sailor in both mind and practice, Smith knew the challenges of unchartered waters. Job One was to surround himself with a trusted crew. He had a budget for one assistant coach, yet he roped together a formidable staff.

There is a blurry photo of Smith's party of six taken in the fall of 1996. It portrays assistant Tom Mutch, equipment man Bob Webster, a couple of volunteer pals from Boston's North Shore, and a BU doctoral student fresh from a playing career in Austria. Of all the treasure mined from Smith's bulging Rolodex, sports psychologist Peter Haberl may have been the brightest.

"When I started my graduate program at Boston University, my advisor Len Zukowsky had known Ben from his time at BU and he thought that Ben might be willing to take me on," said Haberl, who is still amazed that a U.S. Olympic hockey coach would even consider bringing in someone from a mid-level hockey nation.

"I was thinking if an American would come and try an opportunity in Austria skiing, that would never happen," said Haberl. "But in America, that did happen. It was really special to have that opportunity, and I'm grateful to Ben." Haberl found gratitude despite having to commute and coach on his own dime, all while completing his rigorous Ph.D. requirements in Boston.

Smith still needed a home rink to handle his daunting double task: find the best players coast-to-coast, and train the established veterans. The luxury of being centralized by USA Hockey in Lake Placid, with full access to the Olympic Training Center, was still a year away. Smith, his staff and his players were all on a shoe-string budget. This time a hockey lifer named Ted Iorio stepped up. He had recently established a two-sheet hockey complex in the heart of NFL Patriots nation, and he was an early convert to Smith's Olympic cause.

"He was a real benefactor for women's hockey," said Smith of Iorio. "He was the one that gave us great ice time at a pretty cheap price. We ran kind of a quasi revolving door training/tryout session in Walpole, right across the line from Foxborough."

Once he put a semblance of a team together on the ice, Smith got busy implementing his ultimate formula for success. In his mind, every golden aspiration could be achieved by mastering a single skill: "Our goal is to be the best passing team in the world."

If hockey is the primary ingredient in Smith's lifeblood, then passing is his dominant gene. "It comes from the heart," said Smith, who insists that passing is an act of intentional altruism. "You've got to want to pass to a teammate, your teammate knows you passed it to them."

From Smith's point of view, the onus of being the best passing team is not on the passer, but the player on the receiving end. He pounded that message into his players' heads from Day One. "Anybody can propel a puck, but can you catch it? Guys, you can't miss passes. Be a good *receiving* team!"

Even after retirement, Smith continued to stress that fundamental to his youth hockey charges in hometown Gloucester. He's convinced that he left an impact on that '98 Olympic squad. "If you asked any of those players, they probably hear 'be a good receiver' in their dreams. I yelled it so much, 'Be a good receiver! be a good receiver!' I could shatter windows with that."

One of Smith's Walpole coaching volunteers from the fall of '96 was former St. Lawrence stalwart John Gummere, who recalled the manifestation of Smith's mania for passing. "They would give-and-go, back and forth until they virtually worked the puck into the goal," said Gummere. "It was easier for them than snapping home [shots] into the top right corner."

Smith constantly worked the "Contacts" menu on his flip phone, transforming Walpole into a port-of-call for his coaching pals. Keith Allain, a goalie for Smith during their years together at Yale, was fresh from his assistant coaching job with the Washington Capitals when he jumped onto the ice in Walpole. Allain filled a whiteboard with X's and O's connected by arrows with long trails. This was typical fare for NHL veterans, but novel to Smith's charges. Nevertheless, they processed the hieroglyphics and went right to work. "They had outstanding listening skills, and were eager to be coached," said Allain. He shared Smith's devotion to passing, and he exploited Walpole's extra wide Olympic ice sheet. "I remember doing several drills zipping pucks board-to-board on the move with pace, getting it wide with authority to take advantage of the width." The ability to move the puck seamlessly, creating speed in the process, became the trademark of Ben Smith's hockey nomads.

Being in the Boston area was critical. It was the hub of women's college hockey, the source of nearly all of Smith's elite talent. Many of those players put their education on hold in order to prepare for the Olympics a season prior to the Games. America's national players chose to live on the cheap and work secondary jobs in order to chase their Olympic dreams. That scenario raised an issue that continues to plague players and USA Hockey management today: how to compensate national team candidates during non-Olympic years. In 1996, however, players were so exhilarated about living out their five-ring fantasies that no one considered protesting.

Chicago native Sarah Tueting was one of several Ivy League women who became hockey gypsies in Boston. "I lived with a random family in Wellesley until I moved in with Whytey's [Sandra Whyte's] parents in Saugus," said Tueting. "I drove myself out there, I trained, I drove myself around. I think I was working at Seattle's Best Coffee."

Shelley Looney of Michigan had just graduated from Northeastern, with no discretionary income to lay down for a lease. "I remember trying to find a place to live," said Looney. "Myself and Chris Bailey were trying to rent an apartment, and you have to fill out an application, and we didn't know any better. They were like, 'You don't make enough money to live here.' So we had a friend that had a friend that needed roommates. We called her 'The Lady,' because she had a real job, and she actually made enough money to get the apartment. We were very fortunate to have her in our lives because [otherwise] Chris and I would be out on the street."

Karyn Bye chose to forego the Boston experiment in quasi-poverty, and moved up to Lake Placid, working for the Olympic Regional Development Authority (ORDA). She maintained a strict workout regimen at the Olympic Training Center, and skated with North Country Community College under the eye of Tim Gerrish, a respected member of the USA Hockey coaching family.

Bye, a dominant force in the sport, did not concern Smith; he was focused on bottom rung candidates, determined not to let a quality prospect slip through the cracks. He spent his weekends in and around Boston scouting college games, and his weekdays down in Walpole. Hundreds of players from around the country–good and bad—underwent the Ben Smith eye test.

"We had women coming from all corners of the country, firefighters from the state of Washington, people from Alaska," Smith said. "A woman would show up and I could tell she had probably been encouraged by some of the men she had been playing with on a Sunday night league in Phoenix. They see some woman, 'Hey, she's pretty good, if she plays with us, she should be on the Olympic team,' not knowing what the caliber of the top-end players are like."

It didn't take long for Smith to weed out the pretenders once they jumped on the ice and joined the core group for drills. "I would blow the whistle, and pick up the speed, and then, 'OK, thank you very much,' and they'd skate off," said Smith. "You'd thank them and wish them well." It was a revolving door, but it quieted Smith's fears of missing some unpolished gem.

Mired in the internet Stone Age, Smith was barely aware of a teenage prodigy shooting thousands of pucks in Minneapolis. It would be another year before peewee-sized hockey master Jenny Schmidgall would penetrate his radar. More than a thousand miles from the Twin Cities, Smith continued shuffling bodies in and out of Iorio Arena, urgently seeking the next uncut diamond.

Up in Boston, strength trainer Boyle played a critical role in maximizing the value from these raw recruits. Unimposing at 5-foot-9, with thinning hair and a runner's physique, the 38-year-old Boyle was becoming a giant in his field because of results gained from relentless innovation. His reputation as a fitness guru began to spread beyond the sports world. "He had movie stars going in and out of the third floor there," said Jack Parker, whose 1995 NCAA championship trophy had Boyle's fingerprints all over it. Smith had no budget for a world class trainer, but fortunately for USA Hockey, Boyle liked challenges.

"They were all pretty soft looking when they showed up," said Boyle. "None of them looked like they had been on any sort of organized strength and conditioning program." One of Boyle's first projects was a 5-foot-11 beanpole, the poster-child for Team USA's "Before and After" physical transformation.

"Smitty brought me A.J. Mleczko," said Boyle, recalling how Smith introduced him to the Harvard star. "Mike, she's really, really good, got unbelievable skill, but she can't skate a lick." Then Smith left Mleczko with the muscle maestro.

After their introduction, Boyle asked Mleczko to crouch into a deep squat. Getting down was the easy part.

"I can't get up," said Mleczko.

"Huh?"

"Something is wrong because when I squat down I can't get up," the concerned Mleczko said.

"A.J., you have a terrible case of weakness. You're just not very strong."

Twenty-six years later, Boyle was training A.J. 's daughter Jaime. Together they enjoyed frequent laughs over Mom's legendary struggles that he diagnosed in 1996. "She was using a hockey stick that was probably seven feet long because she had no desire to bend her knees at all," Boyle said. "I remember literally making her do body-weight squats, then squats with a sand bag that weighed 20 pounds. The transformation for her was remarkable in terms of when she suddenly got the ability to bend her knees and skate."

A.J. doesn't dispute any of it. "When I walked into the gym, I think he just shook his head, palm to forehead. 'What do I do with this thing?'" Mleczko recalled Boyle saying.

"He completely changed my physique. Not so much what I looked like, but my control, my strength, my fitness, my quickness, all that stuff."

Boyle was introducing Team USA to plyometrics, one of his favorite innovations at the time. He had his women repeatedly leaping onto elevated platforms, though the signature routine of the '98 team was the jump squat. BU sports information offices were directly underneath Boyle's weight room, and Terrier SID Ed Carpenter learned to ignore the thunder over his head, a dozen women exploding back to earth after cleaning as much weight as they dared.

Boyle admired their attitude, and loved the results. "Some of them really bought in," he said. "Shelley Looney, Tricia Dunn, Katie King and A.J."[1] While he has worked with countless athletes, Dunn might be his most gratifying subject. Dunn was a UNH player who was unlikely to make the team until she connected with Boyle. Thus began a season of profound transformation that blew her coach away. "She might be the best skater in the world," Smith later told Boyle.

---

1 Looney was not a particularly fit athlete when she played at Northeastern. Ben Smith was coaching the men's team at the time, and his players specialized in pull-ups, grasping both ends of a towel thrown over the bar, an additional challenge intended to develop grip strength. "They used to do towel pull-ups out in the walkway," Looney said. "We would never go down there." Looney did not master the exercise until she started working with Boyle, the man Smith credits with inventing the towel pull-up. "I probably stole it from someone else," Boyle said.

Meanwhile, north of the border, Team Canada had no Mike Boyle, no formal weight trainer to improve performance. Smith's seemingly bottomless Rolodex in hockey-mad Boston was paying dividends a year ahead of schedule.

Reshaping their bodies wasn't enough for these determined hockey gypsies. When they weren't down in Walpole, they were hustling for ice-time up in Boston. Chris Bailey, Vickie Movsessian, Colleen Coyne, Kelly O'Leary and Looney would set predawn alarms to exploit discounted ice at Valley Sports Arena in suburban Concord. "We would skate at 5:30 in the morning, and we would all show up," said Looney. "We skated early because we all had to go to work." Their motivation to improve was two-pronged: they were terrified of getting surpassed by Finland while also determined to close the gap with Canada. The hockey hustlers begged, borrowed and stole the best on-ice training they could find, cutting deals with the biggest names in the business. "We had Laura Stamm come out and do skating drills with us; we had Greg Carter come out and run us through drills," said Looney. "We would take anybody that would take us."

In October, just as countless students were preparing for midterms in Boston's myriad colleges, Team USA players were also cramming for tests. Their exam hall, however, was a collection of rinks near Ottawa, Ontario; their subject was an IIHF Three Nations tournament. Nagano's three podium favorites would square off multiple times in an Olympic medal-round preview. Whatever gains Team USA had made under Smith and Co. would be assessed on scoreboards throughout Ontario. It was Game On for the dawning of the Ben Smith women's hockey era.

Predictably, the Americans split their first two games: beating Finland and then losing to Canada, both games tightly contested. Game three was in the tiny village of Smiths Falls, an event that locals treated like a Beatles reunion concert: USA vs. Canada, a gold-medal preview in the town of 9,000. Ordinarily, memories of a seemingly insignificant 25-year-old round-robin match would be hazy at best. Smith remembers it because he shares a name with the town. Team USA goaltender Erin Whitten will never forget it.

"The fans were all over, on top of you," said Whitten, referring to the Smiths Falls Memorial Centre. A reported 1,650 fans showed up in a building with a 1,500 seat capacity. "I remember the atmosphere of the game, because it was this tight little rink *packed* with fans. I told my teammates that after the game I was going to celebrate because I knew this was going to be a great one. This was going to live on in my memory."

True to her word, Whitten stood tall against Canada despite the flood of Canadian fans rooting their lungs out for her demise. She allowed the opening goal late in the first period, and was forced to rely on her teammates to bail her out.

Shelley Looney, a Team Canada nemesis, did just that, tying the game late in the second. Then fifteen seconds into sudden death, Looney deflated the red and white balloon with an overtime dagger. Whitten would have her chance to stage the theatrical surprise she had planned after all. A postgame locker room filled with giddy mates provided the ideal stage.

"There was a Saturday Night Live character at the time, a Catholic schoolgirl, Mary Katherine Gallagher," said Whitten with a smile. "Every time she celebrated she did a lunge with her hands in the air. I told my teammates that after the game, if we won that game, that's what I was going to do."

So Whitten seized the moment, and in the center of the crowded locker room she executed the equivalent of a warrior yoga pose, thrusting her arms over her head and shouting out, "Superstar!"

Who could argue? It was just the second time in history that U.S. women had ever beaten Canada's national team. "I remember the laughter and the smiles coming over," said Whitten, still beaming a generation later. "It was one of those games where I had fun from start to finish. I never felt the pressure in that game because I always felt in control of it." Whitten, "America's Goalie," was the overwhelming favorite in the USA goaltending competition.

There was one member of the team, however, who was not reveling in the moment. Sarah Tueting was getting her first start in goal the next day, and she was already in the zone she referred to as "goalie world."

Team USA's hockey caravan crawled into Ottawa the next day for a game that had the makings of a real downer. Playing Finland only attracted a fraction of the audience, and the buzz from the night before had clearly worn off. A reported 250 fans showed up in dumpy Jim Durrell Arena. Coming off the previous night's historic upset, the Americans were facing what gamblers call a "trap game." Tueting would have none of it. The Ivy Leaguer had shelved a promising career in both music and medicine for such an opportunity. For her, this game in a hollow arena was the equivalent of a Stanley Cup showdown.

Tueting needed to be on high alert this night. Her teammates were just coming down from their thrilling upset of Canada less than 24 hours prior, and their energy had nearly flat-lined. In hockey terms, they hung their goalie out to dry.

"There were a ton of 1-on-0's and 2-on-0's," said Tueting, who flashed back to her spectacular ECAC playoff form from seven months prior. "I played really, really well against Finland. We should have lost that game. I think I won Player-of-the-Game." The 4-3 final score in favor of Team USA did not reflect the acrobatic goaltending from the rookie. It was a surprisingly high-stakes contest: Had she lost to Finland the day after Whitten beat Canada, Tueting might have been buried for good on Team USA's goaltending depth chart.

Tueting's performance—dodging a potential disaster through sheer will and skill—was not lost on the woman sitting atop Team USA's goaltending throne. The newcomer will never forget how Whitten spoke to her in the post-game, complaining that Tueting's seat location in the locker room was too close to the center. In Whitten's world, newbies should be relegated to the corner.

"I really want to be happy for you," Whitten said with mock sincerity, "but where you sat in the locker room, that was not OK. *You are still a rookie.*"

Tueting responded with her version of the truth. "I just played one of the best games I ever played. I kept us in the game, the only reason we won that game."

Although Team USA ultimately lost the Three Nations gold medal-game to Canada, it had clearly made the grade in its mid-term exam. By chipping away at Canada and staving off Finland, all metrics were pointing up.

From Team USA's standpoint, the biggest takeaway from the 1996 Three Nations Cup was the surprising development in the competition for sport's most important position. Goaltending was the presumed domain of the platinum blond with that Ellen Barkin[2] crooked smile. A day after Erin Whitten's greatest performance in a USA jersey, 14 months before the final Olympic cuts, she was suddenly facing a threat to her throne. Challenger Sarah Tueting had no intention of backing down.

---

2 Like Hollywood starlet Ellen Barkin, Erin Whitten was America's 'It Girl' of her genre in the 1990s, making national news by playing men's pro hockey in four different leagues. Represented by renowned agent Steve Bartlett, Whitten inked sponsorship deals with both Louisville and Met-Rx, making her a unicorn in women's hockey: She earned a decent living.

Silver Shackles

"In youth sports, everybody's got to get a trophy. I mean, that's ridiculous. If you're a winner, you're a winner and you get a trophy. If you got second place, you don't get anything."

**—Carli Lloyd,
two-time Olympic soccer gold medalist**

Despite Team USA's round-robin shocker in the 1996 Three Nations Cup, Team Canada restored order in international hockey by shutting out its neighbors 1-0 in the gold-medal game. It was a worn-out storyline for the perpetual bridesmaids–a game just close enough to ruin the day for the silver-medal Americans. The fact that the Team USA women had *never* won gold in any competition against Canada was creeping into their heads. "Silver again, silver again!" said Shelley Looney, a veteran who was getting brainwashed by the repetition. "The problem was that we expected that. We try and tell ourselves that we were ready, and ugh, didn't get the job done again."

The formal history between the two women's hockey nations is relatively short, and until 2005, had little nuance. Team Canada had won every World Championship gold medal from 1990 until the United States finally broke through in 2005. When Ben Smith took over Team USA in 1996, he objected to the term "rivalry."

"There's no rivalry," said Smith, who pointed out that rivalries aren't rivalries without competition. "Both teams have to win once in a while."

The first IIHF World Championship was held in Ottawa in 1990, an event with no shortage of pomp and circumstance.[3] Thanks to the Ontario Hockey Association and its tireless leader Fran Rider, Ottawa rolled out a red carpet for this historic event. Eight hockey nations were given royal treatment: entire hotel floors booked for each team, a massage therapist on call, and even some new equipment. "I was in awe," said America's humble scoring ace Cindy Curley. "Even the fact that you got a stick, 'Wow… great!' It was surreal. You couldn't imagine what would come next."

It kept getting better for Curley and company, as they roared into the gold-medal game to face Canada in an arena jammed with 9,000 fans. The Americans scored first, and then Curley slid in a backhand for a 2-0 lead. It was indeed surreal. And then it all came crashing down.

Team USA goalie Kelly Dyer was not sure what hit her when the host nation answered back. "When Canada scored their first goal, the cheering in the stadium was so intense that I could actually feel the vibration in my rib cage," said Dyer, who gave up three more goals in the 5-2 loss. During the official IIHF medal ceremony, the Americans found themselves standing on their own blue line, listening to "O Canada." It was a scene that would be repeated *ad nauseam* from the American standpoint. Team Canada ravaged the Americans in IIHF gold-medal games in the 1990s. After their original 2-0 deficit in Ottawa, the Canadians outscored the Americans 19-3 over the first three World Championships. Canada was a women's hockey force; the red maple leaf represented unquestioned dominance.

---

3 Tournament organizers chose to outfit Team Canada in pink uniforms for the inaugural World Championships, a one-time-only marketing experiment that was widely panned. The 1990 Worlds were also the only IIHF-sanctioned women's competition in which full-ice body checking was allowed, an exemption intended to level the playing field for the four European nations who employed that style at home. Like the pink uniforms, legal body checking was never seen again in women's IIHF games.

Forward Lisa Brown-Miller played in those inaugural 1990 Worlds, and her preconception of Canadian players was driven home. "Being a kid from Michigan, Canada is just across the border, and I'm living with this misnomer that Canadians are better at hockey than the United States," said Brown-Miller, who can never forget being spat upon by a Canadian rival in a youth hockey scrum. "That first World Championship in 1990; they win every time. It gets old. We're just as competitive, we just couldn't pull it together."[4]

Brown-Miller and her mates were clearly *not* competitive at the next World Championships two years later in Finland. Due to a lack of corporate sponsors, the women's Worlds were not an annual event in the 1990s. Although Team USA returned to the gold-medal game in 1992, it found itself outclassed by the rough-and-ready Canucks. "I remember it falling apart," said Dyer, who backed up UNH goaltending star Erin Whitten in the 8-0 massacre. Like their male counterparts, these Canadian players beat you on the scoreboard and in the alleys. "There was bitterness," said Colleen Coyne, who was exposed to the swaggering Canucks for the first time in the 1992 Worlds. "I mean, I don't even want to look at you in the hotel lobby."

In 1994, the IIHF staged the next women's World Championship in America's Miracle venue of Lake Placid. There was a buzz in the air at the Olympic Arena all week; the IOC had granted women's hockey a place in

---

4 The 1990 World Championships was a watershed moment for women's hockey. The eye-popping attendance figures, the bountiful TV ratings in Canada and the high-tempo action on the ice were all components of the presentation Murray Costello, of the Canadian Amateur Hockey Association, made to the IIHF at its annual congress one month later. He sought to instill the World Championships as an annual event and pave the way for women's hockey to be an Olympic medal sport in the future. When presented with highlights from the gold-medal game in Ottawa, the men who ran international hockey literally could not believe their eyes. "I told Murray Costello that I thought the video was speeded up," said future IIHF President Dr. Rene Fasel.

the next Winter Games in Nagano, scheduled for 1998. The Americans were also spurred by two elite stars who had just commuted down from Montreal. Cammi Granato and Karyn Bye had been extending their careers playing at Concordia University in Montreal.

USA Hockey's new Executive Director Dave Ogrean shook his Foundation's piggy bank for the funds to televise the gold-medal game nationally on cable. Fortune seemed to favor the Americans when Granato scored a tie-breaking goal late in the semifinal contest vs. Finland. It was no surprise that Canada would be waiting for them in the gold-medal game, this time bolstered by a 15-year-old wunderkind with the familiar last name: Hayley Wickenheiser.[5]

Barely an hour from the Canadian border, fans clad in red and white took over the house that Herb Brooks built, defeating the Americans comfortably, 6-3, despite highlight-reel goals from both Granato and Bye. Hockey's ubiquitous anthem "O Canada" echoed through America's Olympic Arena, and according to Bye, "silver" was now a four-letter word.

"Even though silver is better than bronze, you lost the game for it," Bye said with an edge in her voice. "You win the game to win the bronze, but you actually lose for silver. It's a tough loss to swallow." Bye, the sport's quintessential power forward, was just beginning her collection of silver medals. A slew of Three Nations and Four Nations tournaments, two Pacific Rim Championships and every IIHF World Championship had the exact same scenario play out at the end of the tournament's final game: Canadian players ducking their heads to receive gold; misty eyed Americans shaking their heads on the blue line. Bye has a shoebox at home, packed with IIHF silver medals that are less valuable to her than candy corn after Halloween. "Yeah, I got plenty of those."

---

5 Doug Wickenheiser, a distant cousin to Hayley, was the first overall National Hockey League draft pick by the Montreal Canadiens in 1980.

The IIHF would stage one more women's World Championship prior to the Nagano Games. April 1997, Kitchener, Ontario was circled on the calendars of every member of these two hockey superpowers. Yes, Ben Smith's new-look Yanks had impressed in the Three Nations event in Ottawa, yet they remained silver surfers once again. It was the presumed outcome every time they battled Canada.

The American girls had to park their respective appetites for revenge until the end of the season. They had plenty of work to do between November and April. In January 1997 the women got a much-needed change of scenery. The Chinese national team invited Team USA over for a series of exhibition games. With the Olympics being held in the Pacific Rim in just over a year, China was eager to invite one of the North American superpowers. It was a two-pronged mission for the hosts: 1) they wanted to drum up publicity for the only team sport in the Winter Games; and 2) they needed to learn whatever they could from the Americans.

From a Team USA player standpoint, it was a chance to experience some team-building on the other side of the planet and escape subsistence living in snow-packed Boston. There were on-ice challenges as well, they would be facing one of the world's great goalies in Guo Hong, the woman known as "The Great Wall of China." She acquired that moniker when she held Canada to a single goal out in San Jose. China's fourth-place finish in the '94 World Championships had its sports federation eager to contend for a medal in the inaugural women's Olympic hockey tournament.

The U.S. players' preconceptions of four-star living in Beijing hotels were soon dashed when the team arrived in China. The 12-day trip became an exercise in spartan living and team-building. Although the Great Wall of China is now the Communists' answer to Disney World, back in 1997, there were no plumbing facilities when Team USA took the one-hour detour to do some sightseeing. The Americans weren't sure if the hole in the floor was meant to substitute for a toilet. After much giggly debate, it took a sophisticated Harvard woman to take the first test-drive. "I was always hydrated," said A.J. Mleczko, who earned a ton of respect from her peers.

Once they finished their excursion, the Americans returned to Beijing Capital Airport in plenty of time for their flight to Harbin, China's winter sports capital. Team USA checked in, visas were processed, and then the players taxied out toward the runway. There they sat, and sat, and then sat some more. "We spent six hours on the tarmac," said Smith. Smoking was permitted on that flight. The athletes and coaches crammed socks and towels over their nose and mouth as masks, but it only got worse. They finally arrived in Harbin, but their equipment did not. For two days. When their gear eventually arrived, they discovered a small problem in their locker room: glass windows facing the street with no coverings. The players were forced to use extra jerseys, towels and old blankets to maintain a semblance of privacy. Team-building indeed.

The American women swept China, legit medal contenders for both the Olympics and the World Championships, a noteworthy accomplishment on the ice. But their shared resilience was the primary benefit from that memorable trip to the Far East.

As soon as Smith touched down in Boston, he intensified his NCAA scouting. He memorized the 60-mile stretch of Route 95 from Boston to Providence. The smallest state in the union paid enormous recruiting dividends for Smith, who had three prospects already penciled in for spots on his World Championship roster.

A mile-and-a-half northwest of the Rhode Island State House lay Providence College, the women's hockey superpower that had produced scoring legends Cindy Curley, Stephanie O'Sullivan and Cammi Granato. This 1996-97 season was the year of another fabulous Friar—Laurie

Baker. The sensational sophomore rang up an astounding 43 goals in 30 games for Providence, including five hat tricks. She was the undisputed women's Player of the Year, but her Friars couldn't beat cross-town rival Brown University.

Led by its firebrand coach Margaret "Digit" Murphy, the Brown Bears went undefeated in the 1996-97 ECAC regular season, defeating Providence twice by a combined score of 10-3. Smith found himself frequently atop College Hill in Providence, scouting in Brown's cavernous Meehan Auditorium. There he spied not one but two forces of nature. The first was Brown senior Katie King, a power forward known as "The Big Train." Her frightening forays down the wing left defenders and goalies scattered in her wake. She would celebrate her goals with a victory sprint on her tiptoes to punctuate the demolition.

Murphy's other dominant skater was a once-in-a-generation talent named Tara Mounsey. The word "awesome" is the most overused adjective in sports, but Mounsey generated awe in everyone who saw her play. And that awe spread to any sport she chose to play. In the world of Brown athletics, Mounsey is held in highest regard for her dominance in field hockey, owning all the career scoring records despite playing only two years. According to veteran New England Sports Network (NESN) broadcaster Bob Norton, Mounsey at age 15 was the best high school pitcher in the state of New Hampshire, male or female. The conjecture by NESN's popular color analyst might be dismissed as hyperbole, but there are also indisputable facts that chronicle Mounsey's greatness. In her senior year at Concord High, she was voted New Hampshire's high school hockey Player of the Year, the state's best, *including* the boys.

Mounsey was sad to miss the full body checking of boys' hockey in her next season at Brown. She toyed with older opponents, touring the ice unhindered. The freshman consistently wowed crowds with her rink-length rushes. As soon as Smith saw her, he was smitten, infatuated with her demeanor as much as her staggering athleticism. A physical brute, a glorious skater, and a ferocious competitor, Mounsey constituted a stunning package. Ivy Leaguers versed in the classics sensed she was created by the Muses, a demigod carved from New Hampshire granite.

Between her senior year at Concord High and her matriculation to Brown, Smith got her onto a national team touring Finland. It only confirmed what he knew in his gut: She was women's hockey's answer to Bobby Orr.

The number four is sacred in Boston, it represents a hockey deity that graced Boston Garden for nine glorious years and two Stanley Cup championships. Old-school fans, coaches, and players use Orr's name to insult cocky upstarts. "Who do you think you are, Bobby Orr?" It stops the posers in their tracks. Count Ben Smith as a member of the old guard who holds Orr as the benchmark of hockey greatness. The understanding is that there will never be another Bobby Orr. Yet Smith has no problem acknowledging that Mounsey is cut from the same cloth. The ability to play on ailing knees accentuates the analogy. "That's right," said Smith of the comparison, "that's who she was."

Smith can't recall if he was at Meehan Auditorium on February 5, 1997, when Digit Murphy's juggernaut bombarded Providence goalie Sara DeCosta with 49 shots, derailing the Friars 4-1 behind two goals from King and another from Mounsey. Murphy was playing chess with two queens, and their dominance propelled her Ivy Leaguers to upstage college hockey's Big Three of Providence, UNH and Northeastern.

Smith knew he had yet another dominant piece for his World Championship chess board, a 16-year-old who needed no scouting. Angela Ruggiero was a junior at the prestigious boarding school, Choate-Rosemary Hall. The 5-foot-9, 175-pound defender was already penciled into Smith's starting lineup. Smith had been awed by her combination of raw-boned strength and elite skating during his women's coaching debut in the summer of 1995, her first international event competing against women. Even at 15 Ruggiero was impossible to ignore. "There was never a reason to scout her after that '95 series in Finland," said Smith.

Ruggiero was yet another one of those multi-sport athletes whom Smith valued so highly. In the springtime, Angela was a shot-putter, Choate's all-time great. Her combination of footwork and power placed her within a fraction of the immortal 40-foot mark before she matriculated to Harvard. It was that strength that Smith was counting on from Ruggiero at the 1997 World Championships. He needed her to neutralize Canada's attack-dog ferocity around Team USA's net. With rugged bookends Mounsey and Ruggiero, physical intimidation would no longer be the Canucks' calling card.

Driving back to Boston, Smith daydreamed about how the addition of these four players—scoring machine Baker from Providence, Brown's dynamic duo of King and Mounsey and cartoon superhero Ruggiero—would impact the upcoming Worlds. The latest IIHF test before the Olympic Winter Games in Nagano was fast approaching. The United States now had the equivalent of a Fantastic Four to help thwart Canada's reign of terror in women's hockey.

IIHF World Championships, Kitchener, Ontario, April 1997

Despite being behind enemy lines, Team USA loved being in Ontario for the Worlds. "You knew that it was Canada," said Ruggiero, a wide-eyed teenager in her first major IIHF event. "That arena was packed, they knew the rules, they appreciated that they were the defending World Champs."

"I never experienced anything like that," said fellow newbie Baker. "I was in awe of the whole thing. To be part of something that everyone is watching. And to put on that jersey… there's no better feeling than to put on that USA jersey."

Baker wasted no time asserting herself in her first World Championship, scoring in Team USA's opener against Norway, a 7-0 romp in front of 3,100 noisy fans. It was a remarkable attendance figure considering the home team was not involved. The next day the Americans were shipped out to Brantford, where they met the dangerous Finns. Entering the third period with a seemingly safe 3-1 lead, goaltender Erin Whitten stumbled, allowing two goals in the final eight minutes, forced to settle for a tie. As fellow contenders in the B group, Finland was now tied with Team USA in the race to win their pool. Total goal-differential would now determine the winner. Losing out to the Finns would likely mean facing Canada in the semifinals, a scenario that had never happened before.

Farmed out to London two nights later for a game with Sweden, the Americans smoked the Scandinavians 10-0, all the while scoreboard-watching Finland versus Norway. The Finns beat their neighbors by an identical 10-0 score to create a razor tight finish in the B group standings. After the final tabulations, the IIHF declared USA the winner of the B group, based on having scored two more goals.

The Americans would face overmatched China in their semifinal, while the Finns would get their crack at Canada in the other semi. As predicted, the Americans easily subdued China, but Finland nearly ruined the party for the local organizers in its single-elimination semifinal with the hosts. Team Canada trailed early, and needed a last-minute goal by Vicki Sunohara to subdue the valiant Finns 2-1. It was the IIHF high-water mark for the Finnish hockey warriors known as the Suomi, who put a major scare into both the United States and Canada.

Despite Finland's gallant effort, the IIHF had its marquee gold-medal matchup: USA vs. Canada. Calling it a border war would not be an exaggeration if you asked Ben Smith. This was before the 2000s when so many

Canadians played NCAA hockey with and against their American counterparts. In the 1990s, the combatants were angry strangers in their high-stakes turf wars.

"The game in Kitchener was a showcase for the sport," said Smith. "I was always concerned about going into a game with Canada. This was never friendly. There was an ugly side of it, just teetering on the edge of "Hudson Bay Rules – guns and knives only."[6]

Canada coach Shannon Miller had scouted the Americans in the preliminary games, and was struck by their size. The four newcomers plus the 5-foot-10 veteran Kelly O'Leary made Team USA practices look like a scene from "Land of the Giants."

"They're putting some big strapping girls on skates out there with that USA jersey," said Miller. "But I'll stack up a skilled, intelligent player that can skate any day against a big bruiser. We'll just go around the Americans."

Game Day. This gold-medal showdown on the cusp of the inaugural women's hockey Olympics was given a massive buildup on Canada's sports network TSN, and over 6,200 lucky fans swarmed into Kitchener Memorial Auditorium for this sold-out event. The fans, most clad in red and white, never stopped cheering from the start of warmups.

Hockey's biggest names flocked to this see-and-be-seen spectacle: Don Cherry from Hockey Night in Canada, Jere Longman of the *New York Times,* and new IIHF President René Fasel all rolled into Kitchener, 67 miles west of Toronto. TSN's executives wore their Sunday best for their

---

6 The term "Hudson Bay Rules" refers to oft-violent hockey in which the referees refuse to blow their whistles, allowing the players to decide the game's outcome. Detroit Red Wings commentator and former NHL star Mickey Redmond suggests the term comes from the on-screen fighting in the classic John Wayne movie *The Quiet Man.*

peacock strut through the auditorium's concourse, delighted that their investment in women's hockey was now commanding the brightest spotlight imaginable.

The production team inside the TSN truck gave this gold-medal game its full international treatment: a pre-game show with highlights galore, patriotic sound bites, and shots of glittery medals under glass. The main event would exceed all expectations.

After warmups, Mounsey was positively geeked. "This is what it's all about," she said. "To go play in Canada is a really special opportunity. The fans, the program, they're so crazy about hockey up there, that's where you want to play." Before taking the ice, she glanced around the room, and made eye contact with Ruggiero. "Players like myself and Angela, we hadn't been embedded in that rivalry, and I think we brought a breath of fresh air in terms of confidence. We hadn't been beat down by Canada over the years, and it was like, 'Yeah, so what? Let's go play!'"

Led by all its young thoroughbreds, Team USA came out galloping, tilting the ice towards the Canadian goal for minutes at a time. But Canadian goaltender Lesley Reddon, the woman who wrested the top spot from the legendary Manon Rheaume, kept the game scoreless. And with just 24 seconds remaining in the period, Nancy Drolet ignited the crowd when she gave the hosts a 1-0 lead heading into the intermission.

The Americans were hardly deflated. Early in the second Alana Blahoski maneuvered a nifty backhander past Reddon to tie the contest. This started what Smith called a "back and forth taffy-pull" of a game. Every time Canada would score, the Americans would answer.

Canada's aging superstar Angela James redirected a puck behind Whitten with an obviously illegal high stick. Despite vehement protests by Smith and his assistant Tom Mutch, the referees allowed the goal to stand. Cameras caught Shannon Miller wearing a smirk, one that was quickly erased by Team USA's Stephanie O'Sullivan. She banged in a power-play goal from the top of the crease, and the game was tied at the second intermission. USA had won the period and had seized the momentum.

But the Canucks opened the third with their own power play, and the opportunistic Drolet pounded in her second goal of the evening to give Canada the lead in the final period. Pandemonium reigned in Kitchener. Heads began to drop on the U.S. bench. The veteran Americans had endured this nightmare too many times before. Canada now had the lead in its own building, playing as if those 20 gold medals in the velvet IIHF display were its birthright. For the Americans, the ticking clock and the tsunamic energy of Hockey Canada were both formidable enemies.

The rookie Baker became disoriented by the bedlam. "I never experienced anything like that," said Baker, her memories rock-solid a quarter century later. "You couldn't hear anything, couldn't hear your teammates in between whistles when you were trying to set something up. Loud, fiery, exciting, things I had never been a part of. I was in awe of the whole thing."

The energy of the young Americans helped flip the script. Three shifts after the Drolet goal, the irrepressible Katie King simply couldn't be moved from atop Reddon's crease, and willed the tying goal into the net. Her response was one that all of Hockey Canada would learn to loathe. The big-boned winger started running on the tips of her skates, sprinting into high gear past her teammates in a raw display of hockey joy. Her Team USA linemate and college rival adores the King celebration. "Seeing her run on her toes, with her hands in the air," said Baker, "it just added to the whole excitement of the tournament and the game. Watching it years later I chuckle every time. I went over to congratulate her and she ran right by me, the runaway train. I *loved* playing with her."

Fueled by newly acquired powerhouses King, Mounsey and Ruggiero, the Americans outmuscled Team Canada for the rest of the regulation, leaning on them, leveraging their size, playing a classic heavy game. There is an isolated highlight of Ruggiero at center ice mauling Canadian veteran Frances St. Louis, pounding her with the body, then finishing her with the stick. It was like a *National Geographic* film clip of a young lion vanquishing the old. It appeared that the Americans' time had finally come.

The horn sounded at the end of regulation with gold still up for grabs. Both teams headed to their respective locker rooms while the packed house simply buzzed in anticipation. "This is the best hockey game of the year, men or women," Fasel said in the concourse to anyone and everyone. Don Cherry gave a double thumbs up to the TSN audience, and the *Times* Longman typed furiously in the press box. Although the players were too engrossed to realize it, everyone else knew they were watching a watershed moment: Canada and the Americans were elevating women's hockey to new heights before their eyes.

There was a contrast of sentiments in the two locker rooms. "We have an opportunity to make history," Miller told the reigning champs before the sudden-death session. "We decide the ending. Let's go!"

The Americans, on the other hand, allowed negative history to creep into their minds during intermission. Rookie goalie Sarah Tueting hadn't played a minute in this tourney, so she studied the room instead. She didn't like what she saw.

"There was an energetic fear," said Tueting. "Katie [King] was one of the rookies, so there were a bunch of us of the younger generation that didn't feel that. But the overarching feeling was like, 'Here it goes again, here it goes again.' I felt it, and it was very strong.

"They're better than us.

"They're better than us.

"They always win.

"They're better than us."

The overtime reinforced all that negativity, when Kitchener's Memorial Auditorium became a house of horrors for the visitors. Canada swarmed Erin Whitten's goal. Team USA got whistled for a pair of penalties, and the fans sensed a kill like a Spanish crowd at a bullfight. Smith sent out veteran warrior Shelley Looney as the only forward on the 5-on-3 penalty kill, desperate to survive the onslaught. Looney nearly didn't make it back to the bench in one piece.

With Canada tightening the noose, the puck came out to Geraldine Heaney at the point for an uncontested slap shot. In desperation, Looney laid out to get in the shooting lane. She did not extend her legs, however; she went head first, like a base-runner trying to beat a throw. She arrived in time to intercept the puck, blocking the shot with her head. A sickening thud silenced the crowd. Looney lay prostrate on the ice, motionless. "She always put herself in front of pucks," said linemate Baker, who had a perfect view of the frightening incident. "It didn't sound good. Oh God, it was concerning."

Trainer Brad Stephens carefully removed her face mask and checked for consciousness. Looney opened her eyes, recognized Stephens, and to his relief, spoke. "Wow, my face really hurts," said Looney, the left side of her head beginning to swell. "I think I got hit with the puck."

She was assisted to the bench, where Ben Smith looked down at the woman he couldn't win without. "Do you know where you are?" Looney gave a tiny nod, which was all the affirmation Smith needed. "OK, you're up next."

Three months later, Looney told Ken Campbell of *The Hockey News* that she remembered sitting on the bench saying to herself, "I'm going to go out and score that goal," while also listening to her own survival instincts. "Oh my God, I can't believe what I'm doing. I hope nobody comes near me."

Looney's display of courage – courage bordering on insanity – hardly surprised her teammates. "That's Shelley," said Baker. "Her legs were fine, her arms were fine, she was going back out. That was just her."

Ultimately, Looney never had to test her injured face, which turned out to be a shattered cheekbone. Canada's latest national hero, Nancy

Drolet, found a loose puck in a frenzied skirmish atop the U.S. crease, punched it in to complete her hat trick, and turned the Auditorium into a red and white madhouse. TSN director Susy Antal flashed a montage of unforgettable images from the post-game mania: Hayley Wickenheiser pumping her arms frantically in a victory dash to the blue line; Shannon Miller, a vision in black, punching the sky with a closed fist; the Canadian flag slowly being hoisted to the rafters. It seemed as if their entire hockey nation belted out the words to *O Canada*.

TSN needed a final "agony of defeat" shot to complete its coverage, and an opportunistic cameraman locked onto Karyn Bye standing sullenly at the blue line, and began a slow zoom into her face. Bye was biting her glove, eyes red rimmed, face flushed. A tear began its slow journey down her cheek. For the umpteenth time, Bye and her mates were shackled in silver chains.

"It was just gut-wrenching," said Bye. "You put your blood and guts and heart into a game, and then you lose? It was so frustrating. Even the parents were like, 'What do we say to the girls?' They didn't even know what to say to us anymore. I think only athletes that have experienced that before can know what you're going through."

Champagne and cigar smoke poured through the Canadian locker room. Old tropes were trotted out, players spoke about having bigger hearts and the superior will to win. Those comments were chopped into sound bites and then broadcast coast-to-coast throughout Canada. But the eyewitnesses knew that there had been a shift in hockey's balance of power. Canada's sporting bible, *The Hockey News,* published it in black and white. "The Americans were the better team. They were faster, stronger, and in superior condition."

USA Hockey executive director Ogrean phrased it more diplomatically when he spoke about their inevitable Olympic rematch. "This gold medal in Nagano is going to be a competition, not a coronation."

Don Cherry, the jingoistic voice of Canadian hockey, lost his heart to the enemy after witnessing Looney's ultimate sacrifice with gold on the line. "I gotta say that I love those American girls," gushed Cherry after this game for the ages.

Team USA didn't have time to contemplate moral victories. The players piled into their bus for the depressing seven-hour ride back to Lake Placid. No one wore their silver medal. Ruggiero needed to be back at prep school the next morning, so after a cat-nap at the National Training Center, she crammed some clothes into a duffel bag and bummed a ride to the Choate School in Wallingford, Connecticut. She arrived just as morning assembly let out.

She hustled up to her advisor, Tom Generous, apologizing for being late and missing classes the past week. Generous had a newspaper tucked under the elbow of his tweed sportscoat. He looked up at Ruggiero and said, "I know exactly where you've been," and proceeded to unfold a fresh copy of that morning's *New York Times*, dated Monday, April 7, 1997. There on the front page of America's newspaper of record was a large picture of Ruggiero in her Team USA jersey for the whole world to see.

A Star
is Made

The undersized eighth-grader paused in the lobby of Braemar Arena in Edina, Minnesota. It was the fall of 1993, and the start of hockey season was just a few weeks away. There was a colorful flier next to all the hockey want ads and beer-league notices. Little Jenny read and then re-read the official notice from USA Hockey: Women's hockey would be a medal sport in the 1998 Winter Olympics. The news struck a chord, one that hummed through her entire being. With no one by her side, the shy tomboy began to speak.

"I'm going to be there," she whispered to herself. "I'm going to be on that team." The fact that she had played only one season of organized hockey didn't mute her ambition, nor did the fact that she hadn't grown an inch since she was measured at 5-foot-3 in fifth grade. Her dad Dwayne would help. Using all the resources available in America's premier hockey state, Jenny Schmidgall would not be deterred.

She already had an athlete's core from living the sporting life in suburban Minneapolis. "Me and my sisters would go to the outdoor rink and skate a lot," said Jenny, who embraced the action far more than her sisters did. "I was the tomboy, loved physical sports, tackle football, hockey. I loved it." In wintertime, the Schmidgall parents would walk their three daughters down to Lewis Park in Edina, one of hundreds of parks in Minnesota with a set of boards for pick-up hockey.

Jenny and her two sisters Stephanie and Amber would fool around with sticks and pucks in the makeshift rink until the older guys would divide into teams and start keeping score. Her big sisters would peel off, making way for the serious recreation that is Minnesota hockey. But not Jenny. Former pros who settled in the area—NHL veterans like Bobby Smith and Gordie Roberts—would frequently be among the neighborhood guys throwing sticks into the middle of the ice. Having pros in the park was business as usual in the Minneapolis suburbs. Little Jenny, unlike her older sisters, was undaunted. "I'm the one that was super passionate, setting my sights toward making that Olympic team."

In the four-year runup to Nagano, Dwayne Schmidgall became his daughter's tireless trainer and advocate as Jenny set out on her quest. The Olympic Dream was her guiding star and the oceans of available ice in the Twin Cities kept her on course.

After his daughter played her first season for the Minnesota Thoroughbreds girls' team, Dwayne Schmidgall signed her up for boys' hockey with Edina's Bantam B squad. But her primary classroom was right in her neighborhood—Lewis Park in the great outdoors. "I basically lived there," said Jenny Schmidgall-Potter, who took her husband Rob's last name. Decades later the two Potters were still taking to the ice to train prospects.

Schmidgall-Potter proudly recalled her days as a rink-rat, the kid who fearlessly jumped into pickup games with men. Hockey was a lot more fun when she possessed the puck, so she dedicated herself to mastering the art.

"It came from playing with a bunch of men all the time. They were all over me, always bigger and faster," said Schmidgall-Potter, who was forced to innovate. "I had to use my brain, my quickness, try to figure out how to get the puck, moving all the time."

With the Olympics on her radar, she and Dwayne poured it on, seeking out open hockey sessions throughout the Twin Cities. "Victory Memorial Ice Arena, Richfield Ice Arena, New Hope Arena, Bloomington Ice Garden," recalled Schmidgall-Potter, reeling off the rinks that now swirl in the helix of her DNA. "Those were your typical rinks where you would play late-night hockey."

Thanks to the lure of Olympic gold, USA Hockey jumped into an arms race with Canada, the two hockey neighbors creating national junior teams to train and then battle in the off-seasons leading up to Nagano. In the summer of 1995 Jenny found herself filling out a roster on America's first girls national junior team, spending a week in July training with strangers from New England before playing Canada up in Ontario. There is a post-practice photo of that inaugural U.S. team, a sea of mostly forgettable faces framed around a handful of future Olympians, including Tara Mounsey and Angela Ruggiero. Jenny was visible smirking in the second row, apparently unsure of where she fit in.

"It would probably be considered a U-18 team now, but it was just a bunch of 15-year-old girls," Schmidgall-Potter said. A week after that photo was taken, Ruggiero was invited to participate with the big girls at Ben Smith's inaugural national team camp; Schmidgall returned to Edina. She was invited back to Lake Placid the following summer, serving once again as fodder for a hockey nation without much depth in the girls' junior ranks. The undersized center did not cast a long shadow. "I never made the national team."

While Jenny continued her anonymous mission back in the Twin Cities, junior-camp colleagues Mounsey and Ruggiero appeared in the monumental 1997 World Championships in Kitchener. Being left off that squad didn't trouble Jenny, she was not concerned with events beyond her control, content to keep her world small. "I was naive and oblivious to it all," said Schmidgall-Potter, who graduated from Edina High six weeks after the thrilling gold-medal game in Kitchener. "I was only 18, just coming out of high school. Being a kid in a small, little world, I just kept it simple."

Simply hockey, that is. For Jenny, the summer of 1997 was an exercise in extremes. The late NBA star Kobe Bryant stoked his legend one year earlier than Schmidgall's summer of growth, training like a fiend in Southern California before his debut with the Lakers. Bryant spent 16-hour days driving up and down the West Coast, seeking out the highest levels of competition while he forged the rough draft of his Hall-of-Fame identity. Ditto Jenny. The only limits to the amount of work Schmidgall put in each day that summer were the 7½ hours of sleep she got each night. Just like Kobe, Jenny's summer of '97 wasn't considered work; it was purely a labor of love.

Monumental life achievements are often accompanied by good fortune, and such was the case with Schmidgall that fateful summer. Jack Blatherwick was one of the world's great sports physiologists, the man Herb Brooks considered indispensable from the moment they connected at the University of Minnesota. Brooks kept Blatherwick at his side with the Gophers, at the Lake Placid Miracle and during his tenure with the NHL's New York Rangers.

In 1997, Blatherwick had just been granted seed money from a USOC grass roots program known as the Community Olympic Development Authority (CODA). This was the inaugural year of a national initiative that pumped up both summer and winter Olympic athletes across America: volleyball in Springfield, Missouri; team handball in Atlanta; and women's hockey in Minneapolis. "An absolute godsend for USA Hockey," said executive director Ogrean. Blatherwick and former Gopher gym rat Rob Potter oversaw 80 of the best girls high school hockey players in the state, endowing them with elite training both on and off the ice.

CODA's first summer session in the Twin Cities featured some of the biggest names in the annals of American women's hockey: future U.S. Hockey Hall-of-Famers Schmidgall, Krissy Wendell and Natalie Darwitz, as well as national team fixture Winny Brodt. As an elder member in this group of high schoolers, Schmidgall became a surrogate counselor while soaking up everything Blatherwick and Potter threw at her. A year later, Potter and Schmidgall began dating, and were later married. But it was hockey, not romance, that quickened Jenny's pulse in the summer of '97.[7]

Her typical day that summer began like most kids, hovering over a bowl of cereal in the kitchen. After dropping her dish in the sink, Jen would glide down to the basement, put on a pair of hockey mitts, and greet her dad, who was wearing goalie pads. "We had an underground garage, he would play goalie," said Potter, recalling fond memories from a generation prior. "I would deke, shoot and stickhandle."

Days were measured by the reduction of the wooden blade on her stick, worn down by thousands of reps in both the basement and the local tennis courts. "We had hard plastic pucks, the kind that slide on smooth cement and the tennis court." After bruising up her dad, the two would hop in the family's silver Geo sedan and make the 20-minute drive to Augsburg University.

Blatherwick and Rob Potter would be waiting every Monday, Wednesday and Friday, looking to employ the latest techniques on this small army of willing subjects. Overspeed training, bodyweight plyometrics, Russian-box passing drills, all innovations at the time, were used to improve strength and performance. Ninety minutes on the ice, a lunch break for a

---

7 "In the winter of 1998-99, we found ourselves sitting next to each other at a fund-raising dinner," said husband Rob. "We started dating after that." Their first child, Madison, was born on January 5, 2001. In her last major tournament as Jennifer Schmidgall, the determined center was the fourth-leading scorer in the 2001 World Championships with 10 points in five games. Her performance came less than four months after giving birth.

peanut-butter sandwich and an apple, and then dry-land shooting drills for an hour were Jen's daily routine.

Future husband Potter demanded constant repetition. "Area shooting, firing pucks into corners, facing your body multiple ways," said Rob, "nothing too fancy." Sports neurologists preach repetition, because after several thousand reps, myelin sheaths are created around the neural passageways from the brain to specific muscle groups. Jenny fired so many pucks that summer that she could literally one-time a shot in her sleep; the sheaths had been formed.

After returning from CODA, Schmidgall would get in some more strength training. "My dad would work with me, he really stressed doing pushups and pull-ups," said Jenny. "Upper body strength is the biggest thing, especially for females." Schmidgall learned that the resulting power had a two-fold effect. "Making myself stronger, not only physically, but mentally."

Dwayne Schmidgall was not a hockey lifer. In fact, he learned to skate from Jen's mom Terri. But he was sports-oriented, and knew how important hockey was in the region. "He taught himself how to play hockey, he loved bike riding, studied a lot of sports, very intuitive," said Jenny, who had earned the equivalent of a hockey Ph.D. herself. "He saw my drive to want to be on that [1998] team, and helped me the best way that he could. Maybe he didn't have all the answers, but he gave me the tools to achieve my dreams."

After all the dry-land and strength work, Jenny replenished back in the kitchen. "My parents were big on having some kind of veggie salad, fruit, and protein for dinner." Then father and daughter each grabbed their bags of gear and jumped back in the Geo. It was time to play with the men.

"My dad played in men's hockey leagues; he brought me into the fold," Schmidgall-Potter said. Dwayne and his "mini-me" daughter would team up and play beer-league hockey deep into the night at Bloomington Ice

Garden. "It might start at nine o'clock, and we'd go as long as they let us, sometimes as long as 11 o'clock." Jenny and Dwayne didn't rush home, either. Filled with endorphins and fading adrenaline, dad might sip a beer while Jen sat quietly absorbing the scene, decompressing to the smells and sounds of hockey.

Her head would hit the pillow a few blinks before midnight, and she would repeat the process all over again the next morning. When CODA wasn't in session, she and her dad would fill those gaps with drop-in hockey on Tuesdays and Thursdays, game action that supplemented her Sunday scrimmages with CODA. Jenny was the alpha leader of the girls, a puck-hunter with the men, and a sponge for every drop of hockey sense that flowed like waterfalls throughout the Twin Cities.

At some point that summer, Schmidgall learned that one of her USA junior coaches, Laura Halldorson, now the first coach of University of Minnesota women, had awarded her the first scholarship ever bequeathed to a female player at the U. The Gophers were commencing on their first varsity women's campaign in 1997-98, and Minneapolis native Halldorson got a sense of Potter's elite skills a few years before the rest of the hockey world. "She was the ultimate rink-rat," said Halldorson with a laugh. "She just loved hockey; that's why she played so long. She was a pond-hockey kid. That's where she got some of her tricks. She was good on the puck."

To any other women's player in the Twin Cities, receiving the first scholarship at Minnesota would have been an historic honor, a thrill of a lifetime. It barely registered with young Schmidgall. She had her Olympic blinders on, and college hockey, even a spot on the vaunted Golden Gophers, meant little to her. Schmidgall, who still looked like a middle-schooler, had narrowed her focus into a laser beam. Surprisingly for someone so committed to an all-encompassing sports goal, there was simply no tension in her game. "I just went out and played; I loved it."

Jenny Schmidgall arrived in Lake Placid on August 20, 1997 for the USA Hockey's Women's National Festival. She had straight blond hair, fair skin and perfectly symmetrical features. Despite girl-next-door looks, Schmidgall kept her smile to herself. She was all business in Lake Placid.

USA's national governing body had rounded up 54 players to divide into three teams. Twenty-five would survive, making up the national team that would eventually be cut down to twenty Olympians before Christmas. Schmidgall, now known as "Schmiggy," was just another body to fill out the ranks, and a small one at that. The official USA Hockey literature listed her generously at 5-foot-4. Going into this Festival, Schmidgall was but an afterthought, barely on the radar among her in-state rivals.

"There were a couple of Minnesotans, Alana Blahoski and Jeanine Sobek," said Potter. "We didn't skate a ton together." Blahoski, who had a noteworthy goal in the recent IIHF World Championship game, would have been a logical skater to compare herself to in the competition for precious Olympic berths. But Schmidgall never played that game. "I didn't know her, I didn't worry about who I needed to beat out. I always had the mentality that I wanted to beat everyone."

There were two days of practice before scrimmages began, and Smith couldn't help but notice the sprite that constantly wedged herself into the front of the drill lines. "She would always be first," Smith said laughing, "annoyingly so to her teammates, which made me like her right away." After practices the women would return to the National Training Center, then maneuver into comfortable social hierarchies based on experience and presumed status. Jenny ignored them all and laced up her roller blades, choosing to tour the paved Adirondack trails on eight wheels rather than gossip with the players. Surrounded by all these sophisticated women from

Eastern colleges, hockey was Jenny's only comfort zone, and she immersed herself. "She would practice as long as I kept a whistle in my hand," said Smith.

Halldorson was at the Festival to help Smith evaluate dozens of women who were essentially strangers to him, hoping to prevent another player like Gretchen Ulion from slipping through the cracks. Halldorson knew Schmidgall's game better than anyone, yet she was surprised at the player Jenny had become after her summer of puck love.

Schmidgall began to control long stretches of the scrimmages when she had the puck in the deep corners of Lake Placid's Olympic-sized ice sheet. "Using her body to shield the puck, it was hard to take it away from her," said Halldorson. "Her strength was her hands. The way she was able to stickhandle and pass the puck, she had a good sense of the game."

But it was Schmidgall's attitude that prompted her ultimate moment from that crucial '97 camp, a moment that helped facilitate her Olympic dream four years earlier than anyone imagined. It came when a fellow candidate, a defender for a different scrimmage team, got injured. Jenny was on Team White, which had the evening off when Team Red and Team Blue squared off towards the end of the Festival. One of the squads would be forced to play shorthanded. The incredibly shy Schmidgall stepped up, and finally spoke. "If you're looking for more players, I'll do it,' said the reticent 18-year-old. "I can play defense."

Potter recalls that turning point with clarity. "I'm sure people were worried that if they played more than somebody else, they might be tired. But I didn't even think about that. I was just, *Hey, I get to play more hockey, I love it!*"

So Schmidgall played defense by night, forward by day. And at the end of the Festival, she was impossible to ignore. Unlike Schmidgall, veteran Lisa Brown-Miller spent her downtime calculating, assessing how many centers could be taken, and the math was not in her favor. She feared her Olympic dream would be shattered by this shy stranger.

"My biggest threat to make the team was Jenny Schmidgall," said Brown-Miller, her angst still resonating a quarter-century later. "I remember thinking at the time, 'Who is this?' I mean, she's played like three weeks of pond hockey and she's a phenom. She was just 15 at the time."

In reality, Schmidgall was a very young looking 18-year-old, having played just four years of organized hockey. Throughout her Hall-of-Fame career, she sat through dozens of national team cut days, most of them are homogenized within her memory. But she will never forget Tuesday August 26, 1997, the stroke of midnight, inside the Olympic Training Center.

"We were in the gymnasium. We're all on the bleachers," said Potter. "They came in to announce who had made the roster. I'm pretty sure it was alphabetical, and my name was towards the bottom. Your heart's beating, your blood is pounding, you can barely hear." Finally, she heard it, the unusual German name that was commonly mispronounced. "Schmidgall." She was the youngest forward selected. The staff decided to keep five centers, accommodating both Lisa Brown-Miller and the precocious teen.

"She wasn't one of the top players that was chosen, but she surprised a lot of people," said Halldorson. "When we were getting down to the tough decisions, she really made a case for herself by the way she played." Four years after setting her outrageous goal at Braemar Arena in Edina, little Jenny had done it, thanks to a summer-long assist from her dad. With Dwayne at her side, she absorbed every nuance, every detail America's State of Hockey had to offer.

Schmidgall and the other 24 players who survived the cut quickly exited the bleachers, dashing off to make calls, celebrate quietly, and escape the stress of the gym. The 29 victims remained seated, talking to Smith and assistant Mutch about what went wrong, quietly pondering the possibility of life without hockey. "It was a shock," said Potter, with a trace of survivor's guilt. Despite the late hour, she ran to one of the two payphones in the lobby. "I couldn't wait to call my parents and share the great news with them." Their elation was tempered due to the immense amount of work Jenny had put in. To the Schmidgalls, their daughter had simply received her just desserts.

"Congratulations," said Dwayne, with no hysteria. "You deserved it, you worked hard." That midnight moment, late in the summer of '97, was the culmination of a remarkable journey for this father-daughter team. Their incessant routines had produced a worthy 1998 Olympic candidate in the short term, and one of America's all-time greats over the long haul.

Early the next morning the Training Center was a hub of emotional transition. A CBS camera crew was setting up in a dorm room adjacent to red-eyed players grabbing duffel bags and exiting to an unfamiliar world colored by uncertainty. Future Team USA captain Krissy Wendell, two weeks shy of her 16th birthday, took a clear-eyed look around before grabbing her ride to Boston's Logan Airport. A budding star, she was secure in the knowledge that she would return.

Not so for Meaghan Sittler, a forward who had played four years for Halldorson at Colby College. Her dad, Hockey Hall-of-Famer Darryl Sittler, was pacing the halls, venting to both Smith and Halldorson at the perceived injustice. Eventually the tremors quieted, peace slowly returned, and the surviving players took turns sitting for their interviews.

Schmidgall spent most of her network debut staring at her shoes, choking out mostly monosyllabic responses. "I was only 18, just coming out of high school," she said. "Who likes public speaking? Not me."

Although few realized it at the time, the career of one of America's all-time greats had just begun. The woman who was inducted into USA Hockey's Hall of Fame in 2021 was en route to the first of her four Olympic tours. To insiders familiar with Potter's level of play in the 2010's, there is little doubt she could have been the first American to play on five

Olympic hockey teams. But she never got the chance to try out for the 2014 Games in Sochi.

Potter was Team USA's leading scorer at the 2010 Games in Vancouver, an irresistible force as a 31-year-old mother of two in her fourth Winter Games. In 2012 she was coaching Trinity College women in Hartford, working out religiously while coaching the Bantams. The *New York Times* featured Potter in a two-page spread, spotlighting her innovative training on a trampoline. But when it came time to head to the 2013 Festival in Lake Placid, she was informed that USA Hockey was committed to a youth movement, and her services, as profound as they might be, were no longer required. She retired as Team USA's all-time leading Olympic scorer.

Team USA missed a gold medal in Sochi by the narrowest of margins. A single goal by Potter against Canada, a hockey nation that both feared and revered her, would have brought home gold for the Yanks. Potter has reconciled whatever injury her pride may have suffered from that missed opportunity, and continued to coach and develop players with the same passion and intensity with which she played.

Prior to her induction into the U.S. Hockey Hall of Fame, Ben Smith praised the prodigy he coached to three Olympic medals. "She was so thorough, just a pure hockey machine," said Smith, a touch of awe in his voice. "I've never come across a player where their love of the game is greater. I'd want her on any team I ever coached."

Golden
Girl

"You think the calm defines her. . . that she is all fragility and grace. But this quiet one is lion-hearted, and when that ferocity wakes she is a warrior without a drop of surrender in her veins."

—Amanda Shea, Poet

Her teammates were already on the ice, loosening up by skating around the rink before a December practice sandwiched between the heartbreaking final roster cuts and a game with the archrival Canadians. Shelley Looney was the last to step onto the ice. A 5-foot-5 veteran of three World Championships, Looney's strawberry blond hair and a smattering of freckles across her button nose disguised her warrior persona. But she was not equipped for the loud encounter with the boss after Ben Smith made a bee-line toward her.

"Why are you late?" her coach asked.

Looney froze. She was surprised by the confrontation because she wasn't late. But she knew the rules – even the unwritten ones in her coach's world. Like, if you aren't early to a practice or a meeting or a team meal, then you're late. And Smith hated tardiness.

"I was waiting for the trainer," Looney said.

"Get off the ice," Smith said. "And leave your jersey on the bench."

Now she was shaken to the core. Team USA was scheduled to play Canada the next night – always a titanic event that every player embraced. Suddenly, Looney wondered if she would ever get a chance to play another game with the national team.

"I thought for sure I was going to get cut," Looney confessed in an interview more than two decades later.

After a restless night tormented by anxiety, Looney showed up for the morning skate – early – only to discover that she would wear "the sit-out jersey" of a player designated to watch from the press box as her teammates competed. She did not skate with her regular linemates. Smith didn't say a word to her during the practice, but that afternoon he summoned Looney to meet with him.

He knew he had pushed one of his better players about as far as he could without causing permanent damage to her fragile psyche. Despite her unique skill set – consider how many other players could be so lethal on the power play at one end of the ice, and on the other be willing to sacrifice herself by blocking an opponent's slapshot *with her face* – Shelley Looney had not been blessed, or burdened, by an overabundance of confidence.

Remarkably, Looney often wondered if she truly belonged among this talented group of women. At times, the chronic self-doubt she suffered would affect her performance to such a point that Smith went out of his way to remind her just how good she was. Looney remembered one such moment. It was the day after the preliminary cuts when her best friend and college roommate, Jeanine Sobek, was sent packing. Looney remains convinced to this day that Sobek should have made the team in her place.

"I was pretty bummed out," Looney recalled, "and at practice the next day we were working on the power play and I wasn't out there and I am wondering, *What is going on?*"

That's when Smith skated over to her and asked, "Do you know who on this team has the most points against Canada?'

"Cammi Granato," Looney quickly responded.

"Nope," Smith said.

"Karyn Bye?"

"Nope."

"Then I don't know," she shrugged. "Who is it?"

"You, Shelley," Smith said. "You have more points against Canada than anyone else on our team."

"Really?" Looney stood there for a moment, not knowing how to respond as Smith skated away.

"Honestly, I had no idea," she said, "because that's not something I would ever pay attention to."

The 30-second conversation worked wonders.

"He knew my state of mind right then," she said. "It was his way of giving me a little kick in the butt and telling me I belonged there and let's get going."

Suddenly, Shelley Looney was feeling pretty good about herself again, and it showed in her performance in Nagano. The best players perform their best in the biggest games, and none were bigger for Team USA than those against that team from Up North.

"So I had a lot of points against Canada," Looney recalled many years later. "Somehow, I guess. . ."

Now Smith was preparing to meet with Looney again after sending her off the ice, sans practice jersey, for being – by his standard – tardy for a practice. He knew full well that his player at that moment would have been more inclined to step off a bridge rather than cross it. Like most successful coaches, he knew which buttons to press on each of his players, how far he could push them in what manner to get them, and his team, where he knew they could be. He also knew Looney was at a precipice.

"So how are you doing?" Smith asked

"I'm trying," she said, fighting and failing to hold back a torrent of tears.

"Look, Shelley, I wish it wasn't you," Smith said, explaining that he felt his team was getting too lax, taking too much for granted when so much was at stake and nothing yet was certain, in terms of selecting a final Olympic roster. He needed to make a point, to send a loud and overt message to every player.

"I didn't want to do it," Smith continued. Then, after breaking her down completely, he began to build her back up. "Shelley, you're like an old dog by my side. You'll always be there for me."

And of course she was. Of that they were both certain.

"He knew I'd always be there," she said, "willing to do anything he asked me to do."

The daughter of a working-class family in a Downriver Detroit suburb, Shelley Looney is proud of her blue-collar roots. Her Tennessee-born father Carl worked at Great Lakes Steel, whose century-plus old blast furnaces made the steel that built America. Her mother Linda, from North Carolina, was a hair-dresser. Both came north, migrating like thousands of other Southern families lured by high-paying jobs in the factories that turned out most of the world's automobiles.

They made their home in Trenton, a city of about 18,000 that borders the Detroit River. Residents can look south across that expansive Great Lakes waterway and see Windsor, Ontario. Canada, where hockey was born and eventually spread across the border into Michigan. But to Linda and Carol Looney, ice hockey was about as foreign as ice fishing.

Trenton, they would soon find out through their children, is serious hockey country in Southeast Michigan. It has produced at least a half-dozen NHL players. It's also the hometown of an improbable young recording artist whose love-letter to Canada stands in stark contrast to the dagger she stuck into the hearts of all Canadian hockey fans when an Olympic gold medal was at stake. As great ironies go, it belongs on Mount Rushmore.

It began when Shelley was eight years old – two years into her own hockey career – when six American diplomats who had evaded capture during the Iran hostage crisis were rescued by a joint CIA-Canadian effort on January 27, 1980.

On that day, those six remained in hiding at the home of the Canadian diplomat John Sheardown, under the protection of Canadian Ambassador Ken Taylor. In late 1979, the government of Prime Minister Joe Clark secretly issued an order allowing Canadian passports to be issued to some American citizens so that they might escape. In cooperation with the CIA, which used the cover story of a film project, two covert agents and the six American diplomats boarded a Swissair flight to Zurich, Switzerland, on January 28. Their rescue from Iran was dramatized in the 2013 Oscar-winning film *Argo*.

Another 52 U.S. diplomats and citizens were held hostage for 444 days, finally released on January 20, 1981, the day Ronald Reagan succeeded Jimmy Carter as President of the United States. But a year earlier, Americans were supremely grateful for the cloak-and-dagger operation that freed those other six who had eluded the Iranian kidnappers.

Renowned local DJ Johnny Williams, whose mammoth 50,000-watt rock station CKLW (AM-800) in Windsor built prolific audiences on both sides of the Detroit River, hatched an idea he knew would play well to every listener in both countries.

He penned a loving thank-you note to Canada, and he figured the hockey-mad little girl down his street would be the perfect voice to deliver it.

"After he wrote it, he came over and asked my mom if I would be willing to record it," Looney said. "I was young and just excited to do something fun."

So at age 8, Looney became a recording artist with a single released by Mercury Records in March 1980. The spoken-word record received some airplay and made Cashbox's Top 100 (two weeks at No. 99) and it bubbled just under the Billboard Top 100 charts, topping at 109 in the States. Here are the lyrics to "(This Is My Country) Thank You, Canada" that she read over a background of schmaltzy patriotic music:

> *Dear Canada,*
>
> *I'm writing this letter to thank you for helping move the six Americans in Iran. I'm not the only one writing you a letter. All my friends are too.*
>
> *Oh yeah, I almost forgot, my name is Shelley, I'm eight years old. Today it seems all Americans are smiling because of what you did. Just when it seemed like we didn't have any friends, there you were!*
>
> *My brother Bill's in the Army. He called home and said Canada was a good friend and in this bad time we need all our friends. I never visited your country, but I've seen pictures of it and it's beautiful — and I do love hockey!*
>
> *I don't know why that man with a beard* [Ayatollah Khomeini] *doesn't like us, but I'm glad you do.*
>
> *Oh-Oh, I have to go cuz my mom's calling me for dinner and I have homework to do. Well, tonight when I go to bed I'll pray to God that he will bless you for what you did.*

P.S. Canada, you have a special place in my heart and my country."

As it turned out, just two years later Canada would break Looney's little heart. It happened during her first visit across the border to play in a hockey tournament. When she was whistled for a penalty, the referee realized that Shelley was the only girl competing with and against all boys, most of them ten years old. She served her penalty, stepped on the ice and was immediately whistled for another penalty. And then a third, by which time even the crowd was yelling, "Let the girl play!"

There was no shortage of irony in the fact that this little cherub, who had honored Canada with a heartfelt and widespread thank-you recording, was being abused by a Canadian official. There she sat in the penalty box crying, wondering, "'Why won't he let me play?' I couldn't figure it out, you know? I was just a hockey player. I wasn't a *female* hockey player back then."

And there began a love-hate relationship between Looney and Canada, one that served her well all the way to Nagano and beyond.

Pressed on vinyl as a 45 rpm single, her recording was well-received and enjoyed moderate success in regional sales. But it was fairly panned by *Billboard* writer Alan Jones.

"The whole record reeks of false sentimentality and runs in at just one minute 28-seconds – appalling value at all levels. Shelley gushes that she hears that Canada is a beautiful country, and in an effort to endear herself to the Canucks says she 'really loves hockey.'"

Unbeknownst to Jones, of course, that might have been the most sincere line in the entire record. Just shy of her 50th birthday, Looney vaguely recalled that she might have made 500 dollars from that recording. Much more memorable, she said, was the fact that she got to be in a parade.

Years and decades followed, during which friends and acquaintances conducting a Google search would occasionally come across that story and her recording.[8] Those from Canada who remember her goal in Nagano find it more than ironic. "Then they really try to stick it to me," said Looney with a sardonic giggle. She had, after all, really stuck it to them.

In August of 2005, months after winning her first IIHF World Championship gold medal, 33-year-old Shelley Looney was cut by Ben Smith for the 2006 Olympic roster. The loyal warrior had played 151 games for USA Hockey, scoring 61 goals and 136 points. Through it all, the only one who dared to question her passion, desire and commitment to the game, was Looney herself, the woman who had scored one of the biggest goals in the history of her sport.

In her final few years with the national team, Looney was already well along in what she hoped might be a second career, one that not only would keep her in the game, but give her an opportunity to pay it forward. By then she had already had plenty of experience working the summer camps and guest-coaching high school players.

After being cut from the national team, Looney returned home to Michigan and put in a call to an old friend, David Quinn, who was coaching the U-17 boys team at the USA Hockey National Team Development Program (NTDP) then based in Ann Arbor, 30 miles northwest of her hometown of Trenton.

Looney had known Quinn since her playing days at Northeastern, when Quinn was assisting men's coach Ben Smith during her senior year. "He was taught by Ben and so was I," said Looney, "so we see the game really similarly."

---

8 On the record label, the writing credit is listed as T. DeAngelis. Tom DeAngelis, who worked at CKLW from 1968-83, was known as Johnny Williams on the air. Mr. DeAngelis died on April 16, 2020 at the age of 68, a victim of COVID-19.

Quinn brought her onto his NTDP staff and immediately laid down the law with his players. "She's your coach, and you're going to listen to her," he told them. Looney could sense the skepticism – until she joined them in drills. "You could just see them go, 'Ohhhh, she plays hockey.'"

In January 2006, Looney joined New Jersey Colonials Youth Hockey Association in Morristown, N.J., where she worked with players of all ages, girls and boys. But her greatest legacy from those years is growing the girls' program.

"When I got there, they only had about three-and-a-half teams. They needed someone to build the program," she said. "By 2012, they had nine teams. We came in third at the nationals one year. Our Mite program had 50 kids and 10 of them were girls. I said, 'Give me a sheet of ice and I'll take those 10 and build it.' We doubled it in a year. Tripled it in another."

While working in New Jersey, Looney also served USA Hockey. In 2010, she was an assistant on the U-18 Women's National Team led by a promising young star named Kendall Coyne (now Coyne Schofield). Looney knew instantly that Coyne had everything it took to reach the highest levels of the game, which she did as an Olympic gold medalist at the Winter Games in PyeongChang, South Korea in 2018. Looney said Coyne reminded her of her Nagano teammates.

"Absolutely. She had that hunger in her eyes back then [in 2010], the passion like nobody else," Looney said. "You just knew she would have a bright future."

Remarkably, Coyne Schofield had no idea about the extent of Looney's playing credentials until years later when the two crossed paths again in St. Louis. The women's national team was barnstorming around the continent in late 2021, preparing for the upcoming Olympic Games in Beijing, and one of their stops was in St. Charles, Missouri, a St. Louis suburb, for a two-game set against Team Canada at the Centene Community Ice Center. That's the home of the Lindenwood Lady Lions, coached by Looney since

2019. After a stirring video tribute cheered by a standing-room-only crowd of more than 2,500, Looney dropped the ceremonial first puck.

A new generation of American stars – including several gold medalists – were inspired again by that 1998 team. "Honestly, I watch their celebration [in Nagano] before every game we play against Canada," forward Brianna Decker said. "I go back and watch the YouTube video. It's something that inspires me to go out and play for our country like they did. They still have an impact on us, the same way we're trying to have an impact on younger girls."

It wasn't until May 2019, when the National Hockey League partnered with Discover Card for a series of commercials featuring hockey at grassroots levels, that Coyne Schofield realized it was Looney, her coach on the U-18 team nine years earlier, who had scored the goal that gave Team USA the gold medal in that inaugural Olympic tournament.

"A lot of us were too young to see that game on TV in '98 in the middle of the night," Coyne Schofield said. "I was probably sleeping. But that team obviously paved the way for us. They lived this dream for us to be sitting here today. All those players, they were the vision that we had. They showed us we could accomplish what they accomplished, that we belong in this game.

"Shelley being one of those. . . It was so great to see her there in St. Louis. It's always an honor when we have the opportunity to get to talk to, and pick the brains of that '98 group. And I always bust her chops about that goal. That was so cool!"

That Discover Card spot, by the way, was inspired by renowned hockey broadcaster Mike (Doc) Emrick, with whom Looney enjoys a special bond. He called her seemingly out of the blue one day asking her for advice on how he might better engage a student in a broadcasting course he was teaching, a woman who had been diagnosed with dyslexia, as Shelley had been as a youngster.

"All I could think about was, 'Mike Emrick is asking *me* for advice?'" she said. "He remembered reading my story and thought I might be able to help."

It was Emrick again who suggested to the NHL that it ought to consider featuring Looney and her work with youngsters for its "Hockey Day in America" celebration in 2019. By then she was in Buffalo, the next stop on her own personal coaching carousel, after leaving New Jersey in 2012.

"At first I thought it was just going to be a little follow-up story after the first one," said Looney, then the hockey director for the Buffalo Bisons. It turned out to be a bigger deal than she could have imagined. First, Looney and a group of young lady skaters posed for a photo with a large, cardboard check for $10,000 to be used to help sustain and grow her program. And then Phil Pritchard, the NHL's "Keeper of the Cup," walked in wearing white gloves and carrying the glistening trophy to the squeals of young girls. Tears flowed freely, but it was especially moving for the coach. She understood that this moment was all about the youngsters she was mentoring.

These are the moments Shelley Looney lives for in her career as a coach. Even at Lindenwood, where she was tasked with rebuilding a Division I program that had been run into the ground. This was her first full-time gig that wasn't about just teaching skills and hockey fundamentals. Her responsibilities ran the gamut from recruiting, to scouting, to executing the X's and O's, and keeping her athletes healthy and academically eligible.

But before she could sustain her program, she first had to build it from pretty much nothing. "That's what I do. When people ask me why I got into coaching, it's because I wanted to help grow hockey," said Looney. "I just wanted to give back to a sport that has given me so much. Everywhere I've gone it's been about building a program from the ground up, and I'm OK with that. I never cared about the glory, about being the best team at the highest level. I've already experienced all that."

The Harshest Cuts

"I wanted to raise my hand and tell him he forgot my name."

—Stephanie O'Sullivan

The giddiness from being on the 25-player national team prepping for the Olympics was soon tempered by the knowledge that five teammates would be sent home by December 20, a noose tightening daily.

But for a few elite stars like Karyn Bye, this pre-Olympic tour was a runway to greatness. "I had a really good tour," she recalled. "I was playing well. Every game, every day, every practice, getting a lot of ice time playing on the power play. It was that mindset to go out there, prove to Coach that he's gotta put me on that Olympic roster."[9]

---

9 Bye was also the team's merry prankster off the ice. She found a way to bring variety and laughter to the long gray days in the Adirondack woods. Photojournalist Bill Rappleye drove up to Lake Placid in search of candid video of Team USA, and discovered Bye leading a charge of players into the Rip van Winkle Bowling Lanes dressed like middle-aged country bumpkins. "We went to the Dollar Store and bought matching outfits," Bye recalled years later. "We had visors and wrote different names on them: Beatrice, Matilda, Agnes, old lady names."

On flights Bye would occasionally commandeer a flight attendant's apron and pushcart, plaster on a smile and then roll down the aisles serving refreshments to her astonished mates. "They were very creative, they knew how to have fun, Karyn especially," said Tom Mutch. "Such a great teammate. I'm sure in the back of their mind they had the feeling, 'Geez, when is this [cut] going to come?' But I think, all-in-all, they really enjoyed the experience along the way."

Bye had the psychology of a hunter stalking its prey. That mindset was in direct contrast to her college teammate and national team pal Erin Whitten. Despite being labeled as "the best women's goalie in the world" by *The Hockey News* at the start of the pre-Olympic tour, Whitten was being hounded by two fresh-faced goalies who paid no attention to her eminence. One in particular was eager to take her throne.

"Sarah Tueting was this young go-getter who, honestly, her goal was just to beat me," said Whitten. "You could tell, her job was to walk in and do whatever she could to earn that role."

In hindsight, Smith saw that Whitten was in a tough spot. He chose a golf analogy to convey her plight: "She was the leader in the clubhouse, and that's not always easy when people are nipping at your heels."

The pressure affected her performance, and she did not distinguish herself on the tour with her play, especially against Canada. Self-doubt crept into her mind, which led to an echo chamber of mediocre games and insecurity. Sponsors only knew of her fame gained from playing men's professional hockey, which only ratcheted up the stress.

A camera crew from U.S. Olympic corporate partner Visa came to Lake Placid to shoot a commercial, and naturally chose to include the attractive blonde goalie with the equally handsome resume. The producers had no idea how Whitten's elite status was now a facade. When the shoot was wrapping up, USA Hockey's PR rep Kris Pleimann made an off-hand remark that Whitten will never forget.

"Well, you better make the team now, because you're in this."

"That stuck with me," said Whitten. "This is pressure." If the world's premier goalie was vulnerable, no one was safe, not Team USA's all-world defender, not their first line left wing.

Shortly after returning from an early December road trip, the team stopped in New York City for a publicity junket before returning home to Lake Placid. The NHL's marketing group, led by Bernadette Mansur, was expanding its reach beyond its players going to Japan. League officials were now pointing their spotlight on the first-ever women's Olympic team. The league donated ice time at Manhattan's Chelsea Piers complex for a feel-good co-ed scrimmage. A group of NYC's well-heeled women's hockey supporters, including actor Tim Robbins, developer Roland Betts, and former Yale star Dave Tewksbury suited up for this battle-of-the-sexes "friendly" against Team USA.

NHL Productions had a video team on the scene, with express orders to capture the story of veteran winger Stephanie O'Sullivan. Orphaned six years prior, O'Sullivan and her 10 siblings from working-class Dorchester, Massachusetts were raising themselves, a real-life version of the popular prime-time sitcom *Party of Five*. The fact that O'Sullivan's brother Chris was a rookie with the NHL Calgary Flames caused a huge stir in Gary Bettman's Sixth Avenue marketing offices: The O'Sullivans were the perfect tandem for the NHL to advance its campaign to invite more women inside hockey's fan tent.

After the game, Pleimann sat down for beers with the NHL staffers. Nearly everyone was glowing after the jovial contest. Thanks to prodding from the league offices, the O'Sullivan story had earned several inches of space in that day's *USA Today* newspaper. This should have been a moment to revel in the fruit of the combined efforts of NHL marketing and USA Hockey public relations, but Pleimann was more dour than delighted. O'Sullivan had been a no-show for an optional appearance, and Pleimann was grumbling. The PR professional held her cards close to her vest, revealing nothing of substance, but she could not hide the fact that she was not on the O'Sullivan bandwagon. It was as if the groundswell of publicity for hockey's ultimate feel-good story was causing her agita. Something didn't add up.

Team USA returned to its fortress in the Adirondack mountains on Wednesday, December 10, exactly 10 days before the dreaded cut-down, five players on the chopping block. To a person, the impending cuts were like a case of tinnitus: barely audible yet increasingly uncomfortable, a hum impossible to ignore. Their immediate concern was the Three Nations tournament commencing that Sunday, a total of five games against medal favorites Finland and Canada. To the hockey world, it was a dress rehearsal for the Nagano Games. For the Team USA players on the bubble, it was a pass/fail final exam.

"We were in the process of buttoning the thing down," Smith said, explaining that the Three Nations Cup "could have solidified a lot of situations, both good and bad at that particular moment." Two days before the tournament opener vs. Finland, Smith called for a meeting. The women trudged up to the second floor conference room, presuming business as usual. "We come in for a team meeting and think it's a chalk talk or whatever," said A.J. Mleczko. The "talk" turned out to be the equivalent of a live grenade for two players. Smith brusquely announced that Barb Gordon and Jeanine Sobek had been cut. No ceremony, no parting gifts.

"It was jarring, because we didn't expect it," said Mleczko. Trimming down his roster was bloodsport, actions that required cold, blunt force. Smith ignored sentiment, his job was to mine gold for his pals Ogrean and Berglund and, most importantly, for his country. His last Olympic experience had been in Calgary in 1988, an assistant coach for a team that was stocked with U.S. Hall-of-Famers. They returned with their ears pinned back, failing to qualify for the medal round. Ditto for his buddy Tim Taylor at Lillehammer in 1994. That failure affected the entire hockey nation, not just individuals. If players had to suffer, so be it. In the case of former Northeastern star Sobek, the pain was contagious.

"My best friend from college was cut, I was just devastated," Looney said of Sobek. "She was only 18 in 1990, the youngest to make the first World Championship roster. I knew the passion she had for the sport. Sometimes I think she loves it more than me. I felt like she deserved it."

Looney expressed a sentiment no men's player would ever utter out loud. "If I could trade places, I would let her go on, and I would go home. I always looked up to her because of that passion she had. We played college four years together, and she got cut, I'll never forget it. It was tough, very tough."

It was only the beginning. Three more cuts were coming, all to be determined on North Country ice: Lake Placid, New York and Burlington, Vermont. The Canada game played at University of Vermont's (UVM) venerable Gutterson Field House was a tragicomedy played out in front of a national TV audience. Legendary broadcaster Mike Emrick called the drama.

Act I was "The Laugher." Team USA jumped out to a three-goal lead, ready to run the world champions out of the old barn and into the Green Mountains. Newly minted stars Katie King and Laurie Baker joined captain Cammi Granato in the scoring parade. The venue known as "The Gut" was throwing a party at the expense of the proud Canucks, the home team leading 4-1. Then came *Act II*, "The Collapse," an act ignited by a game-changing plot point.

With the crowd still buzzing over Granato's tip-in, which gave the Americans a three-goal cushion, Canada's veteran defender Therese Brisson proceeded to sashay around all five USA skaters and scored. She treated the Americans like so many practice cones before calmly depositing the puck behind Whitten. It had taken just fifteen seconds to transform The Gut from Mardi Gras to tension convention. The first shift after a goal is always a barometer of attention to detail. Team USA had blinked, the lead had shrunk to 4-2, and Smith was hot.

The Americans never scored again as Shannon Miller's women in red bled the home team to death, finishing them off 5-4 in a major statement game. Members of the O'Sullivan family watched the contest from their apartment in Dorchester. Stephanie's brother Mark, a former goalie at

Notre Dame, can still remember plays that sank the Americans, like Kelly O'Leary's breakout pass being intercepted in the middle of the ice, a cardinal sin of hockey. "She was in shambles," said Mark O'Sullivan.

In hockey, the last line of defense is in goal, and this was Whitten's game to win or lose. Staked to a three-goal lead, she melted under the hot lights. In her finale against Canada, her nerves betrayed her. "The mind can play some funny tricks on you, and at that position, the funniest kinds of tricks," Smith said two decades later, a trace of sympathy in his voice. "That wasn't a great night for her, that's for sure."

At the time, however, Smith was furious, barely able to maintain his composure following his team's collapse. Their performance was unacceptable and would have its consequences, starting with the return to the locker room. As Smith marched off to meet the press, he barked orders for assistant Tom Mutch to keep the USA dressing room shut tight. *Act III*, "The Lockout," had commenced in this night of light and shadow. Team USA players and their coach were both facing the music, respectively, a hundred feet from each other.

While Smith was busy explaining to two nations' press corps how his club squandered a three-goal lead, down the hall through a set of double doors his players found themselves dazed and confused in a crush outside their own locker room. Squeals of delight from the neighboring enemy, who had just stolen a win on U.S. soil, pierced their ears and overwhelmed their senses. Bitter pills for both the coach and his club.

"So, we're all standing in the hallway," said Shelley Looney. "We hear Canada coming off cheering, all excited how they came back and won, and we're sitting there defeated."

"Oh did they take it to heart," said Mutch. "They were not happy ladies, standing in the hallway listening to that. It was a teaching moment that Ben would not let go by."

"We finally go in the locker room," recalled Looney, "and he [Smith] goes, 'I wanted to make sure you heard that.' It was just burning."

That was the short-term consequence. Long term, heads would roll from this game. A critical exam failed, with another crucial test against Canada three days later in Lake Placid. Dreams of a half-dozen bubble players hung in the balance.

December 20, 1997: Shocking Saturday for three souls, ecstasy for the survivors. The day started at Herb Brooks Arena. Canada and Team USA faced each other in a matinee to determine the winner of the Three Nations Cup. This IIHF gold medal-game also represented last call for several American players, all competing for the right to play in the historic 1998 Olympic Games. Hockey insiders might be forgiven for presuming this game held lesser importance due to Team USA scratching stalwarts Granato, Mounsey and Looney from the lineup. But it was life and death for three distinguished hockey careers.

Twenty-four-year-old memories from one of 13 exhibition games against Canada are hard to extract, even for the Team USA coaching staff. Memories they could recall, however, proved to be quite significant. Ben Smith remembered the play of a young goalie just returning from injury.

"Pretty sure Sara [DeCosta] was in the net," said Smith. "A good statement to shut them out." A statement indeed. In the final game before cuts, DeCosta pitched a shutout to defeat Canada and capture the Three Nations Cup gold medal. It was the first time an American team of women had ever relegated Canada from the top of an IIHF podium. Three days earlier, incumbent Whitten had failed her test against Canada; on cut day, the rookie challenger aced hers.

Tom Mutch couldn't remember who played in goal on December 20, but he recalled a certain left wing inking up the scoresheet. "What did Gretchen Ulion have in that game?" he asked. It was a rhetorical question, even if he didn't recall the details. He was reminded that Ulion scored the first two goals in the 3-0 victory. "Interesting, huh? Scores two goals, you beat Canada 3-0, left shot, left wing," said Mutch, nodding at the memory. "Pretty good. Pretty good showing."

Pretty good indeed. Gretchen Ulion, the woman who was cut in Ben Smith's first tryout camp, notched two goals in a ten-minute span in the second period. There can be no doubt that it was a major factor in her surviving the cut.

Another left-shooting left wing was oblivious to the fact she was even on the bubble. After the post-game meal, Stephanie O'Sullivan strode confidently into the second-floor conference room to hear Ben Smith announce the historic team. Her brothers Mark, Peter and sister Julie had driven up five hours from Dorchester to celebrate with Stephanie after the announcement. "It was like Christmas Eve," said Mark, who had big plans in the works: a book deal and a made-for-TV movie about the O'Sullivan story were both on the table. Both projects were contingent on Steph making the team. The announcement of her name was merely a formality. Until it wasn't.

Smith methodically read through the names of the players he wanted on *his* team. Ulion, who was both a bubble player and one of the last in line alphabetically, was nearly driven to the brink. "Being a 'U' and sitting there for so long, especially since I had been cut before, your mind goes through all sorts of weird things," she said.

The women were so focused on hearing their own names, most of them didn't realize that O'Sullivan was bypassed. Sue Merz had inside information that the final spot on defense was between her and O'Leary.[10] She heard the "M" name before the "O" name, and immediately realized that two fates had been sealed. "The cuts came down to me and one other defenseman," said Merz, "when I heard my name before theirs, I was just fully relieved."

Smith kept his voice neutral, providing no verbal drama. When Ulion's name was finally called, it was all she could do to maintain a grip. *"Am I just imagining he said my name?* I was in disbelief."

When the coach completed his weighty task, he asked the new Olympic team to leave so he could address the players who hadn't made it. Three veterans had been axed, victims of this cruel game of musical chairs. Proud pioneers who had helped build women's hockey in America—Erin Whitten, Kelly O'Leary and Stephanie O'Sullivan, all in their late 20's—had been left on the tarmac. Their reactions spanned the spectrum: anger, resignation, and disbelief.

"I wanted to raise my hand and tell him he forgot my name," said O'Sullivan. "I thought it was a joke. I was on the first line, 22 points in 23 games."

While the joyous survivors scrambled down to the two lobby payphones to spread their joy, Smith remained with the three players who had been brutally cut, thanking them for their contributions to the sport. He offered them all a chance to say their piece, at a time of their choosing.

---

10 Of all the criteria Ben Smith used to evaluate players, pure athleticism ranked at the top. He has never been enamored with "store-bought" hockey players who attend all the skills camps. Although Sue Merz might not have possessed extraordinary hockey talents, Smith never forgot one innocuous act by her before an exhibition game. "In the summer of '97, we were in Finland. I was with Tom Mutch during warm-ups and I remember Sue Merz skating around behind the net. Someone takes a slapshot this high [Smith holds his hand three feet off the ground] going right at her. She jumps straight up, a vertical leap right to there [holds hand out again]. Mutchie and I just look at each other – 'Did you see that!' I remember seeing Merz throw a football, watching her swing a golf club, you just know she's a terrific athlete. I remember saying to myself – there's got to be a place on this team for someone that athletic."

O'Leary, a reigning All-Tournament selection from that year's World Championships, tore into Smith.

"I saw him in the hallway and pointed my finger at him," said O'Leary. "You know I belong on this team!"

"No. No you don't," countered Smith. Weeks later, O'Leary still hadn't found peace, lashing out in nationally syndicated newspaper stories.

"Everybody says you've done so much to be proud of, but none of that means anything anymore," said O'Leary. "There aren't many girls on the team that can even lace my skates."

Whitten, the cover girl of USA Hockey for most of the 1990's, did not fear the reaper. "My husband [Tim Hamlen, fiancé at the time] was there at a hotel, staying because he knew," said Whitten. "I could have told you I was going to get cut. I knew based on how I had played on the pre-Olympic tour." A quarter-century later, Whitten still found solace in her exit from the Olympic Training Center. "When I walked out, I almost didn't want to see anybody." Then she felt the strong hands of Karyn Bye pull her into an embrace.

"You've been my goalie for so long, I don't understand," said Bye. "It's going to be weird for you not to be my goalie."

"That killed me at the time," said Whitten. "I'll always hold onto that, because it was the emotions of having somebody who made it, and her way of saying she was sorry. I'll always appreciate it."

One of the survivors, team elder Lisa Brown-Miller, felt crushed, despite realizing her own dream. "Kelly O'Leary, one of my roommates, her name wasn't called," Brown-Miller said. "I was devastated, I thought she was a shoo-in." She went downstairs to queue up for a payphone, and finally reached her husband. "I got on the phone with John, my biggest confidante, and I was just sobbing."

"What's wrong? Are you OK?"

Brown-Miller shared the news, both good and bad. "Yeah I made it," she sniffed, "but Kelly O'Leary didn't."

The two veterans had known each other for over a decade, they'd been teammates at the inaugural 1990 World Championships. No one embodied survivor syndrome more than Brown-Miller, a residue of experience and hard-earned wisdom.

Angela Ruggiero, the team's youngest player, was unable to contain her teenage jubilation, ignoring the line for payphones in the lobby and dashing outside instead. "I'm just going to run into town," recalled Ruggiero. "I'm a kid. I've got tons of energy." She sprinted half a mile down Newman Road to the phone at the Corner Store Deli. She punched in the Michigan area code and then heralded the breathtaking news to her family. Two weeks shy of her 18th birthday, Ruggiero's four-Olympic odyssey had just begun. Three shell-shocked veterans would never get a taste.

While Ruggiero was scrambling through the Training Center parking lot, she bypassed the players' families. Middle-aged parents and player-siblings were exchanging hugs, congratulations and in the case of the O'Sullivans, condolences. It was in the parking lot that the Dorchester party discovered the sickening news. Several minutes later, Steph crammed into the family sedan alongside her siblings for the darkest ride of her life.

"I've been through tragedy before, and faced a lot of adversity," said O'Sullivan, who lost both her parents to cancer earlier that decade, "but nothing compares to this."

Alana Blahoski, a former roommate and one of O'Sullivan's closest friends on the national team, was baffled by the cut. "I feel there was an injustice," Blahoski said 25 years later. "I took a spot and she didn't. If we were to play one-on-one, she would clobber me."

The O'Sullivan cut was by far the toughest for Smith. Everyone in Boston's tightly interwoven hockey world loved the O'Sullivans; they were hockey bedrock in Beantown. Yet his gut, and more importantly, his eyes, told him that Ulion was the better choice. He had blinders on, ignoring the past, and looking only a month into the future.

"There were players moving forward, slipping ahead, one step forward every day. Every practice, every scrimmage, every game was a tryout situation," said Smith. "Players with great portfolios, O'Leary, O'Sullivan, Whitten. Those were great players in their time. But their time had come to an end in December of 1997. That's the thing that happens, great players get cut."

Boston's hockey nation still struggles to make sense of the O'Sullivan cut. Perhaps the key to solving that riddle is to examine the trio of victims collectively: Whitten, O'Leary and O'Sullivan were all card-carrying members for Team USA's "Silver Shackles Club." They had heard nothing but Canada's national anthem played after every IIHF event in which they ever performed. That runner-up culture was one that goaltender Kelly Dyer, silver-medal goalie in the first two World Championships, knew all too well.

"You look at a team that has only achieved silver in the World Championships, and you're kind of locked into that mentality," said Dyer. "You've got a whole bunch of vets in the room that are thinking, 'Gosh, playing Canada, we're going to win the silver.' Whether you're conscious of thinking that or not, all three of those athletes [O'Sullivan, Whitten, O'Leary] were hard working, driven, giving, all of it. He just needed fresh blood, and the live optimism of youth."

The worst day was now the first day. It was no longer a national team, it was the U.S. Olympic team. "It was hard, but it was also a relief," said Mutch. "We needed to get to this point, we all knew it was coming. What a proud moment, when you saw that team and their smiles and relief. Now you could believe."

The Thrilling Thirteen

"Men are natural warriors, but a woman in battle is truly bloodthirsty."

—Cate Tiernan, author

The dramatic December cuts represented seminal changes to Team USA, as three respected but aging veterans were replaced by next-gen players, all part of America's quest to change the team's culture and close the gap with Canada once and for all. The Three Nations Cup games with Canada that closed out 1997 represented just three of the 13 contests staged by the two superpowers of women's hockey, a live arms race in the runup to Nagano. These contests were hardly exhibitions—they represented the constantly shifting see-saw for world dominance, each game an extension of the brilliant World Championship gold-medal war from that previous April. With the inaugural women's hockey Olympic gold medal as the carrot, the two squads played at a breakneck pace in a series that may never be duplicated.

After the 1998 Winter Games, Canadian players came in droves down to U.S. colleges to take advantage of hundreds of scholarships and bountiful financial aid. National team rivals like Canada's Jen Botterill and Angela Ruggiero became teammates at Harvard, playing many more games with each other than against each other. Almost none of this NCAA cross-pollination had taken place between Canada and the Team USA players prior to '98. Consequently, there were no shared college experiences to mitigate the competitive hostilities between these hockey nations, the hunter and the hunted.

The 13-game Nagano runup was colored by truculence, causing coach Smith to fret over his players' health, a legitimate concern. "This was never friendly," said Smith. "There was an ugly side to it, just teetering on the edge."

The gold-medal battle in Kitchener had sounded the alarm to the entire hockey world that Canada's reign as automatic gold medalist was now in jeopardy. That same hockey world knows how prideful Canada is when it comes to its national sport, regardless of gender. When honor is at stake, as is always the case with Canadian hockey, the response can often be vicious. In 1972, the Team Canada men faced a similar threat from the Soviets in their historic Summit Series. Canada centerman Bobby Clarke responded with his infamous slash heard round the world, a cold-blooded chop that broke the ankle of Red Army star Valeri Kharlamov.

A quarter-century later, Canadian women felt the same threat, but instead of eight games to settle the score as was the case with the Soviets in 1972, Canada and the United States played 13 thrilling games, with the historic Olympic Games as the ultimate payoff. It didn't take long for fans on both sides of the border to sense the heat being generated by this sizzling rivalry. Attendance records were shattered four times in that series. Women stole the spotlight from the men for a full day at the NHL's All-Star weekend, and in one remarkable 10-day stretch women's hockey rocked three different NHL venues.[11] Tens of thousands of fans saw bodies bruised, and nearly broken, in the sport that allegedly prohibits bodychecking.

---

11 Shortly after the 1997 Worlds, a national poll was taken to rank the most popular teams in all of Canada. The list included the NHL's Montreal Canadiens and Toronto Maple Leafs, Major League Baseball's Toronto Blue Jays and the NBA's Toronto Raptors. The women of Team Canada were voted the country's fourth-most-popular team.

Despite the magnitude of these games, players' memories of those 13 USA-Canada matches have faded into a red and white blur. With televised games of women's hockey almost non-existent in the 1990s, this supreme series was in danger of falling into a bottomless crevasse of generic hockey memory, not history. Thankfully, the steadfast archivists of Hockey Canada unearthed all 13 hand-written score sheets, the primary source lifeblood of hockey history. Newspapers were still thriving in the late 1990s, and the work of serious journalists from both countries attribute incendiary quotes to players who have long forgotten ever uttering such statements.

Thanks to off-ice officials and newspapers from a generation ago, a detailed log of the most intense high-stakes series in women's hockey history has been restored: The Thrilling Thirteen.

Salt Lake, 26 October 1997
U.S. 5 Canada 4 (Shootout), *USA leads series 1-0*

More than six months had passed since the hockey world was blown away in Kitchener by the epic World Championship finale, the overtime victory that made every witness stand up and take notice that not only had women's hockey arrived, it was a can't-miss spectacle.

The Saturday night prime-time affair in Salt Lake City's E-Center—America's 2002 Olympic hockey venue—did not disappoint. "Both teams played their hearts out," said Ben Smith. "They picked up where they left off." This Kitchener rematch extended *past* overtime, with none other than Cammi Granato scoring the skate-off goal on the 10th shootout attempt. It sent all 7,306 fans--a U.S. attendance record for women's hockey – home deliriously happy.

A major difference from Kitchener was the starting goaltender for the Americans. Smith used the untested Sarah Tueting instead of Whitten, who entered the season as the frontrunner. Tueting felt lousy about giving up Canada's tying goal, and then went a perfect five-for-five in the shootout. "I was scared and excited," said Tueting. "The fourth goal was my fault." She bailed herself out with her impeccable performance in the shootout.

In the next day's papers, two different writers printed the assumption that Whitten, not Tueting, would be the Team USA starter in Nagano. Whitten had the lengthy resume responsible for the reputation that preceded her. Salt Lake City represented opening day in the runup to Nagano; writers who were learning women's hockey from ground zero simply latched on to a convenient storyline as they began to build their knowledge. With two unknowns and an established favorite, most writers figured the only internal goaltending battle would be for the backup role. This series would prove them all wrong.

Bathurst, New Brunswick, 7 November 1997
Canada 3, U.S. 2, *Series tied 1-1*

Except for a few hundred citizens in Bathurst who filed into the K.C. Irving Regional Centre, this game might be lost to posterity. The score sheet reveals that Tueting got her second straight start, and although she gave up one fewer goal than in her previous game in Salt Lake, she took the loss. She surrendered three consecutive goals after Sandra Whyte staked the Yanks to a 1-0 lead. Shots were 22 apiece.

St. John, New Brunswick, 8 November 1997
Canada 4, U.S. 1, *Canada leads series 2-1*

This was the most lopsided win of the series for Team Canada, "The equivalent of a romp," reported Toronto's *National Post*. Team Canada coach Shannon Miller, who feared that Team USA would close whatever slim margin of superiority her women enjoyed, insisted that there was even more to Canada's game. "We're not showing them everything," a refrain she repeated often. Erin Whitten took the loss, allowing four goals on 32 shots. The two teams were whistled for just seven total penalties.

Kitchener, Ontario, 10 November 1997
USA 3, Canada 2, *Series tied 2-2*

The women's hockey traveling circus had left Canada's sleepy Maritimes and returned to Kitchener, Ontario, well within the blast range of hockey's media capital of Toronto and its grand provocateur Don "Grapes" Cherry, the loudest supporter of women's hockey. Since Canada's epic

World Championship victory, Cherry had become widowed, losing his beloved Rose after 40 years of marriage. Grapes credited his late wife for alerting him to the cause of women's hockey. "Rose was a great supporter of the women's game," said Cherry days before the rematch, "and encouraged me to tell the public that these women should be treated fairly in our national game."

To honor Rose, every Team Canada player wore a commemorative rose on her jersey, adding color to a rivalry that hardly needed it. Canada jumped out to a 2-0 lead, and just four games into this series Team USA found itself in a minor crisis. Including the IIHF gold-medal game in this same building, the Americans had lost three of four games to their rivals, and were outscored 9-1 in the last six periods. The Ben Smith mantra, "It's not a rivalry if the other guy doesn't win once in a while," was dangerously close to becoming a reality.

The Americans finally stopped the bleeding when Karyn Bye, who along with Granato was one of Team USA's two vital ventricles, slipped the disc past Danielle Dube in the second period. The goal allowed the visitors to regroup in the second intermission, trailing only 2-1.

The third period was dominated by the woman who was last seen in Kitchener clutching her broken face. Shelley Looney set up two goals in the final nine minutes of the game, and USA escaped their house of horrors with a 3-2 victory, tying the series at two games apiece. Kitchener was no longer a four-letter word to the Yanks. Smith chose an alternate "F-word" in the post-game.

"It was a lot of *fun* for us to come back here, and for us to win," he said. "A special moment for us." Another newcomer in goal, 20-year-old Sara DeCosta, had just claimed her first victory over Canada on this night of promise.

Smith's injection of young talent was starting to impose itself on the rivalry. "Our youth helps the team," said Tara Mounsey, speaking also for teenagers Angela Ruggiero and Jenny Schmidgall. Her comments were published in a David Levine column that circulated throughout the United States. "The veterans have all gone through big losses [to Canada]. We have no fear of them. It's our turn."

Minneapolis, 4, December 1997
USA 3, Canada 1, *USA leads series 3-2*

This was a Minneapolis homecoming for Schmidgall, and even though the shy playmaker had a pair of assists in the third period to defeat Canada, she cannot recall the game. She does, however, remember an act of kindness that helped bring her into the fold.

Schmidgall and fellow Twin Cities native Alana Blahoski were invited to a state capital function the night before the Canada game, and Jenny had nothing formal to wear, primarily due to her extraordinarily developed lower body. "We had to dress up, and she was having a hard time finding an outfit," said Blahoski. "Pants don't work when your quads are that big."

She felt an immediate affinity for Jenny when she discovered her listening to the hip hop band *Bone Thugs-N-Harmony*. "We went shopping at Marshall's and T.J. Maxx," Blahoski said.

"She was definitely a mentor, very welcoming, a fellow Minnesotan," Schmidgall-Potter said years later. Blahoski, the college grad who had already lived on her own in Boston, took the shy teenager under her wing. The two spent the afternoon searching Minneapolis for a suitable outfit for the rookie.

"I thought she had very good fashion sense" said Schmidgall-Potter.

"Obviously we had two different body types. I was shorter, legs were way bigger. But we had a good time, laughing, trying on many different clothes in stores."

"We finally found something that worked," said Blahoski, who understood she was befriending a young phenom. "Fantastic person, incredible player the way she sees the ice."

That vision resulted in two assists in Team USA's 3-1 taming of Canada, as Schmidgall set up Bye for the game-winner and Katie King for the insurance goal at the buzzer.

Victorious goalie Tueting loved sticking it to Canada. "It was good to come back and slam it down their throats," she said. Tueting had stymied Canada for over 59 minutes before finally letting a goal slip past her. It was her second victory over Canada in three starts, and she was voted the game's Number 1 star. "I can't complain," said Tueting about losing her shutout with 17 ticks left on the clock, but then she reconsidered: "Well I can, but I won't."

The normally reticent Schmidgall loosened up, spewing quotes about the intensity of the Canada games to *The St. Paul Pioneer Press:* "Grueling . . . really rough . . . more physical each time we play."

December 4 was an important date for the Americans in this rivalry: newbies Tueting and Schmidgall played starring roles as Team USA clipped Canada for the third time in five games. The significance was not lost on Karyn Bye. "This is how we're going to improve, by playing Canada and beating them," said the alternate captain, a long-time victim of the silver malaise. "We've lost to them so many times in the past that these games are really boosting our confidence. They beat us 8-0 in the World Championship in 1992. They see we've come a long way, so I think this might scare them a little bit."

There were two other items in the next day's newspapers that made

December 5 a red-letter day for women's hockey: The University of Minnesota women's team was prepping for a series against Princeton in Minneapolis in its inaugural season, and the USA Hockey Foundation announced that it would be giving out the Patty Kazmaier Award to college hockey's female player of the year at the end of the season in Boston. Three institutions that have become massive components of women's hockey in America—the Olympics, the Minnesota Gophers and the Patty Kaz. News of all three crowded the sports sections in Minneapolis and Boston on the same day.

Winnipeg, Manitoba, 6 December 1997
Canada 5 USA 4, *Series tied 3-3*

If the debacle in Burlington was Erin Whitten's Waterloo, then her start in the windswept plains of Manitoba was the equivalent of Napoleon's decision to battle Russia in winter.

There are no newspaper game accounts of Canada's 5-4 win; the two Winnipeg dailies published only short stories regarding Canada's team selections. But there is a note in the scoresheet, written by hand at approximately 9 p.m. CST, that speaks volumes. "12:25 – Second Period, USA CHANGE – DeCosta in for Whitten."

A quick look at the score sheet reveals that at 12:25 of the second period, Whitten had just given up her fifth goal of the night, a fatal short-handed goal by deadeye Hayley Wickenheiser. It was Canada's second "shorty" against Whitten in barely half a game. DeCosta came on in relief and saved all nine shots she faced the rest of the way, but the damage was done.

Forget traditional goaltending stats. When it came to making the grade in goal for Team USA, there was only one metric that mattered—success versus Canada. In less than eight periods vs. the arch enemy, including the World Championship game, Whitten had been torched for 14 goals, losing all three contests. Like Napoleon's return from Moscow, Whitten's reign was coming to a close

Three Nations Cup Round Robin
Lake Placid, 14 December 1997
Canada 3 USA 2, *Canada leads series 4-3*

Canada's Leslie Reddon outplayed Team USA's Sara DeCosta in goal before a sparse Sunday afternoon crowd at the Olympic Centre. The only buzz emanating from the concourse in Lake Placid was about the nationally tele-vised game slated for later that week, a first for American women's hockey.

Three Nations Cup Round Robin
Burlington, Vermont, 17 December 1997
Canada 5 USA 4, *Canada leads series 5-3*

The biggest women's hockey story in *The Burlington Free Press* on December 18 was plastered on the front page, and it wasn't about goals and saves. It focused on how much of the crowd of 2,800 consisted of girls' hockey teams and the ruckus they were making. Hockey-loving teens Samantha Shimel, Molly Sheehan, Heather Bronson and Adrienne Illick of Middlebury were pictured above the fold on the front page of Vermont's largest newspaper, faces painted, mouths agape, sounding joyous screams. Already the next generation was making some noise.

Despite Team USA's collapse, this was a major victory for women's hockey in the United States. Girls across the country got to see women play a thrilling live game, and thousands of fans left Gutterson Field House ecstatic over the experience. Burlington had proven itself a worthy venue for women's hockey, a future host of the IIHF World Championships.

Afterward Erin Whitten showed the courage to face the press after her nationally televised demise. "It was nice to hear fans cheering," Whitten told Ted Ryan of the *Burlington Free Press.* "We're used to playing in front of sellout crowds, but [only] in Canada." These were some of the last words spoken on the record by Whitten while still a candidate for the Olympic Games.

Team Canada coach Shannon Miller made a point of pouring salt in the wounds of the Americans. "We heard the game was televised here," said Miller, "so we wanted to cause a little pain." Three days later those words would come back to haunt her.

Three Nations Cup Gold Medal Game
Lake Placid, 20 December 1997
USA 3 Canada 0, *Canada leads series 5-4*

Fifteen hundred fans scattered throughout the cavernous Olympic Centre were a stark contrast from the jam-packed Gutterson Field House on the campus of UVM. The swaths of empty seats made a poor "studio" for TSN's live production team that Saturday afternoon. The fact that Canada was shut out made it a terrible day in the truck for Paul McLean, Susy Antal and Jon Hynes, elite professionals who beamed the game back to the entire nation of Canada. To make matters worse for Canada's nationalistic women's hockey fans, they were subjected to a song they had never heard before at game's end—*The Star Spangled Banner.* Despite Team USA losing two of three games to Canada in the 1997 Three Nations Cup, the Americans won the gold medal game to spoil the Canucks' party.

Angela Ruggiero, America's happy-go-lucky youngster, spewed the inconvenient truth about her neighbors to the north. "We're walking out with the gold medal, and they only got a silver, which has never happened to them before."

Miller got right to the point: "We played like shit." According to Wayne Scanlan of *The Ottawa Citizen,* moments before facing the press Miller had learned that her team was planning a big alcohol-soaked party for the post-game, their minds on their packed bags and not the game at hand. Miller made her team vow to abstain from alcohol throughout the upcoming holidays.

"They can take that pain with them over Christmas, the pain of standing there on the blue line, listening to the U.S. anthem," said the seething coach. "The U.S. has endured that for years. That's why they're so hungry. Maybe that's what we need."

Miller's worst fear had been realized while facing a U.S. team that had given Cammi Granato and Tara Mounsey the day off. Whatever psychological edge Team Canada had from its run of gold medals had been dashed by losing a Three Nations tournament that it had dominated. As Team USA came to grips with its new team makeup after the emotional cuts in Lake Placid, a sour Canadian team bused towards Montreal, a coach and a club in misery.

Vancouver, 16 January 1998
Canada 2 USA 1 - *Canada leads the series 6-4*

This was much more than a single game on the rapidly flipping pages of the calendar counting down to Nagano. USA-Canada women was a marquee event in the newly formatted NHL All-Star weekend, one that amplified the approaching Winter Games. In addition to seeing NHL All-Stars, most of whom would soon be in Nagano, fans were able to witness a preview of the women's Olympic gold-medal game. Yet another attendance record was shattered as 14,944 piled into GM Place to see the women's game, a gripping, one-goal clash. The Americans may have lost the game, but thanks to their crafty equipment manager Bob Webster, they were winning little victories behind the scenes.

Despite playing up in Canada, Team USA enjoyed the superior locker room, with better access to the ice than host Team Canada. "We are in this locker room that is amazing," said assistant Tom Mutch. "Team Canada is around the corner, further from the ice than they probably should have been. I said, 'Web, how did you get this locker room?'"

"Ah Kid, don't worry about it."

A generation later, Mutch recalled how vital their esteemed equipment manager had become to his team's chances. "Bob Webster was going to make this team the most comfortable team ready to play,"Mutch said.

Meanwhile, the Canadians were still sore over intense media scrutiny due to their loss in Lake Placid. "They're hungry to beat us," Miller said. "You can see that in their eyes." It took Team Canada nearly a month to avenge its embarrassment in the Three Nations final. "They beat us in the last gold-medal game and our pride is hurt," Miller said. "We're like a pack of wolves, going at them hard."

Her wolves generated a nasty hit on USA's vocal leader Karyn Bye, who suffered a minor hematoma after a knee-on-knee collision with Vicky Sunohara in Vancouver. Bye wrote in her journal the next day that it was the first time in memory that she missed a practice due to injury. It would not be her last.

Western Canada's most popular hockey columnist Eric Duhatschek stirred the pot after Canada had prevailed on the big stage when he wrote, "It shows they've got character, some fire in the belly."

On to San Jose.

San Jose, 20 January 1998
USA 4 Canada 3 (OT), *Canada leads the series 6-5*

On Game Day, the hometown Sharks were finishing up their practice when both women's national teams arrived. San Jose tough guy Marty McSorley teased the Team Canada players as they passed in the corridor. "Hey, I bet a beer with [Sharks teammate] Tony Granato that you guys are going to win," he said.

Granato drank for free that night, watching his sister's club win yet another landmark game. For the second time in this series, an American attendance record was set at San Jose's raucous "Shark Tank," as 7,784 fans celebrated throughout, rejoicing over the climactic finish. Mounsey tied the game for the United States with a power-play goal with just eight seconds remaining. Then in the third minute of sudden death, Katie "The Train" King blew behind Canada's defense, taking a perfect cross-ice feed from trusted linemate Laurie Baker before depositing the OT thriller in the back of the net. King punctuated the moment with her patented sprint past Baker, running on her toes. Their connection had become a signature play of the two rookies, and it had devastating effects.

"She'd be screaming down the left wing, I'd be coming down the right," said Baker. "I'd wait until she got a step or two behind the defense, and I'd thread a pass behind the D and she would be on her forehand side. Off she goes, the runaway train, and she always seemed to put it away."

American vet Vickie Movsessian spoke the emerging truth of the new year. "I definitely think these games are giving us momentum," she said.

"Even when we lose, we're learning little things about them. We're setting ourselves up."

Calgary, 26 January 1998
USA 3 Canada 1, *Series tied 6-6*

This was Canada's Olympic sendoff for its women's national team, and the fans in Calgary responded with another record crowd to see women's hockey. The game was held at the spacious Saddledome, home to the NHL Flames, only a 20-minute drive from Team Canada's headquarters at the national Centre of Excellence. Yet prior to the game, Team Canada was spitting mad. When the Canadian players arrived at the rink, they found the Americans luxuriating in the Flames' locker room.

"Team Canada was screaming," said Mutch. "Why are they in the big locker room?"

The culprit, once again, was Webster.

"Web, no way!" Mutch recalled saying to Webster, who replied with a knowing smile.

"Hey, I got the keys!" he responded with a mischievous smile.

An irritable host was treated rudely by the American guests. "Team USA came out and staged a physical assault," wrote Lori Ewing in the *Calgary Herald.* King, Looney and Whyte took care of the scoring for the Yanks, while Tueting minded business between the pipes. At game's end, Team Canada was wondering how it all went so wrong.

"The selfish penalties were unacceptable," said Shannon Miller.

"It's nothing to hang our heads about," said Canadian scoring star Jayna Hefford, "but we can't accept losing to them."

Once again, USA's Bye was injured by team Canada. She insists that Danielle Goyette was the guilty party, deliberately attempting to injure her. "There's a fine line between playing a little dirty, with a little grit here and there. But to intentionally try to injure somebody? To me, that's not good sportsmanship," said Bye. "That's never how I played the game. Hockey's such a great sport, and there's no reason to intentionally go out and injure anybody, ever."

Newspaper accounts point the finger not at Goyette, but at Wickenheiser, who described her role in the play that knocked out Bye. "She came in front of the net, she cut one way and I cut the same way," said the 19-year old firebrand who was whistled for three penalties. Shannon Miller tried to rationalize her star's on-ice truculence. "The intensity and drive to succeed just takes her too far."

Regardless of whether it was Goyette or Wickenheiser, America's most physical forward, Karyn Bye, was now on crutches. As Ewing wrote in the lead to her game story, "OK, this isn't funny anymore."

Colorado Springs, 28 January 1998
Canada 4 USA 2, *Canada leads series 7-6*

In the finale of this series, one that had gone from fun to exhilarating to downright reckless, Team USA finally took its foot off the accelerator. Like Canada's sendoff from two nights earlier, this was essentially a home game for the Americans, who were encamped at their training center in Colorado Springs. And just like the previous game, the visitors spoiled the evening, Canada dominating in both shots (35-21) and goals (4-2).

There was not a single newspaper story covering the game, no quotes to be found, no memories conjured up. It was as if the game were played in a vacuum. Having lost the last two games, Canada clearly had something to prove. With Bye already in street clothes nursing her discolored thigh, Team USA's priority was to stay out of the hospital.

Now, with the historic Winter Games on the horizon, it was time to take inventory after 13 emotional and bruising contests. One could not have divided an odd number of games more evenly: six wins for the United States, seven for Team Canada. And perhaps the most remarkable stat of all was the total goals scored: 37 apiece.

Three months of hockey settled only one thing: There was nothing to choose between the two clubs. Shannon Miller's biggest fear about the length of this exhibition series, the issue that had fueled her protest, had been realized; Canada had lost its psychological edge over its perpetual bridesmaid. This series had seen the Yanks claim six victories over the Canucks, three times as many as they had won combined in their seven-year history. They had heard their anthem played in the house of Herb Brooks. They had beaten Canada in its sacred stronghold of Calgary. The hunter had finally caught the hunted. And Shannon Miller knew it.

"What gap?" she asked Mike Petrie of the *Winnipeg Sun*. "That's the problem, there is no gap."

PART TWO

NAGANO GOLD RUSH

Gearing Up

On the road – and they logged thousands of miles around the globe schlepping their gear and armed with a couple of hockey sticks, they looked like any other adult travel hockey team on a shoestring budget. Proud as they were, though, who could blame them if they felt themselves fighting off a bit of anger, and no small amount of embarrassment by their outward appearances?

After all, these were some of the best hockey players in the world, and their sponsor was the United States of America, the richest nation on the planet. And there they were, looking borderline destitute when they showed up for world tournaments.

Lisa Brown-Miller remembers the inaugural IIHF Women's World Championships in the Canadian capital of Ottawa in 1990. "We had nothing. We were showing up with our rec [hockey gear] bags," Brown-Miller said in an early 2022 interview. "Later, someone's dad got us some really nice bags. Made in Massachusetts, nice, heavy-duty, made out of canvas. I still use mine today."

Still later, the team got jackets and some other apparel, but the women always felt they were getting hand-me-down stuff, things that weren't exactly tailored for them. "It felt like some of it was like, 'What do we have left over?'" she asked, suggesting that after outfitting the U.S. Men's National team, its World Junior team and other more traditional USA Hockey-sponsored teams, they were clearly last in line. "I have gear that was absolutely enormous."

But it fit just fine, she said sarcastically, after she rolled the waist down two or three times, and the leg cuffs up at least that much. "If you look at our uniforms at the '90 World Championships, our gear was just massive," said Cammi Granato. "We all looked so huge. Everything was like two or three sizes too big. My pants were *so* big, the jerseys, everything."

The women knew it was hand-me-down gear from the men's program. They would have preferred second-hand stuff from a youth team because it likely would have fit better. Who could blame them if they occasionally felt like second-class citizens? They were, in the eyes of their sponsor. But they didn't care. They were representing their country and even in those early years many of them had an eye toward Nagano 1998, that first Olympic women's tournament. Little things like matching wardrobes and the quality of their bags was just something they would put up with – because that's what girls always did for the privilege of playing hockey.

And then they arrived in Japan for the Olympics. First stop: Athlete Processing, where what they expected would be a routine visit for the requisite lanyard with photo identification turned out to be something much different. "All of a sudden, you walk into this room and you get a shopping cart for all this USA gear," Granato said. "And it's not just you and your team, but the whole contingency of U.S. athletes. And we're all wearing it together. It just hit us in a different way, the excitement."

They wheeled away an Olympic wardrobe that overflowed their shopping carts.

"That was awesome," Gretchen Ulion told reporter Nathan Clark for a 20th anniversary retrospective. "We had never been given much of anything. USA Hockey gave us some stuff, but nothing like how we needed a shopping cart at the Olympics to get all our SWAG."

Brown-Miller recalled how the players were somewhat confused when they were told to grab a cart and go. "Wait, what? And then we'd go through this big room and they'd say, 'Pick the size that fits you.' We could actually try things on," Brown-Miller said. "They actually fit – for the first time. We were like kids in a candy shop. I just remember thinking, *Is this real?* We'd never had the attention or the care that was given to us. Or the interest."

Some of the women couldn't believe their good fortune. Some were even skeptical, like Katie King. "We get everything? We get all this stuff? Is this for real?" she kept asking herself. "At the end, are they going to be like, 'You are charged $5,000?' Every single one of us was walking through that room in awe. And laughing. And having an unbelievable time. It did make it feel a little more real."

Sarah Tueting remembered the thrill of going through processing and how it was tempered "with a very defined, very real, purpose. After that, you're like a real Olympian. There are Olympic rings on your coat! We were just pinching ourselves the whole time."

To be sure, the success of that inaugural women's Olympic ice hockey championship team had to do with more than just fashion. Thanks to Ben Smith, they also had a world-class strength-and-conditioning coach, one of the best equipment men in the business and a sports psychologist to help them through emotional jams. And the women are quick to suggest all three were paramount to their success. But still, it was nice that someone out there was thinking about them as serious athletes.

"The only company at the time catering to the women's game was Louisville," Brown-Miller said. "They were thinking, 'Maybe we should make these a little bit different, whether it's sticks or pants or shoulder pads.'"[12]

They say clothes make the man, but there's a compelling argument that they make the woman, too. Team USA's women's hockey team schlepped home with all that beautiful gear – and wearing Olympic gold medals, too.

---

12 Kelly Dyer Hayes, Brown-Miller's teammate in the early years of the women's national team, transitioned from hockey to repping Louisville gear in the mid-1990s. Hayes, a goaltender, had a couple of sponsors in her playing days, and Louisville was one of them. Hayes headed a team that created a line of hockey equipment and sticks designed for girls and women. She eventually signed former teammates Cammi Granato, Kelly O'Leary and Brown-Miller, using them as prototypes in Louisville's designs. Brown-Miller was the small.

Fear and Loathing

"The possibility of physical and mental collapse is now very real. Buy the ticket, take the ride."

—Hunter S. Thompson

Shortly after their giddy shopping spree, a fully outfitted Team USA went to the rink for its first test event on Olympic ice, an exhibition with host Japan at Aqua Wing Arena. That match was followed by a Canada-Sweden contest. The games meant nothing, but to a North American press corps, they meant everything.

Taking the temperature of the two women's hockey superpowers following those "meaningless" games revealed two teams heading in opposite directions. The Americans appeared positively carefree, while Team Canada was closing ranks, retreating into what Shannon Miller called, "our little bubble."

In the opener, Team USA enjoyed a 10-1 laugher at the expense of host Japan, with captain Cammi Granato and mates in full, just-happy-to-be-here mode. In her post-game comments, Granato admitted that she was "pleasantly surprised" when asked about women's hockey competing for Olympic medals so early in its existence, and that just being in Nagano was truly a "dream come true."

Three hours later, Canadian dreams were more of the nightmare variety.

Coach Miller's charges were entirely out of sorts in their exhibition with Sweden, settling for a 1-1 tie that was an inch from being a loss when Sweden rang a loud shot off the post midway through the game. The test event was also a chance to go through post-game media protocol, one in which Miller denied access to goal-scorer Hayley Wickenheiser, the one player requested by the media pool. Miller justified her action as an attempt to "protect our people."

Canada's media sharks, already sensing trouble, now smelled blood in the water. They could see their country's superstar distraught in the locker room and, in their minds, eager to talk. That's when Miller slammed the door on all player interviews. A startling development, a shocking response.

"Canada Finds Early Trouble. . . Collars Getting Tight. . . Players Bicker," trumpeted the headlines in the next day's *Calgary Herald*. "What is going wrong? What is happening to this precious team?" penned national writer Roy MacGregor, asking for an entire nation. Miller, the only one to speak on behalf of Team Canada, conceded that she "didn't like the team's body language."

Miller was coaching her team into knots. Having said she was saving a few surprises for the Americans, she had shuffled her lines against Sweden – with disastrous results. Teenage rookie Jayna Hefford, who had blossomed into a scoring sensation alongside Wickenheiser, was left scratching her head.

"Right before the Olympics, all of our lines changed," said Hefford, a memory-scab ripped clean off a generation later. "It was a strange thing, because there was a lot of consistency and obviously chemistry there on our line, but we didn't play at the Olympic Games together."

Hefford, Canada's preeminent goal-scorer in the runup against the United States with 11 snipes in 13 games was forced to play with virtual strangers after arriving in Japan. Of Canada's 29 goals scored at the Olympics, the future Hall-of-Famer was limited to a single tally in Nagano. It seemed a colossal waste of talent. Despite her demotion, however, Hefford holds no grudges.

"Shannon was fair to me," said Hefford. "Maybe she pushed the wrong buttons, but at the end of the day, she worked hard to get the most out of everyone." In Hefford's case, the effort failed.

When it came to dueling with counterpart Ben Smith, Miller may have been in over her head. Smith had already been part of an Olympic coaching staff, had coached dozens of IIHF games in World Junior competition, and was entirely at home in the patriarchal establishment of the five-ring order—blue blazers and button-down shirts. Miller, on the other hand, was a rogue who dressed like Johnny Cash, a lesbian who coached with what she felt was little support of her national governing body. When a major magazine sought a cover photo with Miller and Smith—back-to-back with arms crossed—Smith balked, according to Miller. Regardless, Smith didn't need the spotlight, and certainly didn't need to create a buzz for his rival coach. Although he did not recall the photo request incident, he did confess, "I never called her by her name, just 'the Canadian coach.'"

When it came to media requests, Smith resembled his New England coaching hero. "He was a Bill Belichick guy," said assistant Tom Mutch. "What did he need interaction with Team Canada for? He already knew the significance of Team USA from being around the Olympic Games. He didn't need to interact with that coaching staff. His position was: 'You have your team, I have my team.' I think it was a message: 'This is our team ladies, we're Team USA.'"

On February 8, the two dominant forces of women's hockey began their parallel march toward a loud confrontation in the round-robin finale. Canada rang up 24 goals against the sport's weak sisters, Team USA 26. Both dismissed pesky Finland by identical 4-2 scores. All the obstacles had been cleared away.

When the two squads woke up on Valentine's Day, there would be no more distractions, no more posturing, and certainly no love. Two games remained for both teams, both against one another. The landscape of women's hockey was about to experience its seismic shift.

Oh Captain,
My Captain

*"She served with honor and humility. She will always
be my captain, our captain.'*

—Alana Blahoski, teammate

In the Pantheon of America's greatest female athletes, an iconic few have
risen to such heights that they embody their sport: Lisa Leslie in basketball, Jenny Finch in softball and Mia Hamm in soccer. But the fore-
most example of a woman being synonymous with her sport is hockey's
Cammi Granato.

Before we tell her story, though, we must first talk about that name:
Cammi, as the whole world knows her. Last name not required. For
starters, we can just disregard what it might say on her birth certificate.
"No one calls me Catharine," she says. "Well, maybe on the first day of
school or something, or a doctor I haven't seen before. It's always been
Cammi." Always. Starting with the day Catharine Michelle Granato was
brought home from the hospital and introduced to a house full of siblings.
Cammi. Period.

A dark-eyed brunette with a serene, confident smile that quickly puts
those around her at ease, Cammi explains how she became, well, Cammi.
"I was named after my mother's two sisters, Catharine and Michelle. They
just combined my first and middle names."

Cammi is the daughter of Natalie and Don Granato, whose first date – you can't make this stuff up – was attending a Chicago Blackhawks game. She grew up in suburban Chicago among six siblings, a sister, Christina, and four boys: Tony, who enjoyed a standout career in the National Hockey League; Don, a career coach who ascended to the NHL with the Buffalo Sabres; Rob, who played hockey at the University of Wisconsin; and Joe, the baby of the family born, somehow, with a natural immunity to the game.

"He's the smart one," Cammi explained. "He wanted to be President of the United States by the time he was three. He's on another level. Whenever any of us had any questions, we were relying on him – since he was about five. He's just too smart for hockey. Him and my sister, and even our brother Rob, they don't get a lot of attention, but they've always been there for us."

Christina played a little hockey as a youngster but quickly grew out of it. Cammi, conversely, fell head over heels in love with it, playing with as much joy and passion as her older brothers – whether on the ice or in their basement, where the action could get a little rough. Like a generation of American youngsters, the Granato kids were inspired by the 1980 Miracle on Ice game at the Lake Placid Olympics, when a team of college players upset the dominant Soviet Union en route to the gold medal.

In those intense basement games of shinny, Cammi and her brothers would reenact plays by some of the stars of that team, like captain Mike Eruzione, who scored the game-winner against the Soviets, Bill Baker, Mark Pavelich or Jack O'Callahan, who eventually wound up playing for the hometown Blackhawks. She cherished every minute of it – even the bumps and bruises and fat lips from errant shoulders and elbows.

"I was a huge fan of that 1980 team. Then I watched my brother play [in the Calgary Winter Games] in 1988. It was surreal," Granato said. That's when it hit her like a thunderbolt: She wanted desperately to be an

Olympic athlete. So much so that she was willing to give up hockey to get there. Maybe basketball would be her ticket. Perhaps volleyball? She considered both seriously.

"Then two years later I'm pulling on the jersey for the 1990 Worlds," she said. Granato would also wear the Team USA colors in the next IIHF World Championships in 1992, a watershed moment for her as she surpassed fellow Providence Friar Cindy Curley as America's premier women's player. She rang up eight goals in five games for the silver medalists, and won the prestigious IIHF Directorate Award as the team's best player.

"Cammi is a player that is hard to replicate," said Curley, a U.S. Hockey Hall of Famer in her own right. "She had that Wayne Gretzky hockey sense: Wherever she was, the puck found her. I wish I had that sense."

Being recognized as a world-class athlete was not what drove Granato. She wanted to participate in the Olympics, something that was a hot rumor while she was at the World Championships in the spring of '92. That rumor was confirmed by summer, but Cammi, a rising senior at Providence College, calculated that she would have to tread water for four more seasons if she were to even get a shot at the 1998 Winter Games in Nagano. A rare case of self-doubt crept into her mind.

USA Hockey assistant coach Laura Halldorson was in Lake Placid helping run the women's camp when the Nagano news became official. She will never forget her subsequent conversation with Granato. It was in the second-floor conference room at their Training Center.

"I remember talking to Cammi about the Olympics," said Halldorson, who recalled Granato's ambivalence.

"Geez, it's still so far away," said Granato. "Can I hang on?"

Halldorson had coached Colby College the previous three years against Granato's PC Friars, all games in which Granato had dominated.

"I have every confidence in the world you will make it," said Halldorson. "You're the best player in the country. I think you can make it Cammi."

Granato thanked Halldorson and went downstairs to her dorm room. Her dream was still alive, but it required a plan. She had another sensational year for Providence, captained Team USA to its third World Championship silver medal in 1994, and then spent two seasons up in Montreal, playing hockey for Concordia University while taking graduate courses. Following in the footsteps of Karyn Bye, Granato had found an unorthodox solution to closing the gap in the lead-up to the 1998 games.

"They wanted to keep playing and training," said Halldorson about Granato and Bye, "and there weren't a lot of opportunities. I don't know if a lot of people would have thought about doing that, an interesting move."

Captain America swooped down for one more World Championship in 1997, and finally it was mission accomplished when she arrived in Nagano, Japan.

"A dream-come-true," she said. "The timing of it all was so seamless. I had all these dreams. I didn't think I could take them that far, and all of a sudden I'm wearing the Team USA jersey at my first Olympic Games."

And on that sweater, on the upper left chest, was the letter "C" that designated her as captain of her team. By the 1998 Games in Nagano, she had been wearing it for about a half-dozen years, an honor bestowed upon her by her peers.

"Because it was team-voted, I felt comfortable that that's what the team wanted," she said. "From my perspective, I had been kind of primed by my brothers – by my entire family, actually – who taught me that team-first mentality, never getting your feet too high off the ground, everything is for the team.

"The leadership that I had in front of me, my brothers and sister and my parents, I think that primed me to feel like I could just naturally do that…Definitely, there is that thought of the extra stuff you have to do. You can't just focus on you. At first it was a little harder to maneuver, but then I realized that by being myself – I mean, that's why the team picked me – I assumed they picked me for just being me. So I didn't have to change. I think my strengths were probably in managing, for me, it was about personal relationships. Anyone who was struggling or needed any kind of help, that's where I was probably the most aware."

The players all knew they were lucky to have such a natural-born leader wearing the "C." "She was not the most vocal, but she didn't have to be," said Alana Blahoski. "There's a humility about her. She served with honor, never took it for granted. We were able to do some amazing things with her leadership."

Jenny Schmidgall was the second-youngest member of Team USA in Nagano, but already a hardened little hockey warrior. Never one for flattery, Schmidgall simply adored her captain. "I played on a line with her; Cammi has a special piece of my heart," Schmidgall-Potter said a generation later. "One of the great leaders on Team USA."

And leading her mates onto the ice in the inaugural Olympic women's ice hockey tournament in Nagano remains an unforgettable experience. "The best thing about it is the memories," Granato said. "They can take you back in a flash."

She remembered the walk from the locker room to the ice before that first game against China, all the flags from the myriad competing countries, the noise of thousands of fans, many waving flags of their home nations. "I took that first lap in warm-up thinking, *We're here. We made it. We're in a game at the Olympics, right now. This is really happening!* That was a really cool moment I will never forget."

Then, at 7:39 of the first period, with assists from Gretchen Ulion and Schmidgall, Cammi Granato scored the first goal in her nation's first-ever Olympic women's hockey game. No big deal, right? In fact, that was Granato's first instinct. "That was kind of the job that I had, that our team relies on, as one of the offensive players," she acknowledged. "But then, as I skated over to the bench, I started thinking, *I just scored in the Olympics!*

How surreal is that? In my wildest dreams I never thought anything like that would ever happen. It was a really neat moment."

Like many of her teammates, Granato credits coach Ben Smith as being the right coach at the right moment to lead that group. Virtually every move Smith made seemed to work, and his players responded fervently. Between players and coach, trust was implicit and unshakable.

"He came in at the perfect time for us," Granato said. "We all gravitated to his style. He ran a lot of skill-based practices that really improved our team day to day. Our passing – we were a really good passing team, and a really good skating team. And from a fitness standpoint, strength and conditioning, we were in really good shape.

"We all took to that. He was passionate about the game. His experience in the men's game really helped, and it carried over to us. It was obvious he was kind of intrigued by the fact that he was coaching women. He would say things like, 'You guys listen so well, you ask questions, your attention to detail and work ethic is there.' He seemed excited about that. We just had a great relationship with him."

The relationship between Granato and Smith, captain and coach, would thrive as they combined forces to reach their sport's zenith. But how long would it last?

Sleeping With
The Enemy

*"We stand in silence for another moment and I real-
ize how lucky I am to have someone I can be myself
around in all my melancholy glory."*

—Marisa Calin, actress

The last thing Shannon Miller needed in the midst of the most intense,
pressure-packed and tumultuous two weeks of her life was to hear
the confession of one of her players seeking advice on an issue that had
the potential to divide teammates and explode into headlines at the worst
possible time. Her player, it turns out, had struck up a relationship with
someone on Team USA, and she probably wasn't alone. Teammates on
both sides were aware of it. Some didn't like it at all.

"That just really bugged me," said Team USA forward Lisa Brown-
Miller, the oldest player on the team at 31. "I mean, 'Are you kidding me?
They are not our friends. We don't hang out with them.' We had to ask
those players to take a step back from that."

If indeed there is a thin line between the emotions of love and hate, as
scientists have confirmed from studies of brain functions, then for some of
the world's greatest hockey players that line is red, 12 inches wide and sep-
arates the two halves of the standard North American hockey rink. Some
players wouldn't dream of crossing it, ever.

And for others, well, sleeping with the enemy just wasn't a big deal – though their timing may have been quite reasonably called into question.

"Some of our players were friendly, or even friends with, some of the Canadian girls. I was not," said goaltender Sarah Tueting, 21 during the Nagano games. "I wanted nothing to do with any of them, on or off the ice. We're not friends. They are the enemy. . . and there was hate. To me, it felt disloyal to the team. Most of what happened, I really don't know. It didn't affect me one way or the other very strongly, but I do remember some of us would say, 'That's not cool. That's not right.'"

But it's not necessarily wrong, either. At least that's how Shannon Miller viewed it. "There was one relationship that I knew of, and to be honest I was grateful that my player trusted me enough – and that she felt safe enough – to talk with me about it," she acknowledged.

"How do you feel about relationships with players on the other team?" the player asked.

"I don't care at all," Miller responded.

"Good, because I'm dating 'So-and-so.'"

"Fine, just don't let Ben Smith know about it. And you have to ask your roommate. Make sure it's OK there. And I would be careful about the hallways, people seeing you. Just be discreet and be careful."

Naturally, in that environment the rumor mill was in overdrive. "There were all kinds of stories being told, and most of them weren't true," Miller said. "I felt like I was in a circus. But I just didn't think there was anything wrong with people having relationships with someone who lived in another country. Obviously, Ben Smith and I were on opposite ends of the spectrum. From what I understand, he forbade his players to have relationships with anybody on Team Canada. My players talked to me about it, and I just said, 'That's ridiculous. You're all adults. I don't care who you date, but obviously when you suit up, you go to war.'"

Smith, as it happened, tried to impose similar guidelines with Team

USA. "We had had some boundary issues," he said. "One of the things I made clear was not to put people in difficult situations in regards to hotel rooms. If you have a friend, boyfriend or girlfriend, it's unfair to your roommate to bring them into the group's living quarters. I made that pretty clear, pretty early."

But he also acknowledged the concern of some of his players who were adamantly opposed to cross-border fraternization, like Tueting. "I can see why she would object. I find it difficult in regards to confidentialities amongst the teammates," Smith said. "I can understand that. I hope I'm not being sexist or any type of 'phobic,' but I can see why people don't want outsiders in the midst of our group."

Miller theorized that because so many players on either side had been with their national teams for years, had played one another so often in competitions at the highest levels of their sport – including their 13-game runup to the Nagano Games – that familiarity bred more than contempt. It also triggered a kind of reverence that some players found difficult to resist.

"It's a really strong rivalry, yes," Miller said. "And a lot of it has to do with how often those two teams ended up playing one another at the end. For some of them, the rivalry builds and the intensity builds. For others, it softens them, personally."

And for some, the rivalry can serve as an incubator for love – the "in sickness and in health, 'til death do you part" kind of love.

Remarkably – and at the same time perhaps not so surprisingly – the epic tug-of-war between Canada and the USA for supremacy in women's ice hockey has produced three marriages.

Jayna Hefford, one of Canadian Hockey's most prolific scorers and a four-time Olympic gold medalist, and Kathleen Kauth, a bronze medalist on America's 2006 team in Torino, Italy, have been partners since about 2005. They have two daughters and a son. Hefford, of Kingston, Ontario, scored the golden goal in the 2002 games in Salt Lake City, when Canada beat Team USA after losing all 13 games to the Yanks in the runup to the Winter Games. Kauth, of Saratoga Springs, New York, lost her father, Don, who was on the 85th floor of the second World Trade Center tower that was attacked by terrorists on September 11, 2001. A few months later she was one of the final cuts for that 2002 Olympic squad. Inspired by her father's death, she persevered and made the 2006 team that lost in a shootout to Sweden in the semifinals and settled for the bronze.

The couple played against one another in the 2005 IIHF World Championships in Sweden, and at no time was Hefford ever aware that her partner was even on the ice.

"No, no. It never enters your mind," she said. "You just play. You see the jersey, that's all you see. As athletes, we're all competitive. You want to win all the time; it doesn't matter who you're playing against. You don't want to give anyone an edge. You can be competing against your best friend, but you're competing for bragging rights, for excellence, and all those things you train your entire life for.

"I think it's a very old-school thought, that because you hate the team you can't talk to them, you can't have a relationship. Whether it's a relationship or a friendship, you don't hate the people, you hate the competition. I don't think the hatred is ever personal."

Toronto's Gillian Apps is a descendant of hockey royalty. Her grandfather, Syl Apps, was a three-time Stanley Cup champion with the Maple Leafs and he was inducted into the Hockey Hall of Fame in 1961. She and

Meghan Duggan competed against one another for several years. Both were forwards. Both wore No. 10. Both captained their teams. They faced off twice in the Olympic Games, in 2010 and 2014. Each time Apps skated away with the gold medal, Duggan the silver. But Duggan, of Danvers, Massachusetts, finally got her Olympic gold in 2018. The following September, in a gorgeous ceremony chronicled in photos posted on their social media pages, the couple was married. They have two children, a son and a daughter.

Duggan recalled being aware of the rivalry between the women of Canada and the United States since she was ten years old. And later she spent 14 years right in the middle of it.

"People always want to talk about the hate," she said. "but it's a rivalry I admire and respect. It's so exciting to be a part of, such dynamic pressure, such high stakes. A lot of times it comes down to one huge goal every four years. I've been on both ends of it. On a personal level, I know we have our own unique story – I married one of my deepest rivals."

Losing to Apps and the Canadians, especially being so close to a gold medal in 2014 was something that riles Duggan to this day. "That was tough, I'm not going to sugarcoat it. It was unbelievably tough, one of the most heartbreaking experiences in our lives. It certainly was one of the most difficult things I've ever been through in sports.

"As much as you try to separate your professional life and your personal life – and I know a lot of people have to do that – it's not easy. We needed some space for a long period of time.But at the end of the day, this is my family after all."

Eight years later, when the rivalry was again celebrated at the Winter Games in Beijing, the couple still needed a little space. Duggan welcomed many of her American friends to her home to watch the game. Her wife was not invited.

Caroline Ouellette, a French-Canadian from Montreal, and Julie Chu, an Asian-American from Fairfield, Connecticut, have also been a couple since the mid 2000s. Both were captains of their teams. Both wore No. 13. Three times they competed for Olympic gold. Chu, a brilliant, two-way center who played on both special teams, won silver thrice and a bronze once. But Chu is also a five-time gold-medalist in the IIHF World Championships. Ouellette, along with teammates Jayna Hefford and Hayley Wickenheiser, is one of only five athletes to win gold in four consecutive Olympic games.

Chu and Ouellette were first introduced at a hockey camp for youth in Peterborough, Ontario, in the summer of 2003. They had been invited by their teammate, Jennifer Botterill. Chu and Botterill were teammates at Harvard. Botterill was Ouellette's longtime center on Canada's national team. Coincidentally, Chu and Ouellette had crossed paths a few months earlier in the handshake line after the NCAA championship game when Chu's Harvard team lost to Ouellette and the University of Minnesota-Duluth, coached by Shannon Miller. UMD prevailed in double-overtime, 4-3, in what is widely considered to be the greatest women's college hockey game of all time. Ouellette was named the tournament MVP.

Then in Peterborough the magic happened. At least for Ouellette. She locked eyes with Chu and her knees buckled. "I fell in love with her from the moment I saw her," Ouellette said. "I think it was her laugh, her smile that got me right away. She has such a beautiful and kind personality, and she is so wonderful. She just adds life and energy in any room she's in, and she is the kindest person you will ever meet."

They became fast friends, but it took awhile for a more intimate relationship to develop. "I was actually dating someone else at the time and wasn't really having an eye for anyone else," Chu said. "Not long after we broke up, it went from there."

Ouellette wound up spending 16 years with Canada's national women's team. Chu spent 14 years with USA Hockey's national team. She is one of three siblings of a Chinese father, Wah, who immigrated to America with his mother when he was 16, and mother Miriam, whose father is Chinese and whose mother is Puerto Rican. The games between the two nations provided some of the fiercest, most exhilarating competition the women had ever experienced.

And yes, both agreed, there was definitely hate involved.

"It was the kind of culture where, to beat them you have to hate them," Ouellette said. "It's one of the greatest rivalries in sports, in my opinion. I wish that every game in my career was against the U.S. That's how much I loved it."

That love-hate thing again, eh?

The couple played against one another too many times to count, and they were frequently on the ice together, battling for the puck, for their team, for the honor and glory of their country. Difficult? A little bit. Particularly when Canada went on the power play and Chu was killing the penalty for the Americans.

"If we're going after the puck and I give Caroline a shot in the ribs to get it, it's not because it's Caroline," Chu said. "But I think we both secretly wished, maybe hoped, that I wasn't lined up on Caroline's side when she was winding up for a one-timer from the point."

But even then – perhaps *especially* then – their relationship took a backseat to their dreams and goals.

"I think what helped us along, the way we were able to compete against one another, is that we both were really committed to our teams – and our teammates knew that," Chu said. "They knew we loved our teams. That was really important to our teammates. Even though Caro and I were dating, nothing changed in terms of how we prepared, how we were going to play, that we were going to try and do everything possible to make our teams successful.

"As competitors – and as people – we take pride in what we do and what we commit to. I think it helped that neither of us are the dirty ones on the ice, the kind that get under the other team's skin a lot. I know I'm not good at trash talk and I've never heard you chirp," Chu added, glancing at her partner.

Caroline responded with a grin. "Well, maybe a little bit," Chu conceded.

With the stakes so high, the passion and the commitment so intense, two people under the same roof chasing the same goals and dreams, how can they possibly handle the enormous heartbreak for one while the other is celebrating reaching the Olympic summit with a gold medal? No matter the result, one is deliriously happy and the other profoundly disappointed.

"And Sochi is one of those moments," Chu confessed.

For the Team USA captain, it was a soul-crushing defeat in Russia at the 2014 Winter Games. The Americans led in the gold-medal game, 2-0, with less than four minutes to play in regulation. But Canada cut its deficit in half with a goal from Brianna Jenner at the 56:34 mark, then tied it on a goal by Marie-Philip Poulin with just 55 seconds remaining to send it into overtime. Poulin won it with her golden goal on a five-on-three power play at 68:10. Both Jocelyne Lamoureaux (slashing) and Hilary Knight (cross-checking) were in the penalty box. Chu was one of three skaters defending. She wound up with silver. Again. Ouellette won gold. Again.

"It took awhile to get over that moment," Chu said. "But that's just the reality of sport. You dedicate yourself to being the best in the world, and you fall short. On the flip side, we love each other and we felt a great balance of understanding how we could support each other. I have a best friend who knew everything I was going through. I had someone who understood the highs and the lows and what it was like to go through those things. It's about respecting each other – for me allowing Caroline to celebrate and for Caroline also knowing that she cares for me and that I'm hurting, finding ways to still acknowledge that we care about each other. We celebrate with our teammates – and after the game we feel for our partner, who we love."

Ouellette learned of the power of such support from her parents. She got her love of sports from her father, Andre, though he discouraged her interest in hockey. He feared it would be too rough for her. It was her mother, Nicole, who gets credit for two of the most important moments in Caroline's life. After two years of begging her father, to no avail, it was her mother who took her to the rink, traded in her figure skates for a pair of hockey skates and turned her daughter loose to compete with boys.

Nicole Ouellette also told her daughter: "If someone is beautiful to you and you love them, then you should tell them." And so she did. But she and Chu kept their relationship under wraps for years while they were still competing against one another at the highest levels of their sport.

While their teammates knew they were partners, the couple chose not to come out publicly because they wanted people, particularly the media, to speak and write about their game, to focus on their teams, Oullette said. "And when we finally did [come out], we didn't have any idea about the impact that it could have on young girls – and young boys," she added. "They reached out to us and told us, 'You're an inspiration. You have no idea how much this helps me.'"

The couple also was heartened to see the needle moving, if only slightly, on the men's side. In September 2020, then 17-year-old New Brunswicker Yanic Duplessis, an elite junior prospect, revealed he was gay after he was outed at a party he didn't attend. "It was a struggle for me, and it shouldn't be," he said in an interview with CBC's Quebec AM. "It shouldn't be a big deal." But it was headline news throughout Canada.

And in August 2021, Luke Prokop, a third-round draft pick of the Nashville Predators, came out, saying he felt like "a new version of himself."

"That was huge, *huge* for men's hockey," Ouellette said. "Today in the female game I see young girls in their teenage years, and they feel comfortable coming out. They feel comfortable telling their parents, telling their friends. But on the men's side, on the boys' side of hockey, it has always been very close-minded."

Ouellette and Chu experienced that close-minded chill at the Winter Games in Sochi, Russia, in 2014, when they were among only about a half-dozen openly gay athletes. They had been warned in advance by Russia's minister of sports, Vitaly L. Mutko, that athletes of "nontraditional" sexual orientation were welcome to compete, but they would be expected to obey a new Russian law banning "homosexual propaganda" or face criminal prosecution. Mutko was speaking for his boss, President Vladimir Putin, and it cast a pall over the entire experience for the athletes.

"For sure it was difficult as a gay couple, and for other players on our team who were openly gay at the time," Chu said. "When we spoke about it as a team and what we could actually do, we just reminded ourselves what the Olympic Games actually stand for. It goes beyond one person, or even one country's vision. Hopefully, we could ensure that acceptance, that inclusion, is shown in the way we carry ourselves when we're at the Olympics. That's what's going to be able to change minds and break down barriers."

On their retirement and into their marriage, they've strived to maintain that attitude as coaches and as parents of two little girls. It is their touchstone with the youth they inspire and with the players they coach with their Concordia University Stingers team. They often take their daughter, Liv, a little social butterfly among the players. That's where the idea crystallized for them that it is the adults who can and must set the standard for how we treat one another.

"That's our power as parents, as adults, in shaping our younger generation to be more open and accepting," Chu told an interviewer on *whereparentstalk.com.* "Caroline runs a not-for-profit hockey celebration, and what was so important to us is that these girls are so excited to be around us, to be around our daughter. And they don't even bat an eyelid that we're a gay couple. It's just, 'Oooh, it's Baby Liv, and it's Caroline and Julie and they're together and. . . okay!' That wouldn't happen when we were growing up. There just weren't that many role models, or many people that were outwardly gay with families in our everyday lives."

In their Montreal home so full of love, Caroline Ouellette and Julie Chu still find room to celebrate an epic rivalry that will forever be part of their lives. Their daughters – Liv, carried by Caroline, and Tessa, carried by Julie – each have plenty of cute little outfits from both Team Canada and Team USA. But at certain times, like when the intensity gets ratcheted up during the World Championships or the Olympics, that clothing stays in the dresser.

"That's when we bring out our Stingers' stuff," Chu said.

Meanwhile, former teammates like A.J. Mleczko, who transitioned to broadcasting after her playing career, remain in awe of what Ouellette and Chu have built together.

"How weird is it that members of this bitter rivalry have crossed over, married and started families?" Mleczko asked. "It's amazing that they were able to rise above that and find such beautiful lives together. It speaks volumes about the respect of the two countries and the rivalry. I know if I'm Julie Chu and I'm married to someone that has four gold medals that I wanted, and I've got three silvers and a bronze – that's tough. And she's living in Canada, where Ouellette is a legend. What an amazing relationship. What an amazing family they're creating. And what a great thing that is for our sport."

In early 1998, Alana Blahoski was a 23-year-old forward helping Team USA win gold in Nagano. As the 25th year anniversary of that epic event approached, she was in her late 40s and pursuing a master's degree in sports psychology. Coincidentally, one of her graduate courses was called Sports and Society, in which students delved into the history of sport and how it still revolves, as she described it, "around this white heterosexual male identity – and it has to be very macho."

For women in sports, she said, there is more tolerance regarding sexual identity, but there remains some negative stereotypes. "If you play college softball or hockey, then right away you're labeled a lesbian. If you're a white male athlete, you're just seen as heterosexual, and there's nothing that can change that. And for a long time, if you were a female athlete you were just labeled as gay. That's the way it was; luckily, things are changing."

When she was with the women's national team, the topic felt almost taboo. "It wasn't really spoken about when I played, and it was not addressed by USA Hockey at all. You were expected to keep it on the hush-hush. You had your private life and you had your hockey life."

All of which seemed rather naïve, considering society's modern-day demographics, she said. "Statistically speaking, you're going to have a couple of gay people on every team, male or female. The fact that you had to keep it hidden for so long – you're training, you're playing. And hockey is such a small world; it's the same circle, especially if you're a female athlete in training. That could be another reason these players are taking a liking to one another, and then exploring that. It kind of makes it easy because you have the same schedule, you're going for the same thing, you have a shared passion. But the girls who did that, and there weren't many, I think when I played there were one or two, it was always handled in the most professional way. It was never a problem. Really never."

That there have been unions like Hefford and Kauth, Chi and Ouellette and Apps and Duggan is hardly surprising to Blahoski.

"It speaks to the passion of the sport and the rivalry," Blahoski said. "These girls, yes they compete for different countries, but a lot of them attend the same university, where they have more time playing together as teammates than as rivals. They see each other every day for four years, as opposed to a sprinkling of international tournaments."

The bottom line, however, Blahoski continued, is that sports – including and especially hockey – remain in the dark ages with respect to gender equity.

"Hockey, I feel, is so far behind in embracing that part of the game," she said. "It's [the NHL] the last sports league to have a male player come out as openly gay. And it exists. I wouldn't be shocked if there were teammates that were dating. But of course that's such a taboo thing to even mention. People don't want to see that. Attitudes are changing. There is definitely more of an acceptance. But it's been much slower for the male athlete."

Few have understood this rivalry between the women of Team Canada and Team USA – and the enormous effect it has on the individual competitors – like Austrian-born psychologist Peter Haberl. His work with the 1998 American team led to a full-time position with the U.S. Olympic Committee. He ranks the women's USA-Canada hockey rivalry among the greatest the world has ever seen.

"It's more intense than Germany-Brazil in men's soccer, maybe England and Germany, 1966, at Wembley [Stadium], maybe Celtics-Lakers," Haberl said. "As you watch the Canadian and U.S. women over the ages, I think there comes an understanding of how much each side has benefitted from the rivalry. In sports psychology, you find competition not as triumphing over somebody, but coming back to the Latin root *competere*, which is to seek excellence together. So if you want to be really good at something, you actually want to have a rival – and be blessed by your rival – because that rival can bring out the best in you."

That explains why an iconic athlete like Caroline Ouellette says she wishes every game she ever played could have been against the Americans: Because it forced her to be better, to be the greatest version of her hockey-playing self. Clearly it affected the way she viewed members of the opposition.

"What's interesting, and what we're alluding to here with those cross-border relationships, is perhaps we can learn something from them," Haberl said. "That despite the fierceness of that rivalry, love is possible."

Angela Ruggiero understands that now, after a brilliant 14-year career with Team USA's national team. In 1998, she was the youngest player on the team and had little media training before being thrown into the spotlight. She found herself just following along with reporters when they lobbed cliché questions in her direction.

"'Do you hate them?' I remember getting that question all the time as an 18-year-old," Ruggiero said. "And I just went along and said, 'Yeah, I hate them.' But did I? People tried to manufacture this enemy."

But the more she played against Canada, the greater appreciation she had for her rival.

"I know I always walked bigger in the lobby when I passed the Canadians," she said. "I wanted to let them know I was here. I was ready. I was fit. You just conducted yourself, you carried yourself a little differently when Canada was around. But eventually you realize that we're all in it together. Women's sports are all in it together.

"I rose to the occasion when I played Canada. I loved playing Canada. We needed each other, to push each other in the gym even when we're alone. It's hard to train. You need that rivalry. All these things you bring to the table – the red-white-and-blue vs. the leaf. But there's more in common than there is different.

"It's hard to peel that back when the world is telling you that they're your biggest enemy, when in some ways they're actually your best friend. It's not even love-hate; you just want to win. I was so competitive, every little piece of the ice – even off the ice – I wanted to prove what I could do. And I loved it. It's what drove me to be better."

So while the teen-aged Angela Ruggiero just smiled, nodded and said, 'Yeah, I hate them,' when asked about her rivals to the north, the 40-something Ruggiero who competed on four Olympic teams and later served eight years on the IOC's executive board, was quick to reassess that notion.

"Did I really hate them?" she asked. "I actually loved them in some bizarre way because they got me amped up. They got me ready. They gave me the target that I was shooting for. And that helped the game."

The Miracle Man

"Hey coach, I just wanted to see if you had any magic left. There's got to be a little more Miracle in you."

—Assistant coach Tom Mutch

B en Smith is a hockey raconteur, a man who loves to regale listeners with clever stories, witty yarns, and forgotten fragments of the sport's history. He is a stickler for accuracy, whether it pertains to Jack Parker, Hobey Baker or the architecture of the original Boston Arena. To use one of his own pet phrases, the man knows his onions.

He stumps a lot of tavern dwellers with this trivia item: How many Olympic teams did Herb Brooks coach? A novice will answer one, a veteran might offer two. Smith has won a lot of sudsy pints by revealing the correct answer: three. In addition to coaching the 1980 and 2002 U.S. men's teams, Brooks found himself in Nagano coaching the French national team, thanks to timely recruiting by expat Jimmy Tibbetts, a Bostonian who has been playing, coaching and managing hockey in France since the late 1970s.

Brooks was scouting for the NHL Penguins in 1997 when Tibbetts pitched him to coach Team France. Brooks got permission from Pittsburgh GM Craig Patrick—his right-hand man at the Miracle on Ice—to take the gig on the condition that he keep an eye out for international prospects while he was at it.

So unbeknownst to most fans, Brooks coached at the 1998 Winter Games in Nagano, representing France despite not knowing a word of the native tongue. According to Team France GM Tibbetts, Brooks spent no time at the French pavilion within the Olympic Village, preferring to hang out in the cafeteria instead. He was the only person in the Village with no national team garb, having given all of it away to his final cut from Team France. For a guy known as the architect of the greatest moment in American sports Olympics history, he found himself as an outsider, a loner in a fading green trench coat in the midst of abundant color.

"He was kind of a lost soul," said Smith, whose observations proved to be accurate. One might presume Brooks socially would have latched on with the Team USA men, the latest variation of the group he guided to fame and glory in Lake Placid. But there was a problem. Team USA coach Ron Wilson still had a festering wound from being cut by Brooks' University of Minnesota team a generation prior, a memory so painful that Wilson actually detested the sight of Brooks.

So there was the Miracle coach, one of the most recognizable figures in Olympic history, standing alone with his lunch tray in the Village cafeteria, the proverbial sixth-grader at a new school. And then Brooks spotted Bob Webster, his trusty equipment man from 1980, and the lonely coach found safe harbor—the crew from Team USA women. Brooks' colleague Tibbetts was pals with fellow Bostonians Smith and Tom Mutch, and along with Webster, the five of them became their own coffee klatch for two weeks in Nagano.

Smith, an early riser by nature, began most days with a cup of joe and conversation with the GM of Team France.

"Where's Herb, have you seen Herb?" Tibbetts would ask with a hint of desperation.

"Yeah, don't worry Jimmy, he was with Mutchie and Webbie last night."

Smith sensed that Brooks was a "pariah" to the men's team, so he and his crew made a point of including him in all their downtime activities. "Herb was there by himself, he wasn't speaking French," said Smith. "Every time we went out, we would just grab Herb. We'd go to the games together because Webbie could always scrounge up a car. Bobby [Webster] was magnificent in the off-ice stuff: transportation, libations, all sorts of different things." Webster was the perfect facilitator at these international events, a veteran who got things done with both modesty and efficiency.

Every day Herb took his coffee and lunch with his new gang, a comfortable perch from which to admire all the athletes and celebrities who were in constant motion throughout the Village. Smith seized on the opportunity to pick the brain of the Miracle mastermind, eager to learn whatever he could from the man who glistened gold. Smith came right out and asked Brooks for the recipe to his secret sauce.

"What are the keys to winning?" asked Smith.

"Make sure you know how to rebound," said Brooks with a sly grin. "It's going to come down to rebounding."

"You mean the paint? The crease?" asked Smith, nonplussed. "We're not playing basketball, coach."

"No, no, no!" said Brooks. "What happens when things go bad? How do you rebound when they do?" Smith never forgot the lesson. "Herb was big on rebounding."

Smith and Mutch continued to press Brooks on how to win the Olympics. Decades later Smith quotes the Miracle Man. "The lesson I learned from Herb, the one we always recite is: 'Rule Number 1: Don't beat yourself.'

"Mutchie goes, 'What's Rule Number 2?' We never figured that out, but that's a good one," said Smith, laughing hard at the memory. "Rule Number 1 is good!"

Mutch loved shouldering up next to Brooks' celebrity in the cafeteria, especially when stars and starlets in their national team tracksuits plopped their trays down to visit with the man with the golden aura.

"I was in awe of where I was," said Mutch. "We sit down with Ben and Coach Brooks, and here comes Mary Lou Retton." The American gymnastics legend sat and compared notes with Brooks for a short time before leaving. Mutch was star-struck as he followed Brooks out of the cafeteria with Smith in his wake. Brooks was off to reconnoiter with Tibbetts, and Smith and Mutch needed to get to Aqua Wing. As the two parties shook hands and splintered off, Mutch was struck by a brainstorm.

"We take a couple of steps, and I spin back. 'Hey Coach!'"

"What's up Mutchie?" Brooks responded.

The exuberant assistant reached out for another handshake, and while grasping his paw, manipulated Brooks 180 degrees. The two men were now back-to-back. Smith will never forget the ensuing scene, one straight out of the Three Stooges' playbook.

"We're at the transportation center and Herb's wishing us luck, and all of a sudden Mutchie skooches over and puts his shoulder behind Herb's waist. He rubs his coat all the way to Herb's shoulders."

Mutch, a natural-born cutup with a healthy appetite for the inane, described this scene as if it were commonplace.

"I reach out and spin him, and I'm rubbing backs with him," said Mutch, who then spent several seconds back-to-back with the middle-aged man, rubbing up and down with the confused Brooks. "Hey coach," said the fired-up Mutch, "Just wanted to see if you had any magic left. There's gotta be a little more Miracle in you."

Brooks' dour look softened, staring first at Mutch and then Smith before speaking.

"You guys are good."

With that, Brooks spun away to meet up with his team of foreigners, a rare smile splitting his face.

Wonder Woman

"I am woman, I am strong, I am invincible."

—Helen Reddy, recording artist

Twenty-four years to the day – February 8, 2022 – A.J. Mleczko and Angela Ruggiero were teammates again.

In 1998, they wore their country's colors as stalwarts on Team USA playing its first-ever game in the Olympics' inaugural women's ice hockey tournament. They defeated China, 5-0, that day. Now they were reunited, working as color TV commentators for NBC as it broadcast the Winter Games from Beijing. And there was Mleczko, breaking down the action on a faded highlight clip of their teammate, captain Cammi Granato, scoring two goals. Another highlight showed Mleczko herself, muscling a Chinese player to the ice – an act that earned A.J. a trip to the penalty box.

Great fun, certainly, but what NBC's producers failed to show were any highlights of Team USA defender Tara Mounsey, who set up Karyn Bye for a power play goal before scoring one of her own. In other words, NBC missed an open net from close range, blowing an opportunity to showcase one of the sport's all-time greats.

Team USA coach Ben Smith says so. Smith has never been shy in his praise of Mounsey. A self-proclaimed "low-profile" personality, Mounsey was a giant to her teammates and coaches. Smith puts her on USA

Hockey's Mount Rushmore of Olympic hockey legends. Right alongside John Mayasich, who led the American men to their first Olympic gold in 1960. Mayasich is the player he often compares to Mounsey when he considers their star-quality and importance to their respective golden teams.

Smith's assistant Tom Mutch compares Mounsey to another Hall-of-Famer. "Brian Leetch," said Mutch, recalling the New York Rangers All-Star who competed with the Team USA's men in Nagano. "Both lefties, both used Easton sticks, both had confidence and swagger. Two similar players, that's how I envision Tara and Leetch: shoot it well, pass it well, defend well. If you have the puck the whole time, that's defending."

Mounsey and Leetch also wore the same number, leading to some good-natured chirping when Leetch arrived in Nagano a week after Mounsey.

"The men's team comes in, and the joke was, 'We already have a Number 2 out here,'" said Mutch. "The boys were teasing Leetch because they were like, 'Wow, look at *this* Number 2 play!'"

Lofty praise from a team of NHL stars.

Like Lee Johnson before her, Mounsey was a once-in-a-generation Wonder Woman, a powerful force who controlled the action, regardless of the competition, regardless of gender. Mounsey led the Concord, New Hampshire boys' high school team to the 1996 state championship, earning Player-of-the Year honors along the way. Her thrilling rink-length rushes made Mounsey impossible to ignore, conjuring up memories of Bobby Orr and even the other legend who played prep hockey in Concord—Hobey Baker of the St. Paul's School.

After high school, Mounsey carried Brown University to the 1997 ECAC championship game, and then donned the red, white and blue at the World Championships in Kitchener. The games against Canada were much more physical than college play, which pleased Mounsey immensely.

With Ruggiero, an equally physical bookend on the blue line, the Americans finally had some muscle of their own.

"I absolutely loved the physicality of it!" said Mounsey. "It was exactly like playing high school boys, and that's why I loved it. You watch a [USA-Canada] women's game and you would think that there was body checking."

Shortly after Mounsey joined the national team for the 1997-98 season, Smith realized he had to make a major adjustment to her game, and it had nothing to do with her passion for physical contact. She needed a better understanding of hockey as a team game.

"Growing up, I was able to carry the puck end-to-end, lug it, and walk through people," said Mounsey. "Then you get to this new level, I'm a 19-year-old kid, and I think I can still do that."

Those mad dashes were Mounsey's calling card, both in practice and games, and although they may have delighted fans, they turned her teammates into statues. So in the middle of a practice down in Walpole, Smith blew his whistle and halted the action. He cleared the ice of everyone except Mounsey, himself, and a single puck. Mounsey was confused, her teammates silent.

"All of a sudden he stops practice and puts me on the goal line," said Mounsey, vividly recalling the scene.

"Alright," said Smith, loud enough for everyone to hear. "I'm going to blow the whistle, and you're going to go. I want to see if you can beat this puck to the other end of the ice."

The players on the bench perked up. This was going to be interesting. The coach and the budding superstar were involved in some kind of dramatic tension as Mounsey got into a crouched stance, ready to sprint.

"So he was going to shoot the puck to the other end, and I had to skate and beat the puck," said Mounsey. "Sure. I jumped on the goal line."

Smith blew his whistle, Mounsey took off, and then the coach proceeded to fire a slapshot the length of the ice.

"I'm barely three strides off the goal line, and the puck is hitting the boards at the other end." Mounsey stopped when she heard the puck crash into the boards nearly 200 feet away. The middle-aged guy with the whistle stared her down.

"Move the puck!" he said. "The puck goes much faster than you can skate."

"Ooooh," said Mounsey, the light bulb switching on overhead. "Good point."

Mounsey made the adjustment, of course. Sadly, Olympic hockey fans never got to see a woman emulating Bobby Orr in Nagano. But they did see Tara Mounsey in her prime, a swashbuckler who put Team Canada on its heels while at the same time raising the level of her teammates.

Among the least surprised was coach Smith. From the instant he saw Tara Mounsey play, he knew he was witnessing the dominant chess piece needed to checkmate the champs.

"She was," Smith said, "the lynchpin of the whole thing."

A Bag of Doughnuts

"Women should do a lot more fighting. I don't think it's fair that we can't get into a good bar fight once in a while. We'd get out a lot of stuff we're supposed to repress."

—Sandra Bullock

By the time Team Canada and Team USA met for their round-robin match, it had already been established that the rivals would meet with Olympic gold at stake. The United States had won each of its first four games by a margin of 26-3; Canada won its four by a combined score of 24-5. No one was surprised.

The gold-medal game would be epic. But that preliminary contest? Fairly meaningless, eh? A good moment to showcase the women's game to all the young girls around the world watching and wondering about what the sport might hold for them – a kind of love-letter to them from the sport of hockey, on Valentine's Day. At least that's what an International Ice Hockey Federation official had in mind when he brought the two coaches together for a meeting the day before that game.

Although Ben Smith has no recollection of it, Canada's coach Shannon Miller remembers trying to be friendly. She also recalls Smith refusing to even make eye contact with her.

"Listen," the IIHF official said, according to Miller, "I would ask you both to have a very sportsmanlike game. Then, in the gold-medal game, you can come out guns a-blazing."

He then asked the coaches to shake hands, which they did. Reluctantly, Miller said.

Smith tells a different version. Faced with the hypothetical of such a request to "play it friendly," Smith was as direct as a right cross. "I would never tell my kids to pull back. I might tell my players to be careful to stay out of the box, because the refs will be calling the game tighter."

Miller sticks by her story. "I told my boss about the meeting and what was said, and I also told my team what happened; that was a mistake. I was young enough to drink the Kool Aid, so I told them that this would be a fun, competitive match. No rough stuff. No retaliation. Blah, blah, blah. I made the mistake of believing that's how both teams were going to play.

"That's not what happened. What happened was, they beat the shit out of us, and we came away from that game extremely injured."

The scoresheet suggests that the Americans were paying dearly for their transgressions. Canada built a 4-1 lead. Each of its goals were scored on power plays. Canada's Lori Dupuis opened the scoring three minutes into the second period, and Cammi Granato responded for the Americans. Midway through the period, in a move predetermined by Smith, Sara DeCosta replaced Sarah Tueting in goal.

In the final minute of the middle period, Vicki Movsessian was whistled for high-sticking after the blade of her stick caught Canada's Danielle Goyette in the throat. While Goyette skated to the bench in obvious pain, Movsessian took up residence in the penalty box for a double-minor, all but 10 seconds of which would bleed over into the third period.

"We had a lot of penalties," said Sandra Whyte. "I was a penalty killer, and I just felt like that's all we were doing, PK, PK, PK."

The teams ratcheted up the intensity to start the third period. The

Canadians made the best use of their manpower advantage and went on a roll – and the Americans continued with the penalties. They were far from playing their best hockey, Lisa Brown-Miller acknowledged, but no one on her side was giving up. "We were just getting hammered with penalties," she said. "I remember thinking, 'Come on! Stop with the whistles.'"

Six minutes into the third period, Canada had built what seemed to everyone in the arena to be an insurmountable lead. Three straight power-play goals, one of them on a 5-on-3 advantage, gave the Canadians a 4-1 lead. The last of the three – a shot from the blue line by Therese Brisson, beat DeCosta between the pads.

"If you're ever down to Canada 4-1, you're not coming back, no chance," captain Cammi Granato said. "Never in our history of playing them have we been able to do something like that."

Smith didn't care as much about the win or the loss as much as he cared about his team continuing to play within itself and not fall into disarray ahead of the gold-medal game. So shortly after Brisson's goal with 14:07 remaining in regulation, he called a time out, which still stands as one of the momentous coaching decisions of his career. This was all about getting his team to "rebound" from adversity – the lesson he learned just a few days earlier from Herb Brooks.

"I could just sense what was going on on the ice, and more importantly on the bench, and how we were squeezing the sticks, how tight we were," Smith said. "I always thought our team had some cool to it, some swagger to it, and we had anything but that."

Assistant coach Tom Mutch could see the pressure in the eyes and shoulders of the players as Smith began his memorable chat. "Ladies, this game is worth a bag of doughnuts," he said, reminding them that the only thing at stake was their own pride. "Let's go back to Burlington."

That single word – Burlington – was reminder enough of one of their darkest moments as a team when they were locked out of their dressing room – by their own coach – who wanted to rub their noses in the sounds of Team Canada players boisterously celebrating after a Team USA meltdown on national TV. It was like a slap in the face his team desperately needed.

"They heard that message," Mutch said, recalling that inexcusable loss in Burlington. "They didn't forget. That's how Ben thinks. . . Bang!"

Now was the moment, Smith thought as he called that time out, to plant a stake in the ground. "I just wanted to remind them to play like who we are. Never mind the other team. Never mind the score. Let's just get back to being who we are, because I knew there was another game coming."

Then he explained, in the simplest terms, how they were going to climb that mountain. "For starters, stay out of the box," he implored his team, "and then, score a goal. Just one goal, then let's see what happens. Go play now. And don't be nervous."

A simple, subtle message: Be yourselves. Play your own game. Show why you belong here, in this moment. And have fun. Mutch could see how it registered with the players.

"It pumped their tires up so big," he said. "It relieved the pressure. It was like, whoa. That message was so subtle, but the players had been around Ben, so they understood. He could have gone the other way during that time out and really gotten after them. But he knew what he had seen all tour long, that the team was not playing the way they could. He relaxed them."

What followed was something straight out of Hollywood: just under 15 minutes that would forever change the trajectory of this extraordinary rivalry – and forge strikingly different memories among the combatants.

"Just thinking about it now, my body is full of goosebumps," Brown-Miller recalled nearly 24 years later.

As Canada's Miller described it, her pulse seemed to quicken, her voice tinged with anger and regret. "We were winning and it was late when Ben called the timeout. Some of our players had kind of stopped playing, which you never do. Some were coasting, not really competing. Some were physically intimidated. And unfortunately for us, and for [goaltender] Leslie Reddon, everything they shot went in."

In a span of 6:32, the Americans tied the game with goals by Laurie Baker, Granato and Jenny Schmidgall. In the midst of that flurry, Team Canada had a glorious chance to restore order and retake a commanding lead, but goaltender Sara DeCosta made the biggest save of her career at that critical juncture.

"She has to stop a partial breakaway at 4-2," Smith said. "If they score, the air comes out of the balloon, but she made a great save."

After Schmidgall tied it, there remained nearly 7½ minutes yet to play. Canada was on the ropes, and the Americans were feeling one of those rare moments that are impossible to describe.

"We scored a goal, then another goal, then another goal," Brown-Miller recalled. "It was like you're a surfer and you're riding a wave and you can see for miles and miles. It was just. . . working. Things were starting to crumble for them, and our confidence just kept building and building and building."

Tricia Dunn put Team USA ahead just 23 seconds after Schmidgall tied it, followed in the closing minutes by two more, one by Brown-Miller and an empty-netter by Baker. Six straight goals with the crowd of 5,782 at the Aqua Wing Arena chanting "USA! USA!" Final score, 7-4.

Although this was not a medal-round game, the Canada-Team USA round-robin matchup had major reverberations throughout the United States. CBS re-aired long segments of the game and a variety of highlight packages over the middle weekend of its Olympic coverage. Millions of Americans saw the stirring comeback, two of the goals coming from the American captain. After years of toiling in near anonymity, Cammi Granato was taking her star turn, an Olympic triumph on network television. With the eyes of the world turned squarely on Team USA, Granato enjoyed her finest hour.

But it was more than just the goals that had such a devastating effect on Team Canada, Miller said. It was the brutality with which the Americans closed out the game, a game that was supposed to be a "friendly" display of hockey, that left her team shaken.

"They changed strategy, and that's when they beat the shit out of us, and everybody knows it," Miller said. "We came away from that game extremely injured. Our captain, Stacy Wilson, was in the hospital with internal bleeding. She was checked from behind after a whistle. Hayley Wickenheiser, our top shooter, somebody two-handed her elbow and broke it open. Danielle Goyette just got beat up to death, and she was playing on our top line with Hayley. Another player had a cracked ankle after a two-hander. We limped into the gold-medal game, that's the unfortunate part."

Goyette dished out as much as she got. She was a focal point of the Americans for what they perceived as dirty play, provocative, unnecessary and unbecoming of a rivalry between two immensely skilled teams. Sandra Whyte accused Goyette of a gratuitous slash she perceived as a deliberate attempt to injure – not at all unlike the aforementioned sadistic slash by the Philadelphia Flyers captain Bobby Clarke on the Soviet Union's best player, Valeri Kharlamov in the iconic 1972 Summit Series between Team Canada and the U.S.S.R. The NHL stars were down, 3-1-1 in the series, when Clarke slashed Kharlamov and broke his ankle in Game 6. Kharlamov missed Game 7 and played injured in Game 8 as the Canadians rebounded to win the series.

Bye was still sore at Goyette from their vicious battles during the 13-game runup. "Not good," Bye said. More than two decades later she remains infuriated by the play of some Canadian players.

Three days after that round-robin loss to the Americans, however, it was Miller who was struggling to ice a team with so many injured players. She had already made up her lineup card for the gold-medal game – without her captain – when she got a call that Wilson had been released from the hospital. "She stopped peeing blood," Miller said. "She played. But each of those players needed cortisone shots in order to play the gold-medal game, and that had never happened before."

Which explains why, whenever she's asked what she might have done differently during her Nagano experience as she remembers it, Miller's reply is quick and blunt: "Not be so naïve. Don't do exactly what you've been asked. The U.S. sure didn't. It's just a fact."

As soon as the game ended, Brown-Miller wanted a rematch. "I just remember I had so much energy, knowing that we could come back like that. And to see Canada's disappointment at falling apart. I told my teammates, 'I wish we could play them tomorrow. We're in their heads. They were used to playing an American team that would just roll over and go through the motions. Not anymore.'"

Then she joined the handshake line, where the conflict between the two sides took a disturbing turn. Halfway through one of the most honorable traditions in sports, Goyette bolted from the line and, with tears streaming down her cheeks, skated to the boards, turning to her coach as the teams were still shaking hands.

It had been an emotional tournament for the veteran forward from French-speaking Canada. On the day of Opening Ceremonies, she learned of the passing of her father, a victim of Alzheimer's. And within minutes after this intolerable loss to the Americans, she told her coach she heard someone make what she thought was an offensive comment about the loss of her father – and she pointed the finger at Sandra Whyte. The accusation shocked the Americans; Whyte has been universally described as the least likely member of their team to say anything like that.

"You have to know Whytie," said Sarah Tueting, her roommate in

Nagano and one of her closest friends on the team. "She might have said something like whatever gets said a dozen times during any given hockey game. But she would never – and I mean *never* – say something about another player's family."

Immediately, Shannon Miller, who took a leave of absence from her job in law enforcement, went into cop mode and began her own investigation. "Everybody is always quick to say, 'you know, there are two sides to every story.' No there isn't. I was a police officer. There's only the truth."

Miller first tried to corroborate Goyette's allegation. She spoke to the person behind Goyette in the line of Canadian players, and that player seemed to confirm Goyette's version of the story. Then Miller waved Granato, the American captain, over for a word.

"I told her what my player had just told me," Miller said. "And then I said, 'We're above this. It's not who we are, and there's no place for it in our game.' And Cammi said, 'I agree Coach, and I'll address it.' I'll never forget that conversation. So it is what it is, and if people have a problem with that, it's their problem."

After Granato told her teammates about Goyette's accusation, they collectively dismissed it – primarily because they knew Whyte. At the same time, they were willing to give Goyette the benefit of the doubt, suggesting that as a native French speaker she may have misunderstood what Whyte had said.

"Yeah, I said something, but it was just regular trash talk – just like it occurs in any hockey game at all levels," Whyte said. "And afterward it was, 'Hey, she said you said something about her father.' I'm like, What? I have no idea where that came from. I have no idea if that's what she thought she heard. I did not speak French. I did not speak loudly. Maybe she didn't hear me clearly.

"The thing that bothered me most about it was that it was very out of character for me to even open my mouth at all. I never, ever, ever, ever trash talk. But I was really upset about an incident on the ice where I felt she was intentionally trying to – I don't know if I'd go so far as to say injure – but it was intentional. She took a swipe at me that made me furious. It was in the third period. I don't usually bring that up because there's no justification. I just say that stuff [retaliatory trash talk] happens in hockey. But deep down, I feel that me opening my mouth was wrong because I'm just not that type of person. I try not to speak badly about anybody or say things that are not nice. That's what upsets me most about it – that I did that. So I blame myself. . . But I have no idea how it went to where it did."

Indeed, what might have started as a controlled burn, a distraction by the Canadians after their melt-down to try to rock the psyche of the Americans, had become a fire raging out of control. Without question, that "meaningless" round-robin game had devolved into exactly the kind of ruthless play Ben Smith liked to describe as "Hudson Bay Rules" – guns and knives – only with words that hurt as much as bullets and blades. What should have been a pivotal victory for the Americans in this rivalry was being manipulated in a way that left one of Team USA's most important players psychologically shaken.

As dawn rose the next morning over the mountains of northern Japan, damage control was in full force. The American women were pointing the finger at the Canadian coach, who they felt went out of her way to torch the issue to distract the media – and perhaps her own players – from the embarrassment they had just experienced by giving up six goals in just over a half-period of hockey to lose a game they had well in hand.

"It was probably a ploy," Brown-Miller said. "But what was surprising was that she picked the wrong person. Sandra Whyte is a classy character. We all knew that Danielle had just lost her father, but nobody on our team would have said anything like that."

In fact, as Mary Turco described in her book *Crashing the Net*, the entire American team signed a sympathy card and delivered it to Goyette after hearing of her loss. That's why the Americans were certain the issue was fabricated – for what it was worth.

"I don't know what could have knocked us off our game at that point," Brown-Miller said, "but that was nothing."

Truth be told, however, it nearly knocked Whyte off her game. In the three days between games, she received hundreds of vicious, hateful emails. Some included death threats, which drew the attention of IOC security and the FBI. It saddened her teammates, who knew better.

"Here's the thing: The player they picked – whoever made this whole thing up – Sandra Whyte was the sweetest player," said Bye. "She never said a bad word about anybody."

Whyte, who was among the group of teammates who called themselves LPs, low-profile players, was blindsided by the media storm that followed.

"It was overwhelming to be all of a sudden in this position where I had to answer questions regarding that. And it was particularly frustrating because I don't think that in men's hockey this would ever be an issue. No one asks the men, 'Oh, what did you say to him?' Please, c'mon. That's just ridiculous. So yes, it was challenging."

Wrought with anguish over all the negative attention, the emails, the death threats, Whyte withdrew even further into herself, growing even quieter. Her teammates worried about her. She needed help, and it arrived just in time.

The Bat
Signal

Two days prior to the tumultuous USA-Canada round-robin game, USA Hockey's executive director Dave Ogrean and veteran equipment manager Bob Webster were slaking their thirst at a Western-style pub in downtown Nagano. Hours earlier, Team USA had thrashed host Japan 10-0, a result that guaranteed the Americans a berth in the gold-medal game. Shortly after the USA-Japan game, Team Canada dispensed with Finland, guaranteeing the all-North American gold-medal matchup so longed for by the hockey world.

America's two veteran hockey men were pleased. After all, this was exactly where they hoped to be at these historic Winter Games—playing one game for a gold medal. But they were far from giddy because conventional wisdom held that women's hockey was a two-team race, one in which a silver medal represented last place. Ogrean's mind was working, knowing what a gigantic difference there was between silver and gold. He swigged his last sip of beer and stared into the bottom of his glass, searching for answers. He looked up and turned toward Webster, a guy who knew first-hand about winning Olympic gold back in Lake Placid.

"I don't want to go home with a silver medal and say, 'Geez, maybe we should have done this instead,'" said Ogrean to his bar mate. "Is there any rock we haven't turned over Bob? I don't want to leave anything behind if it's going to be a difference-maker."

The two men spent several seconds lost in thought. Webster looked up and uttered a single name: "Haberl." They immediately locked eyes.

"Do you have his number?" Ogrean asked. Webster nodded emphatically, reaching for his phone.

Sports psychologist Peter Haberl was the final piece to Team USA's puzzle, an integral part of the team's well-being. Yet somehow he was the odd-man-out in the inevitable tug-of-war for credentials with the local organizing committee. Ogrean thought, *screw it,* we'll figure it out later, and proceeded to pull out his cell phone and hurriedly punch a dozen numbers.

Midnight Thursday in Nagano was 10 a.m. at the Boston University science labs. Haberl picked up his ringing phone.

"Hello?"

"It's Dave. Any chance you can take the week off?"

"Can I ask why?"

"I want you to come over here. Don't tell anyone you're coming. We have 48 hours after you get here before the gold-medal game. You can spend that time getting everyone's head in the right place."

The two men had no idea how urgent this commute would come to be, and how critical his presence would become in Team USA's rush for gold. As was his nature, Haberl moved with deliberate efficiency. "It was very exciting to get that call," said Haberl, a USOC staffer 24 years later. "On the logistics end, I needed someone to step in for me to teach at BU."

After securing his replacement, the next logistical piece of the puzzle was how to get himself from Tokyo to Nagano – fast. After all, he would be stepping into a strange city after a 17-hour flight. In 1998, there was no English signage on either light or heavy rail in Tokyo, and Haberl needed a seamless transition from Haneda International Airport into the heart of the city if he hoped to connect with the proper bullet train. Without boots on the ground, the degree of difficulty would be prohibitive.

This is where the fates asserted themselves: Peter had an older brother working and living in Tokyo. When the jetlagged psychologist wobbled through customs, Dieter Haberl collected little brother and whisked him into Tokyo's transportation hub. Moments later the younger Haberl had his ticket and was seated on the proper train for the two-hour sprint to Nagano.

Unbeknownst to Haberl, while he was crossing the International Date Line at 30,000 feet, one of his favorite players was engulfed by media fire. By the time Haberl boarded his train to Nagano, Team Canada's incendiary comments had fanned the flames into a four-alarm blaze, threatening to turn all of Team USA's hard-earned confidence and concentration into ashes. Sandra Whyte was receiving a barrage of hate mail and death threats at the normally cozy Surf Shack internet cafe. With just two days until the gold-medal game, Whyte needed her head adjusted, ASAP. Enter Peter Haberl.

"He walked into the Village cafeteria, where the team was having breakfast," said Ogrean, who witnessed the scene. "They didn't know he was coming. It was mayhem: hugging, tears, joy, all this stuff."

Whyte was not in the cafeteria, however, choosing to snack in her dorm room while seeking refuge. Peter was briefed as soon as he was shuttled into the Athletes Village. "It was really nice to see the joy that they experienced seeing my face," said Haberl. "It felt really good."

Haberl's enthusiasm was tempered after meeting with Smith. The psychologist had crucial work in front of him: Whyte would be meeting the press after that morning's practice, one that had the makings of a feeding frenzy. Every reporter from Toronto to Vancouver would be getting a crack at her, seeking to extend the life of this sensational story of trash-talking gone sideways. Whyte needed her head in a good place if she were to survive the ordeal.

"Ben took me up into one of the rooms," said Haberl, "and I got to meet Sandra there." Whyte's eyes were red-rimmed, but they brightened at the sight of Haberl. "Oh my God, he was sent here just for me!" said Whyte recalling her immediate reaction that morning in the Athletes Village. "I remember being really upset, and sort of being in tears about it. I can't imagine who else I would have allowed…I was really grateful."

Whyte did not have time just then for a session with Peter. She had a practice and a press conference to contend with. But she was incredibly relieved to see her confidante. They agreed to visit between practice and presser, but that window would be very tight. Although Whyte would be facing the music alone, she was buoyed by the knowledge that Peter was there to pick up the pieces if she cracked.

The media throng at Big Hat that morning paralleled one typical of the Stanley Cup Finals. Anticipation of the USA-Canada women's gold medal game had reached fever pitch, capturing the imagination of both hockey nations. Since the American and Canadian men's teams were both underachieving, this women's showdown was reaching blockbuster status. Add a raging controversy, and *L'Affaire de Goyette* vaulted women's hockey above the men on the media food chain. Even non-hockey writers crowded into the mixed zone hoping to gather quotes from Whyte, the unlikeliest lightning rod imaginable.

Once Team USA wrapped up practice, Smith walked into the mixed zone to say his piece. Webster and a team assistant swapped credentials to get Haberl into Big Hat, allowing him to connect with Whyte. They didn't have time to speak in any meaningful way, but Haberl's mere presence provided Whyte with an emotional safe harbor. After Smith completed his thoughts, it was time for the main act. Whyte looked at the throngs, and exhaled.

"It was a big group of media, so I have no idea who was asking questions," said Whyte, who faced all varieties of the same question: How had her trash-talking in the handshake line erupted into an international incident? She firmly denied the accusation of disparaging Goyette's deceased father, but admitted to trash-talking in response to a late-game slash from Goyette. Then the Harvard grad proceeded to question the interrogators.

"This is ridiculous, would you be asking a man these same questions?" asked Whyte. For this introvert, chastising the media scrum was as likely as Wayne Gretzky streaking naked across the ice. "I don't say that because we think like men, or want to be men, but it is the sport of hockey. Am I saying women should do that [trash-talk]? No. Do women do that? Yes."

Her theme, that there shouldn't be a double-standard for trash-talking, no matter how unseemly, was indisputable.

Then she was asked why anyone would accuse her of such a remark to Goyette, and the Ivy Leaguer with the Boston accent managed to flip the script, suggesting that the Goyette accusation, "was a psychological tactic" from the other side. Now the newspapers from Toronto, French Canada and Boston all had new material with which to tee up the gold-medal showdown.

Haberl was proud of his subject. He would meet with Whyte after she had lunch with roommates Gretchen Ulion and Sarah Tueting. Haberl had spent the last two seasons working with Whyte on occasion, forging a relationship ideal for the task at hand. "It helps to have a connection, a sense of trust," said Haberl, who diagnosed the scenario as "intentional chaos" sewn by Team Canada.

"Basically, there was a strategy to get inside a player's head," said Haberl. "In my territory as a sports psychologist, maybe we can diffuse that, allow that player to not get trapped in that setup."

There were no Team USA players more level-headed than Whyte, but she clearly needed Haberl's guidance after a full day of absorbing the wrath of Canada's online hockey trolls. "I didn't spend hours and hours talking to him, we just sat down and had a conversation," Whyte said. "He just told me to put everything in perspective, to see what was really happening."

Haberl mentioned more extreme examples to drive home the point, contrasting her misfortune to a neighbor dying of cancer.

"It was just one of those moments. I needed to have a readjustment, and focus on what we were there to do as a team."

After the meeting, Whyte made a point of bypassing the now toxic Surf Shack. She had more than a day to process her conversation with Haberl, and was already feeling a great weight lifting.

The gold-medal game would be the last competitive contest of Whyte's remarkable career. Few could have possibly imagined what kind of farewell act was in store from this willowy introvert.

Woman
in Black

At one point in the second period, with the score tied at 1, a rough check to the boards by a U.S. defenseman prompted Canada coach Shannon Miller, an on-leave Calgary cop, to stare down her rival, U.S. coach Ben Smith, with a glare that could melt Plexiglas.

When she finally caught his eye, Miller shouted an obscenity that even non-English speakers were able to lip read, then translate.

She probably didn't realize she was on camera, and her two-word salute became a two-story-high testimonial on the Aqua Wing's Jumbotron. Even our Japanese hosts knew what she said, and the crowd — equally divided between mouth-foaming Americans and Canadians — went wild.

"What can I say?" an unapologetic Miller asked with a wink and smile after the [post-game media] scrum. "I'm a hockey coach, eh?'

—Seattle Times columnist Ron C. Judd

On the afternoon before the biggest game of her young career, Shannon Miller heard a knock at her door in the Olympic Village in Nagano, Japan. When she opened it, an elderly Japanese man bracing himself on a cane bowed elegantly and asked, through his niece acting as his interpreter, to be received.

Miller motioned him inside. After taking a seat on the edge of her bed, the man begged for a moment to share something immensely important to him. Then he began to recount a story about how his native Hiroshima, a thriving 20th-century metropolis, was forever changed on August 6, 1945 at 8:15 a.m., when the United States Army Air Forces dropped the first atomic bomb – "Little Boy." Most of the city was destroyed, and by the end of the year an estimated 140,000 of the city's 350,000 people had died as a result of the blast and its effects.

"I *hate* the Americans," the man said. "Please, *please* do not let them win your game tomorrow. Not here. Not on Japanese soil. Please."

With those words and a few more, he bowed again, wishing Miller and her team the best, and departed.

"After they left I just sat there on my bed, not knowing what to think," Miller said in a series of fall 2021 interviews. "But to this day, it still rocks my world.

"I mean, as if there's not enough pressure, eh? There I was, a woman, young, openly gay, and I'm just getting hammered everywhere I turn. But that was an awesome moment. Talk about perspective. The biggest game that year, and my God, Hiroshima? I laid awake half the frickin' night thinking about that guy. I mean, I was young, but I was old enough to understand what he was talking about."

As it turned out, it was just one more in a months-long series of restless nights that began almost immediately after she took leave as an Alberta police officer to coach Canada's national women's hockey team. What should have been a joyful experience turned out to be about as pleasant as a daily root canal.

Shannon Miller was born in 1963 and raised in Melfort, Saskatchewan, a small town about 50 miles southwest of Prince Albert known as the "City of Northern Lights" for the spectacular auroras dancing in the night skies for much of the year. She was the second oldest of four siblings.

"But I'm the boss," she said, explaining that her older sister Sherry was born prematurely. As a result, she was much smaller than the other kids in school and was frequently bullied. Shannon wasn't much bigger, but by the force of her outsized personality she became Sherry's protector.

Miller began playing hockey at age 11 on an all-girls team that included players from grades 6-12. They competed against other girls' teams. It was an idyllic life until she was 13 and her father died. Suddenly, she learned that there were more important things in life than hockey. Her family moved and she hung up her skates to share the burden of caring for her siblings.

She didn't play hockey again until she enrolled in the University of Saskatchewan, where she had her mind set on making the school's volleyball team. She had survived the first round of cuts when she saw a notice on a bulletin board that the university was starting its first-ever women's hockey team and calling for tryouts.

"I went nuts," Miller said. "I hadn't played for five years, but I called my mom and told her exactly where my skates were. I asked her to box them up with my hockey gloves, and she sent them to me – on a bus. I went out and bought a stick for ten bucks at Canadian Tire. I didn't have a helmet, and it was full body checking. Didn't matter to me."

During tryouts, she sustained a cut over her eye when someone pitch-forked her, slicing through her eyebrow, blackening the eye. She had to leave practice to get stitched up at a local hospital. "I didn't care. I was tough as shit then," she said. "They nicknamed me 'Killer Miller.' I made the team and had the best years ever."

As soon as she saw her name on the hockey roster, she quit volleyball. The coach thought she was crazy. "I was being scouted for Team Canada. All I could say was, 'I'm sorry. I can't explain it. I love hockey.' And that was it."

During her university years, the Canadian provinces were beginning to form all-star teams to compete against one another. Miller eventually played for Saskatchewan and competed for national championships. She played until she moved to Alberta to begin her career as a police officer, which she loved nearly as much as hockey. But she never left the sport.

After her shift as a cop, she would return home, change out of her uniform and begin her labor of love—coaching. "I'd put a baseball cap on backwards, grab a Diet Coke and a Mars bar, and work on hockey. I was coaching minor hockey, kids at the time, volunteering. It took a lot of time. Five nights a week, three practices and two games. And I just *loved* it. I couldn't watch enough videos or read enough books. I mean, really, how do you explain the love of the game?"

In 1989, Miller and two friends started a women's hockey team in Calgary. They needed 12 players to fill a roster, and when it came to recruiting she knew no limits. "I was a cop on patrol one day and I saw this girl rollerblading down the road," she said. "So I pulled her over and told her if she could rollerblade like that she could certainly skate, and she could join our team. She wound up being our 12th player. Women's hockey wasn't booming across Canada, but it existed in pockets around the country."

A year later, in 1990, Canadian Amateur Hockey Association (which merged with Hockey Canada in 1994) President Murray Costello hired Bob Nicholson as its vice president of hockey operations, tasking him with two primary responsibilities: rejuvenate the country's World Junior program and build the team that would represent Canada in the IIHF's first World Women's Championships. At the time, Canada had more ambition than money to throw at such programs.

"When I look back at that very first national team and that tournament and how we picked our players," Nicholson said, pausing to laugh, "we actually charged them to come to our tryout camp – $250 each."

It was the best team money couldn't buy. Coached by Dave McMaster, that Team Canada rolled through the preliminary round by beating Sweden, West Germany and Japan by a combined score of 50-1. The Canadians were severely tested, however, by Finland in the semifinals, surviving 6-5, before going on to beat Team USA, 5-2 for the gold.

Canada followed a similar script in the next two World Championships, capturing gold with two different coaches, Rick Polutnick in 1992 and Les Lawton in 1994. Meantime, Miller kept her head down and continued building her resume with the Women's High Performance Program, a commitment by Hockey Canada to develop elite female coaches. Gradually, Miller rose in the coaching ranks until she found herself as an assistant with Team Alberta, which won the gold medal at the Canada Winter Games on Prince Edward Island in 1991. A spectacular 12-year-old named Hayley Wickenheiser—who would eventually win widespread acclaim as the greatest women's hockey player—scored the winning goal.

That tournament was a harbinger for the force known simply as "Wick," the national team superstar who rewrote Canada's record book. Seven years later, Miller and Wickenheiser would lead Team Canada to Nagano as the favorite to win the gold medal in the newest Olympic sport.

But Miller had some work to do first. While she was the highest-ranking women in the Hockey Canada coaching fraternity, she labored as a national team assistant for several more seasons, jockeying for position against some male coaches who were vying for a job behind the bench.

Finally, she was named head coach of Canada's women in 1995—still as an unpaid volunteer. And there was no guarantee that she would retain the job when Canada sent its team to the Winter Games in Japan. Certainly, Miller was taking nothing for granted. But she knew if Canada kept winning it would be hard to replace her.

Despite standing just 5-foot-3, Miller could tower over nearly anyone she encountered by the sheer force of her cop's personality. She rarely appeared in public wearing anything but black to match her short-cropped hair. And her eyes, bluish-green or greenish-blue depending on her disposition, were quick to soften in a moment of compassion or twinkle when her mood turned humorous. But they could just as quickly buckle the knees of anyone she felt warranted her wrath. They were as much a weapon as the service revolver she carried on her other job. If looks could kill. . . And it worked for her. Canada won a lot.

Ben Smith had been on the job as head coach of the United States women's Olympic program for nearly a year, appointed on June 3, 1996, before Canada finally got serious about hiring its coach. Miller knew she was on the short list. She had heard whispers that she was the leading candidate, that if Canada won the 1997 Worlds she would likely be named, so she submitted her formal application. During that tournament in Kitchener, she remembers reading a newspaper story suggesting that she would be the Olympic coach if Canada won.

In the epic finale on April 6, Nancy Drolet completed her hat trick, scoring at 12:59 of overtime to lift Canada to a 4-3 victory over the United States to win the IIHF gold medal. The powers at Hockey Canada had seen enough.

"We did a thorough search at that time, and while there were some male coaches that had good qualities to coach that team, Shannon Miller had really been a builder of the female game," said Nicholson, praising Miller's leadership skills, motivational ability and hockey acumen. "Shannon had really done her part. She was the obvious choice for the job."

Eighteen days after Kitchener, Miller became the first-ever, full-time salaried head coach of the National Women's Team – and the only full-time female head coach of a national women's team in the world. It was her first paying coaching gig. Her record as Canada's head coach to that point: 18-2. She was 33 years old.

Miller built a powerful Canadian team, but she bristled over the 13-game schedule with Team USA in the runup to Nagano. "I didn't like that at all," Miller said. "First of all, nobody ever consulted me. And I pushed back, many times, because I thought that in the end it would favor them, not us. We had far more to lose."

Twenty-five years later, Nicholson remained steadfast in his belief that the extended series between the two rivals, with host cities split nearly evenly between the two countries, was essential to promoting the game and building the sport of women's ice hockey. He eventually conceded that there were probably too many games vs. the United States.

As Miller had feared, the series created a monster of a rivalry. Prior to Nagano, Canada held a slim 7-6 advantage in the series, but the margin for error grew slimmer with each contest. Team USA seemed to improve with every match, and the competition between the new archrivals became increasingly edgy and physical. Acrimony on both sides intensified.

But when they weren't playing Team USA, well, the Canadians had a tendency to drift, as they did during a trip to Helsinki for some friendly matches. In one game, she ordered her team back onto the ice during an intermission to skate sprints – to the confusion of the sparse crowd.

"I was unhappy with my team. Players were drinking and partying when Hockey Canada was spending so much money to go to Finland and play someone other than the USA," Miller explained. "I gave them the talk before we left, but we had a problem with a very, very small group of players who were very social. They had a big party and they were hung-over when we played the next day."

The party ended in no uncertain terms with her players gasping for air after a hard skate between periods of the game. Every established hockey coach has conducted such punishing "bag skates," but Miller is the only one on record to have ever demanded one *in the middle of a game.* True to form, she did what she felt needed to do to get her team's attention.

"It wasn't about humiliation. I wanted to make a point, so instead of talking about it I brought them out during the intermission and bag-skated them for five minutes," she said. "It was an exhibition game. There might have been 12 people in the stands. But my message was clear: When you put that jersey on, you're representing your country."

While some of her players might have resented it at the moment, it worked.

"You're never going to please every one of your players all the time, but in that moment she was doing what she thought was best for the team," said Fiona Smith-Bell, a defender on that 1998 Canadian team. "I have the utmost respect for Shannon. She demanded a lot from her players, but what successful coach doesn't? She knew how to motivate us and she demanded excellence every day. And she was a person who truly cared about her players. She would always go to bat for us."

And if that included hurling two-word epithets across the benches at the opposing coach, so be it. The relationship between the two programs boiled over in the handshake line after the Americans scored six unanswered goals in their shocking round-robin victory. Somebody said something. Somebody heard something. And one of Miller's players sprinted to the bench in tears. Miller addressed it privately with Team USA captain Cammi Granato, and that's how Miller intended it to end. She blamed the media for fanning the flames, with global headlines over the next three days that resulted in two Americans receiving an avalanche of hate email, including death threats.

Meantime, Canada's epic meltdown in the preliminary match had become all but forgotten. The Americans considered the handshake-line incident a vastly overblown sideshow, created to distract. To the Canadians, Goyette's pain was visceral. More than two decades later, neither side was budging on how they viewed it.

Overblown or not, distraction or not, the forthcoming gold-medal game between the two sides was epic. Tightly contested, physical, hard fought. And the result was unthinkable – even just a few weeks before when the teams landed in Nagano.

"We got to the gold-medal game," Miller said, "and we lost."

In the hallway outside her team's locker room, she had a minor meltdown. "I wasn't crying because we lost," she said. "I was crying because I just hurt so deeply. I wanted so badly to win for the players, for everyone in Canada who loved the game so much, for all the little girls who looked up to us. I just broke down."

Miller managed to pull it together enough to get through the post-game press conference. She was calm and spoke deliberately, recalling some things clearly: an impossible toe save on a puck headed toward an open net, a slapshot that clanged off the crossbar with the puck landing on the goal line but not crossing it. Had either of those shots found the back of the net, it would have changed everything. But that, she also understood, is the undeniable beauty of the game she loved.

Miller also spoke eloquently about how emotional she felt seeing a woman lean forward to accept a gold medal around her neck. The fact that it was American captain Cammi Granato and not her own player didn't matter so much; this was a transcendent moment for women's hockey, and Miller felt proud to be a part of it all.

Afterward, even just a few hours later, she couldn't recall a single thing from that press conference. All she wanted, with her entire being, was to put some distance between herself and what she felt was a miserable experience after fighting so hard for her women to be treated more equitably.

"I was just happy it was over," she said. "I remember that I was heartbroken about absolutely everything – including the loss, but not specifically the loss. I was exhausted and angry. I just couldn't wait to get on the plane and go home and be free of all that."

Bracing herself for the worst on her return to Canada after Nagano, Miller was pleasantly surprised. "People were fantastic," she said. "A lot of people recognized me, and I'd say 90 percent were very positive and celebrated us. But when you lose, it divides people. There were some mean comments, being called a dyke. . . and worse."

Being the only female head coach of an Olympic team – and being openly gay – was at times a heavy burden. Miller experienced harsh treatment, seemingly from all directions, but worst of all, she said, was the media. "Asking questions about my sexuality and even if I'm in the locker room when the players are changing, stuff like that," she said. "Just stupid, horrible shit that embarrasses you, offends you, and wears you down."

Shannon Miller didn't stay in Canada long. Ironically, she was the beneficiary of the groundswell of support and interest in women's hockey in the United States, thanks to Team USA's gold medal victory. "I took a job in the States after that," she said. "I left Canada. I left my country. I needed a fresh start, and it was the right decision for me. And I got to start a program from scratch. It was amazing to have that privilege."

Just two months after leaving Nagano, on April 20, 1998, she was hired as the first head coach for the University of Minnesota-Duluth's women's team. "A commitment to hockey was made – that's the biggest difference in the U.S. for women in the college game," she said. "That's what drew me to the States after Nagano, that they're getting scholarships to play hockey. Women! It was crazy in a good way, and I was so impressed.

"But what was missing in women's college hockey in the States was there were no Europeans. I just thought, 'Oh my God, what a chance to help develop the global game.' Here the Americans are, willing to put money and resources into women's college hockey. What an opportunity, not only to have Canadians, but to bring over the best Europeans. Then we're growing the game globally. So I went over to Finland and Sweden, Switzerland and Germany, and picked up some of their best players. That's how we were so good right out of the gate. We were strong immediately. But mostly, you know what? This is what's best for the game globally."

Miller held her position in Duluth for 17 seasons. In that time, she became the most successful NCAA women's hockey coach in Frozen Four tournament wins (11) and NCAA Division I national championships (five). She reached her 250th and 300th career wins faster than any other head coach in NCAA Division I history. On October 5, 2013, Miller became the third coach in NCAA history to reach 350 career wins. Her final record at Duluth: 383-144-50.

During the 2014-15 season, with her team ranked sixth in the country among the NCAA's 34 Division 1 women's teams, after her team had won 12 of its final 13 games, Miller was fired. More accurately, her contract was not renewed. By then, it had been five years since her team had won a season title; five years since it won a WCHA tournament title; five years since its last Frozen Four appearance; and its most recent NCAA tournament win was in 2011. The university mentioned neither wins nor losses as its justification for the firing, citing instead the need to narrow a $4.5 million budget deficit.

True to form, Miller left with guns blazing. In September 2015, she and two other former UMD coaches filed suit against the university's board of regents alleging that the university had created a hostile work environment, violated equal pay laws and violated Title IX of the United States Education Amendment of 1972, which prohibits sexual discrimination in education programs receiving federal financial assistance.

"I was fired because I was gay. No doubt about it," she said. "People took my name tag off my door and put up a yellow sticky note that said 'Dyke.' They put mail in my mailbox saying, 'Go home, Dyke!'"

In December 2019, the university agreed to a settlement with Miller totaling more than $4.5million – $2.1 million to her and $2.4 million to her attorneys.

After her Duluth experience, Miller got as far away from hockey and the frigid temperatures of Northern Minnesota as she could, metaphorically and literally, settling near the desert in Palm Springs, California. She started a business, the game she loved in a distant, rearview mirror. But hockey tracked her down six years later. On November 21, 2021, Miller was named Vice President, Branding and Community Relations, for the Oak View Group, owner of the Coachella Valley Arena and the American Hockey League affiliate of the NHL's Seattle Kraken.

Shannon Miller was back in hockey with arguably the most diverse franchise in sports. The Kraken previously had made Cammi Granato the first female pro scout in the National Hockey League. So for a few months, until Granato joined the Vancouver Canucks as an assistant general manager, Miller and Granato were finally on the same team. Go figure.

By then at least some Team USA members like A.J. Mleczko were beginning to soften their opinions about the Darth Vader-like character who coached that Canadian team in Nagano.

"We hated her, like they hated Ben Smith, right?" said Mleczko. "She was salty. She always wore black. But there was a lot of pressure on her. A lot. If she didn't win gold, she was losing her job with Team Canada. And she did.

"But I've gotten to know her a little bit since [Nagano], and I actually have a lot of respect for her now. I think she's done a lot for our game. She was great up in Duluth. She's a very good coach."

A hockey coach, eh?

A Golden
Showdown

"Champions keep playing until they get it right."

—Billie Jean King

If football is a game of inches – "and inches make the champion," as Vince Lombardi always said – then hockey is a game of millimeters, where a tiny fraction of an inch can dictate fortunes.

A screened shot from distance labeled for the back of the net because the goaltender can't see it nicks a shin-guard and pings off the crossbar and out of harm's way. A cross-crease pass caroms off a defenseman's skate blade and eludes the unsuspecting goalie for a score. A game of millimeters. The kind of millimeters that can create champions – and change lives.

So it was at the Big Hat Arena, with thousands in the crowd of 8,626 chanting "USA! USA!" and the Americans pinned in their own zone desperately clinging to a 2-1 lead with just over two minutes to play in regulation. Team USA lost the puck behind its own net and a Canadian player passed to a teammate for a point-blank shot into a yawning net that would have tied the game and likely created the kind of momentum that would have been difficult for the underdog Americans to overcome. Again.

If Karyn Bye hadn't seen it for herself, she wouldn't have believed it.

"It was a toe save," Bye said. "I don't know how she extended that leg out and made the save, but it was the save of the game."

The save of her life, to be more precise, but don't ask goaltender Sarah Tueting to explain it. She cannot.

"Canada passed it out and they shot lower right side," Tueting said. "What I remember about it was, I didn't do that. I don't know how that happened, but I didn't do that. I remember feeling so lucky. Thank you God, thank you body or thank you whatever. That wasn't me, but I sure am grateful."

As play continued, Tueting, as she is prone to do, was caught up in one of those uncanny existential moments, a whisper from deep within that said, "Look at the mind, being surprised about the body doing something on its own. Then there was something behind that: Look at the witness watching the mind being surprised about the body doing something on its own.

"And then I very consciously remember being like, *'Oh shit, the game is still going. C'mon, back into the body, the game is still happening.'* That moment is more real to me than any of these other memories I have a hard time conjuring up."

Seconds later, Sandra Whyte had the puck on her stick crossing the enemy blue line and staring at a four-by-six-foot target – 2,229,672.96 square millimeters to be exact – that had been vacated by Canadian goaltender Manon Rheaume for an extra attacker. Whyte wouldn't miss, and finally everyone on the American side could take another breath.

There were three long days between that stunning Valentine's Day comeback that ended the round-robin portion of the women's tournament and the gold-medal game the following Tuesday. As amped up as the players were after that 7-4 victory, coach Ben Smith was there to remind them often, and in no uncertain terms, that they hadn't won anything yet. He recalls having to pull back a bit during some spirited practices. That smell of victory – especially after a big game, can be intoxicating.

When they weren't at the rink preparing, they used the time to decompress and rejuvenate their bodies and minds ahead of the biggest game of their lives. They spent their idle hours divided between people watching and the internet café known as the Surf Shack.

"Email was just sort of getting started when we were over there," Lisa Brown-Miller said. "We'd write emails to family back home to share what was going on, and they were emailing back telling us what a great sensation we were. None of us could believe it. Really? It seemed like everybody was sending me messages. I have boxes and boxes of emails still; I'm not sure what I'll do with them all."

It was also a time when those with ill-intentions were just learning how convenient the internet could be for spreading innuendo and lies, hatred and threats. And the Americans, particularly Whyte and Shelley Looney, had been singled out by a cyberspace mob for wild and unsubstantiated rumors that Whyte had said something unbecoming – and frankly unthinkable – in the handshake line after the round-robin game with the Canadians. In other words, the confrontation went viral before viral was a thing.

As difficult as it was, Whyte and Looney eventually were able to shake it off, Whyte with an assist from team psychologist Peter Haberl. Both benefited from the wisdom of teammate Sara DeCosta, who reminded them that the haters sending those emails were just trying to distract them, get them off their game ahead of the coming gold-medal match with Team Canada.

Meantime, they all did their share of people watching, especially starstruck Angela Ruggiero, the youngest player on the team who had turned 18 a month before the Nagano Games.

"Oh my God, there's Wayne Gretzky! He's right here in the village!

I have to go tell him my little kid story," Ruggiero recalled. And she proceeded to reintroduce herself to the Great One and remind him about the time they were photographed together on the cover of *Sports Illustrated for Kids* when she was representing a group from Los Angeles and he was captain of the National Hockey League's Kings.

Gretzky posed for another photo with Ruggiero and signed his autograph for her. "Just a nice man," she said. "He was playing for the Canadians, but I didn't hold that against him."

Suddenly, she thought of herself differently. "Now I'm a peer, a fellow Olympian, so that was the coolest for me," she said. "The other one was seeing Jaromir Jagr [another NHL star competing with the Czech team]. They had a really cool arcade there to kill some time, and he was in there on a motorcycle. It was just so cool to see guys that you look up to on the NHL side."

And that's when young Angela Ruggiero began to understand the enormous potential beneath the platform that was beginning to take shape beneath her boots. "Why did I want to be Wayne Gretzky when I was growing up learning to play hockey?" she asked. "I should have wanted to be Cammi Granato, but I didn't know who she was. Now I was so proud that I could come home, even as an 18-year-old, and be a role model – which is crazy. I never thought of myself that way.

"It was about having an impact – not just for little girls, but for little boys, too, and what that can do for society – having strong female role models visible, something that I didn't have as a kid."

The Athletes Village during Olympics is full of such role models, many of them unaware, as Ruggiero had been, of their budding potential. Among them in Nagano that February was 15-year-old Tara Lipinski, the figure skater often seen sitting at a cafeteria table by herself. The women hockey players would wonder what it must be like, how challenging and stressful it must be for Lipinski, knowing that the greatest threat to win the gold medal came from fellow American, Michelle Kwan, who had opted to stay in a local hotel rather than the Athletes Village.

Anxieties seemed to rise exponentially as the gold-medal game approached. Katie King tried to keep her teammates loose and laughing by visiting their rooms and playing a song for each of them. "Reach" by Gloria Estefan, one of the two official songs of the Atlanta Olympics in 1996, was a team favorite. Sleep became a challenge. The walls were so thin between the rooms in the Athletes Village that some players wore ear plugs to help them drift off.

At the last practice before the finale, the goalies still didn't know who would get the start. And when the word finally came, it seemed almost like an afterthought. No formal meeting between the coach and his goaltenders. No solemn words to either – one of them thrilled, the other crushed. Ben Smith simply skated by Tueting and said, "You're on for tomorrow." That was it. Not a lot of time for either goalie to obsess about the decision.

On the ride to the rink before the gold-medal game, players watched a short video prepared by Peter Haberl. It showed the many highlights of their games against Canada – the great goals they scored, the amazing saves by the goaltenders. By the time they arrived outside the Big Hat Arena, the players were so high they needed parachutes to step off the bus.

Captain Cammi Granato felt a good vibe from her team, an intense focus – not from pressure but from sheer passion that had engulfed her team. Especially from Tueting.

"Sarah Tueting was literally like 'Bring it on,'" Granato told writer Nathan Clark. "When your goalie is feeling like that, things are good. She was like, 'Bring whatever you want at me and I'll save it.'"

That's how Tueting remembered it, as well. "I always wanted the start," she said. "I do know some goalies, they're afraid. But for me, possibly to my detriment in terms of interpersonal situations, I wanted it. I wanted the start. My entire mindset was always, 'Fucking bring it. Give me your best shot.'"

In the locker room before the game, Ruggiero, the youngest and most irreverent member of the team, did what she always did before games. She danced.

"I loved to dance in the locker room and they allowed me to act my age in a lot of ways," Ruggiero said. "It was like I had 19 older sisters. They made fun of me a lot. I was a kid, of course. I didn't get treated like an adult. I enjoyed being the youngest."

Karyn Bye remembers sitting in her stall when a staffer came by and handed her a telegram from Minnesotan Bill Baker, who played on the 1980 U.S. Olympic team that had upset the Soviets at Lake Placid. Somehow, likely during a TV interview, Baker had found out that Bye often pretended to be No. 6, Bill Baker, when she played hockey in her basement as a kid.

"Good luck," the telegram said. "Bring home the gold!"

"Holy buckets!" Bye thought to herself. *"This is huge, right? This is amazing!"*

She taped the telegram up in her locker.

Defenseman Tara Mounsey was sequestered in the trainer's room with team Doctor Sandra Glasson. Tara's left knee was swollen and pockmarked, still recovering from a torn ACL she suffered in high school. Glasson found a patch of fresh flesh and injected a syringe full of Toradol, a liquid anti-inflammatory. Then her knee was firmly taped to enhance her stability. "It was a medical team effort," said Mounsey.

Insulated from the music and nervous energy in the locker room next door, this was a time of quiet introspection for Mounsey, the star defenseman coach Smith counted on to help neutralize Canada. Mounsey stared at her knee in silence, willing it to support her for the final game of the season. "It wasn't pain-free, probably 85 percent," she said. "It wasn't that far from being good to go, it just wasn't pain-free." Forty-five minutes to warmups. Eighty-five per cent would have to be enough.

Back inside the dressing room, Sarah Tueting's routine was interrupted by a teammate – a cardinal sin in a pre-game hockey locker room. You don't talk to starting pitchers as they are preparing for their baseball games. You don't talk to starting goalies in hockey. Ever. You just don't. But this interruption came from Sara DeCosta, Tueting's goaltending partner. She wanted Tueting to wear her good-luck charm, a guardian angel pin that DeCosta had received from her parents.

So while the interruption forced a slight deviation from her pregame routine, Tueting was moved by such a kind and generous gesture. DeCosta pinned it on the back of her equipment.

When Tueting led Team USA onto the ice for warm-ups, fans were already on their feet cheering wildly and waving the American flag. When Granato hit the ice, she felt more as though she were flying than skating. Sue Merz was in line behind Alana Blahoski at the start of pregame drills, the looks in their eyes said it all. Their bodies were literally quaking with energy, nerves, excitement – they didn't know exactly what it was, and they didn't care – but that feeling was incomparable and indescribable.

"It's time to open a can of whoop-ass," Blahoski said.

"A can of whoop-ass!" Merz repeated. And they both laughed, feeling their nerves melting away.

Then, at the opening face-off, a bit of a surprise to some of the players, a rather familiar face there in stripes and orange armbands was there at center ice to greet them.

Nine days after referee Marina Zenk stood at center ice and dropped the puck on the newest sport in the Olympic Winter Games – Finland would beat Sweden, 6-0, in that inaugural game before 2,208 fans at the Aqua Wing Arena – she was back at center ice to officiate the gold-medal game. Now she was on an even bigger stage in the much-larger Big Hat Arena, where the men played their tournament, and there were 8,626 fans on hand to witness this remarkable chapter in the women's game.

That Zenk, a Canadian from Gloucester, Ontario, was there to call the game was in itself notable. After failing to advance enough to call medal-round games in the 1997 World Championships, she nearly blew the whistle on her own career. But she persevered, pushing herself to excel at the selection camps in Lake Placid and Andorra, Spain, winning an invitation to the Nagano Winter Games as one of two female Canadian referees.

Though she made history refereeing that opening game, Zenk wanted desperately to work the gold-medal game. But the IIHF rulebook was quite clear: The gold-medal finale could not be officiated by a referee from either of the two countries playing for the championship. And as expected, the final was between Canada and the United States. The best she could hope to do in the Olympics was to manage the bronze-medal game between Finland and China.

And then fate intervened. At breakfast that morning, she was approached by IIHF supervisor of officials Bob Nadin, who asked how she was feeling. When she told him she felt fine, he said, "Good, because you're doing the gold-medal game."

Nadin was scrambling for help after Manuela Groger-Schneider of Germany who was scheduled to work the game became sick. Then alternate Sandra Dombrowski of Switzerland also reported she was too ill to work the game. Zenk was the obvious, most-capable candidate to replace them. There was, however, some concern that the Americans might protest having a Canadian official refereeing the finale.

Team USA coach Ben Smith put an abrupt end to a potential

controversy in a hastily called meeting. The IIHF needed USA Hockey's authorization. Smith said, quite simply, "I want the best referee available to call this game." And so it was Zenk standing at center ice when the teams gathered for the opening face-off of the gold-medal game.

Zenk dropped the puck and play began as these kinds of games often go – choppy, with little flow, both teams nervous, over-cautious, everyone worried about making the tiniest mistake that would lead to a penalty or an opposing goal. It was a tense and tentative process typical of most winner-take-all events, like Game 7 of the Stanley Cup Finals.

One critical factor: After a 14-game runup to the gold-medal game, including that wild comeback victory by Team USA in the round-robin, the teams knew everything there was to know about the opposition. The Americans knew Team Canada would play a physical game. Canadians at every level play that way; it's how they were raised. The Canadians knew enough to try to avoid the penalty box because the Yanks had a devastating power play.

"It wasn't like we didn't have an idea how each other played," Looney said. "It was more feeling out the ref, trying to see how the game was being called."

Zenk played her role perfectly. "It was probably an advantage for both teams, having a Canadian ref," Looney said. "We were able to play the game we knew how to play. We always loved to play against each other. It was great that she understood that and let us play."

The first period ended scoreless, Team Canada outshooting the Americans, 9-8. Both teams had a turn on the power play; neither team scored. But when Canada was down a player, the American coaches noticed that their opponent had made some tactical changes that revealed a chink in their defensive armor. Between periods, assistant coach Tom Mutch took the team's power-play quarterback Sandra Whyte aside and said simply, "Gretchen's open back door."' Whyte nodded an OK, silently processing.

Forty-three seconds into the second period, Canada's Nancy Drolet was whistled for tripping, a two-minute penalty. She served all but six seconds. The Americans converted on a tic-tac-toe power play – Sue Merz whipped the puck to Whyte, who one-timed a sharp pass to Gretchen Ulion at the back door. Ulion finished, and Team USA had a 1-0 lead.

"Bam, bam, bam! Just like he told me to do it," Whyte said. "How did my brain take that in so quickly and go there?" This from the woman who had spent the previous 72 hours in crisis mode. "It's amazing. I get a kick out of that because I did exactly what Coach [Mutch] told me to do. He should get some credit, too. He called the play."

Remarkably, neither of the other two women on that scoring play was even expected to be in Nagano; Merz and Ulion had both taken spots from USA Hockey stalwarts on that final cut day back in December. Merz's raw athleticism gave her the tiniest edge over Kelly O'Leary in the competition for the final spot on defense, while Ulion needed a two-goal outburst against Canada to surpass hard-luck Stephanie O'Sullivan at the wire. Ulion's playing career had also been on the brink of extinction back in 1996. If not for Dartmouth coach George Crowe throwing her a lifeline – convincing Smith to give his former star a second look – Ulion would have been back in the States watching the game on television, not ripping a one-timer high over Manon Rheaume's glove. The undersized survivor ended up scoring the historic first goal in the women's inaugural Olympic gold medal game.

For Merz, having the Americans convert a power play to open the scoring felt perfectly natural. "That was the whole point, to be as normal as we had been," she told Clark. "Getting on the scoreboard first was huge, and being a part of the goal felt special." It was also Team USA's seventh straight goal against Canada, the momentum spilling over from their round-robin shocker.

The second period ended, 1-0, the Americans holding a 19-13 advantage in shots. But they knew they hadn't yet seen Canada's best; that would come in the opening minutes of the third period and the fierce, punishing battle would continue until the final horn. Bodies colliding all over the ice, elbows raised, sticks up, tempers barely in check. A European referee might have whistled a parade to the penalty box, but as Zenk recognized that these athletes were playing the game of their lives, she refereed the game of her life – Canadian to the core, allowing the players to determine the outcome, not the officiating.

Midway through the final period, the hitting intensified. Finally, at 9:37, Zenk raised her arm and sent Canada's leading goal-scorer, Danielle Goyette, off for body checking. As intense as she was talented, Goyette seemed to be a lightning rod for the controversies that bubbled between the two teams. She also had a knack for singling out Team USA's best players for borderline dirty hits. This time, the player she battered at center ice was Shelley Looney.

Not a coincidence, Looney figured. After all, it was she who stepped between teammate Sandra Whyte and Goyette in the handshake line after Team USA's shocking comeback victory three days earlier. Which also explains all the hateful emails Looney was receiving leading up to the gold medal game. It was hardly a case of mistaken identity, as some have suggested.

Looney headed for the bench after she was hit even though her unit was about to start the power play. She wasn't hurt; she just needed a breather after her shift. Smith sent captain Cammi Granato out in Looney's place. As she sat there catching her breath, Smith leaned over and spoke to her.

"Alright, you're going to play in Cammi's spot," he said. "Just stay in front of the net."

"OK," Looney said, and immediately thought to herself: *"Oh, man, I can't mess this up."*

Then she quickly shook it off; she reminded herself she had experience playing that role. She knew exactly how to respond when Smith sent her back out to join the power play.

"Just a matter of doing what we practiced every day," she said. "Stay in the far corner and pull their D away from the slot. Just sit there in the back door trying to draw them out." Then Whyte – with a telepathy of immense subtlety – hit Looney with a slap-pass right to the blade of Looney's stick as she broke in from the back door. "As the puck starts to move, I kind of move to create an open space and the puck just comes to me," said Looney. "I swung and hit it. I didn't get all of it. It kind of rolled. I remember it very slowly rolling over Manon's pads."

Her penalty terminating 20 seconds early, Goyette took the unpleasant "skate of shame" out of the penalty box. Her team was now trailing 2-0 with less than a half a period to play in regulation.

To be clear, this historic goal wasn't one of those miracle shots from long distance through traffic that eluded a backup goaltender, as was the shot taken by Team USA captain Mike Eruzione that beat the Soviets in Lake Placid. No, this goal would blend the perfect combination of passing, playmaking and courage, featuring Looney breaking toward the crease from her corner position. One of the best power forwards of her era, Looney was at home in that hard area around the net where so few dare to venture when the temperature rises. Right time, right place is how she would describe the play a million times from that moment. Looney's blade made gentle contact with Whyte's slap-pass, redirecting the puck on its slow-motion tumble into the back of Team Canada's net.

It was Whyte's second consecutive primary assist, teeing up goals for her opportunistic mates. This was in addition to her job on the other side of the puck—tracking Hayley Wickenheiser's every move. Whyte was having the game of her life with a gold medal on the line.

Now the Americans owned a two-goal advantage, which any experienced player will tell you is the worst lead in hockey. If the opposition scores, it can steal the momentum and use it to tie the game. Or worse. Suffice it to say that no one on the American side was feeling comfortable. If anything, the Americans were wise enough to expect another big push from Team Canada, which is exactly what happened. Nine minutes and three seconds remained in regulation, and the Canadians, a proud and noble group of women, found yet another level – and soon had the Americans on their heels.

With just 4:10 remaining, and Canadian coach Miller contemplating pulling her goaltender for an extra attacker, Mounsey – Team USA's most physical player – was whistled for bodychecking. Guilty, she pleaded in a 2021 interview – but proud of it nonetheless. And forever grateful to her teammates for bailing her out.

"If you're going to teach bodychecking, it's like a picture-perfect bodycheck," said Mounsey, noting that it's among her family's favorite plays in her digitized highlight video. "Absolutely! I remember that moment probably better than I remember any moment in my career. It was one of the best-executed bodychecks I've ever done – a defensive play at the blue line, good gap control. . . yet it may be one of the worst decisions I ever made."

She was in the penalty box for just nine seconds before Canada sliced Team USA's lead in half on a goal by Goyette, her tournament-leading eighth. "I put my team in jeopardy," Mounsey said. "but thankfully it's a team sport, and my team competed until the end."

With the score 2-1, it was anybody's game – and everyone on both sides knew it. They played at a furious pace, the Canadians leaning heavily on the Americans, who couldn't seem to clear the puck out of their zone. The play was behind the net. Tueting took a quick glance and saw that Lisa Brown-Miller had the puck. And then she didn't. Something happened – Tueting had no idea what – but Canada's Karen Nystrom had regained possession and threw the puck out front onto the stick of her captain Stacy Wilson.

To suggest Tueting was caught by surprise would be an understatement. With at least half the goal to her right unguarded, she was scrambling to cover it when the puck came toward her destined for the back of the net. Somehow – don't ask her to explain or she'll get all metaphysical again – she threw out her right leg and the puck caromed off the toe of her hockey boot and out of harm's way. Just one millimeter more. . .

Play continued, Canada still pressing, both teams playing to their highest levels, fighting each other with all the frantic joy and passion typically reserved for a rival they respect, however grudgingly. For much of the second half of the period, the Americans had shortened their shifts – 45 seconds at the most, more typically 30 seconds, on-and-off. All hands on deck trying to stem the Canadian tide.

"It was a matter of digging deeper and playing harder," Karyn Bye recalled, "just emptying the tank, because at this point what do you have to save it for?"

Still, when players returned to the bench and looked up toward the clock, it felt like time was standing still, especially after Canada trimmed the lead to 2-1. Finally, the clock ticking down to the last dozen seconds, and with the Canadian net empty in favor of an extra attacker, Whyte provided the golden *coup de grace*. She intercepted the puck just outside the Team USA zone, managed to chip it to herself off the boards at center ice while sidestepping a defender, and raced into Canada's zone by herself, a gaping net before her. With eight seconds remaining, Sandra Whyte – the American who could have buckled under the enormity of all that ugly hate mail from Canada the previous three days – scored the unassisted goal to make it 3-1.

The third act of her offensive trilogy completed her remarkable ledger: a goal and two assists in a 3-1 victory. Equally important, she neutralized Wickenheiser on the defensive end. An impeccable performance on the world's biggest stage. Whyte's empty-netter allowed her teammates to celebrate their miraculous achievement

"Holy buckets!" screamed Bye. "We're gold medalists!" She joined teammates on the bench, jumping up and down, just waiting for the clock to expire, to finally, mercifully, hit double-zeroes so they could scramble over the boards and celebrate. "It was exhilarating."

Up in the broadcast booth, Mike (Doc) Emrick captured the moment for a worldwide television audience. "This is no miracle," he screamed into his microphone. "It's an arrival for women's hockey!"

Many years later, Tueting was still struggling to recall specific events from that game, so focused was she on seeing the puck – and keeping that little intruder out of her net.

"I. . . remember a big save with two minutes left, one that would have allowed Canada to tie the game at 2-2," Tueting wrote for her website. "Mostly, I don't remember anything about the game until Whytie, my roommate, teammate and friend, scored an open-net goal to make it 3-1.

"In that moment, the game ends. Joy possesses my body. I jump up and down, kicking my legs, arms flailing in relief, joy, disbelief and pride. There are eight seconds left, we line up, the puck drops and the buzzer sounds. I'm knocked down and piled on by my teammates. I can't breathe. I'm literally crushed. I'm so happy. We disentangle, hugging, throwing our hands up in joy, crying. I find my family in the stands and wave."

Bye, an accomplished stage manager in another world, emerged from the scrum and sprinted to the bench, where Bob Webster presented her with a colorful three-pound bundle. She had waited for this very moment to unveil the mother of all production elements: A 5-by-8-foot American flag.

"I brought it from home," she said. "The reason I did that is that every time Canada would beat us in the Worlds, they would grab their Canadian flags, wrap them around themselves and skate around. It was almost like they were kind of in your face, *and it killed me.* It killed me to be standing at that blue line and get that silver medal and look over there and see them with that Canadian flag.

"So I'm like, you know what? I'm going to win a gold, and I'm going to take the American flag, and I'm going to wrap it around myself."

Which is exactly what she did, sharing it with teammates, many of them frozen in time with cherished photos of themselves draped in Old Glory. And just as they did three days earlier, the teams lined up for the post-game handshake. Unmitigated joy and soul-crushing heartbreak, passing like ships in the night.

Decades later, the Canadians still feel visceral pain from having left Nagano with silver medals. Cassie Campbell-Pascall, the star-turned-broadcaster, is convinced the Team USA comeback three days prior is what doomed the Canucks in the gold-medal game. "You know, I just don't think we ever recovered from the whole round-robin," said Campbell-Pascall in an interview with TSN. "We just melted down, we just fell apart. From our goaltender to our defense like myself, to our forwards. We couldn't stop the floodgates from opening. We couldn't. . . we didn't know what to do."

One of the heroes for the victorious Americans typified the selflessness that coursed through Team USA. At some point well after the game – Looney cannot recall exactly when it was – someone mentioned to her that she had scored the golden goal, the one that gave Team USA the gold medal in the first-ever Olympic women's ice hockey tournament. Her response was typical Looney.

"Oh really?" she shrugged. "Cool."

Mike Eruzione never played another meaningful hockey game after his Miracle gold-medal run in Lake Placid. As the guy who scored the goal that beat the Soviets, he was content being "America's guest." Not only did he never have to pay for his own dinner or drinks wherever he went, but he could command serious appearance fees just for showing up.

And Looney? Well, when someone asked her what post-Olympic plans she had, she really didn't know. "I might take the fireman's exam," she said, adding that she would probably return to Massachusetts, where her belongings were stored with a friend, perhaps go job-hunting around Boston. She also needed surgery on her injured left shoulder.

And of course, she has spent much of her post-Olympic life downplaying her own golden goal. "It really didn't matter who put the puck in the net," she said. "That's how our team was. Everybody knew their role and we all were willing to play our roles." Twist her arm a bit, and she will admit one thing: "I wish I had Mike Eruzione's bank account."

On the scoresheet, Sandra Whyte had an epic game, climaxed by the cold-blooded dagger into Canada's empty net. Fellow Bostonian Tony Amonte had scored the winning goal in the World Cup of Hockey 18 months prior, joining Eruzione and 1960 legend Bill Cleary in the pantheon of international sporting heroes from hockey's Hub. It was time to make room in the club for another skater with a Boston accent, the irrepressible Sandra Whyte. Unlike her Beantown brethren, however, she had spent her days prior to the gold-medal game managing a media shit storm. Her partner in that task, Peter Haberl, had invested time, energy and a piece of his heart in getting Sandra's head on straight. He's convinced that Whyte's two-way excellence had made her a target.

"It made sense to me how that controversy happened, how there was an attempt [by Team Canada] to get her off her game," Haberl said. "Obviously that didn't work; her performance was exceptional."

"She was MVP of the game that night," said Smith, "a goal, two assists and marking their top line." Smith was just as impressed with how she handled the swirling controversy in the days leading up to that gold medal game. "Along with Peter Haberl, she was able to put that [controversy] in a little drawer, to fuel that energy. She's extremely intelligent, one of those great athletes."

Whyte dismisses the idea of having played a perfect game. "I don't know that any high-level athlete ever feels, 'I was perfect,'" she said. "But I can't say I've ever had a better outcome. Those years playing, to have finally gotten there, that weight off your shoulders and that relief. To feel like it was finally accomplished was amazing."

Smith allowed himself a brief moment of satisfaction as the celebration unfolded before him. "From a personal side, I was pleased that my idea of hockey was something that could be put into practice," said Smith, who gained entry into both the IIHF and U.S. Hockey Halls of Fame from that golden moment. "We worked on the right stuff, played the right way, played with a flair of confidence, weren't afraid of the puck. We played like a hockey team, you know?"

A man versed in history, Smith knew how far his American pioneers had come before carving their names into the record book. "The sacrifices they had to endure to perform, to go to a rink and put a bandana on so their hair wouldn't come out of their helmet, the things they had to overcome, it's so rewarding. To see the culmination of their efforts, hey, I knew it was something pretty neat."

Granato flashed back to her childhood fantasies from days competing in the basement with her brothers. "It's always about the celebrations, right?" she said, "You think about winning, watching the Olympics, the Stanley Cup Finals and you see these champions, you watch the celebrations. I always wondered what it is like to feel that way, to jump on your teammates and celebrate like that. And we did. We did that.

"And then we're in the locker room and someone says, 'Hey, now we need to go out and get our medals.' Oh my gosh yes, our medals. And we can keep them forever! They're ours."

Then they donned the perfectly fitting podium jackets they had tried on hours after their arrival in Nagano two weeks earlier. Having yet to play a game, they had slipped on those jackets and posed for a photo on Day One, their Olympic dreams still distant, but drawing ever-closer. Now the Olympic champions stood in a line on the ice for the medal ceremony, watching a woman walking toward them carrying a tray. It's Anita DeFrantz, a U.S. Olympian who won a bronze medal in rowing at the Montreal Games in 1976. In 1997, she became the first female vice-president of the IOC's executive committee. Her duty on this day was to deliver a hard-earned keepsake.

"All I saw was this bright, sparkly metal coming in our direction," Granato said. "I immediately started almost hyperventilating. OK, hyperventilating may be too dramatic, but I felt like I was losing my breath – like I couldn't breathe when I saw it."

The tray stopped in front of Granato. And with the world watching, she leaned forward and accepted the first Olympic gold medal ever awarded to a female hockey player.

"When Cammi Granato had the gold medal put around her neck, a feeling of joy went through my body," said defeated Canadian head coach Shannon Miller, in a moment of grace and dignity. "An Olympic gold medal was hung around the neck of a woman hockey player. I couldn't believe the impact that had on me. It almost took my breath away." She was hardly alone. Women's hockey would never be the same. And now it had a face.

By the time the teams lined up to shake hands, referee Marina Zenk had quietly left the ice, as officials tend to do. But she did not go unnoticed. "I remember getting off the ice and René Fasel [IIHF president] is there,"

Zenk later told a reporter. "He was grinning from ear to ear. He shook my hand. It was probably out of a sense of relief. It was the first time an official from a [finalist] country had refereed the final and nothing happened."

In fact, something quite remarkable had happened. Zenk distinguished herself with a well-called game with so much at stake between two teams whose animosity had spilled over in the past. A game played at an extraordinarily fast pace, that was as physical as hockey gets between women, but also relatively clean. Zenk assessed Team USA four minor penalties and Canada three. A few days later, Zenk met Canadian women's head coach Shannon Miller, who also congratulated her for a game well-managed.

Goaltender Sara DeCosta joined her teammates on the blue line during the gold medal ceremony. As they waited for the first notes of the Star-Spangled Banner, their hands dropped down to grasp the hand of a teammate on either side while their eyes rose to the stands. DeCosta remembers seeing U.S. mothers huddled together, crying, fathers high-fiving one another, siblings trying to climb over the glass.

"It was such an emotional moment," DeCosta told an interviewer on her return years later to her alma mater, Providence. "There we were, joined hand-in-hand for a moment that you'll never forget. It's actually hard to explain to people."

As was the loss for the Canadians. "It's painful still to this day, and it's been 20 years," said Campbell-Pascall, who eventually was able to find an upside to the loss more than two decades later. "I can say this now: them winning the gold in '98 was probably the best thing that happened to our sport, because we did have some attention. It was always Canada's game; we were getting support and it was fun. But I mean, you win a gold medal in the United States of America, it just takes your sport, your profile to a whole other level."

Curiously, the newly minted gold medalists had no idea about the headlines they were making back home, as the late-night talk shows began booking some of them as guests to show off their historic medals. The hysteria lasted for three days. Mercifully, at least for USA Hockey, it overshadowed the news of the Team USA men's hockey team vandalizing their Athletes Village dorm rooms and furniture.

Then, on Feb. 20, two days before the closing ceremonies in Nagano, the 15-year-old figure skating wunderkind Lipinski stunned the world by upsetting teammate Kwan in Ladies' Singles, becoming the youngest ever female gold medalist in an individual event, a record that had stood since Sonja Henie of Norway won the same event, also aged 15, in St. Moritz in 1928. The media mob quickly became fixated on the next new shiny object.

No worries. By then Team USA's women's ice hockey team was planning a 10-day blowout trip to Hawaii. And in their own subtle ways, both privately and professionally, they've been celebrating ever since.

Lee Johnson (right), the Hobey Baker of women's hockey, never got to perform in the Olympics because her epic career peaked in the 1970s. She did, however, get her hands on Sandra Whyte's Nagano gold medal when the stars teamed up during an exhibition game in 2006. *(Joyce Inserra)*

Not only was Karyn Bye Team USA's alternate captain, but she was also its designated cut-up. Teammates never forgot when she convinced a flight crew to lend her attendants garb and started taking drink orders. *(Karyn Bye Collection)*

Living for six months in Lake Placid can be pretty dull for two-dozen renaissance women. In a day of inspiration, (from left) Michelle Amidon, Tricia Dunn, A.J. Mleczko and Karyn Bye shopped a dollar store for costumes and then invaded the local bowling alley to inject some variety into their routine. (*Karyn Bye Collection*)

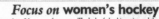

Focus on women's hockey

A miracle on ice: It's a goon-free game. The lack of checking, size and the absence of booming slapshots are the biggest differences from the men's game. It's alot like watching women's below-the-hoop basketball. Nice bounce passes, no slam dunks. The emphasis is on skating, passing, stickhandling and playmaking.

An Olympic 'league of their own'

By Jeff Schultz
STAFF WRITER

Salt Lake City

If we are to believe history books in the northern provinces, the women hockey players bound for Nagano will be 109 years too late to be considered among the sport's pioneers. In 1889, Canada's Lord Stanley flooded his front lawn so that it would freeze into a sheet of ice and enable his two daughters to practice their stickhandling.

So there.

But it seems safe in assuming that the men whose name adorns the NHL's championship trophy did not foresee what will take place halfway across the globe in three months. Women on skates. Women with pads and sticks and helmets and sometimes even an attitude. Women representing their countries, trying to win a medal in the Olympics.

This isn't old-time hockey.

"Many people won't be able to tell the difference from men's hockey, except that a lot of the players have ponytails hanging down out of their helmets," said Ben Smith, the long-time men's collegiate coach who now oversees the U.S. women of pucks. "I must admit, it still strikes me when one of our players takes off

The immovable object meets the irresistible force. In a series reminiscent of the classic 1972 men's Summit Series between Canada and the Soviet Union, the Team USA women battled Canada for 13 games leading up to the 1998 Olympics. The series captured the imagination of prominent newspapers from both sides of the border. (*Atlanta Journal-Constitution*)

Former Northeastern University men's coach Ben Smith was poached by USA Hockey executives to become America's first women's Olympic hockey coach. Their belief in Smith was well-founded. (*USA Hockey*)

Team Canada Coach Shannon Miller flashes a smile with her team, which failed to win the gold medal despite the vow she'd made in Vancouver just before leaving for Japan. (*Hockey Canada*)

Defense partners Colleen Coyne and 'Wonder Woman' Tara
Mounsey, brandishing gold. *(Colleen Coyne Collection)*

Team USA's goaltending tandem of Sarah Tueting (left) and
Sara DeCosta generated both victories and an unshakeable
friendship. Each earned wins over Canada in Nagano.
(Sarah Tueting Collection)

The Sprint. Karyn Bye emerges from the Team USA celebration to collect her American flag. She and her teammates used Old Glory as a backdrop in their respective victory laps. *(Colleen Coyne Collection)*

Best pals and Nagano roommates Sarah Tueting (left and Sandra Whyte share a golden glow after their sensational performances against Canada. *(Sarah Tueting Collection)*

Game officials, including referee Maria Zenk in the orange
arm bands, stand by during one of the greatest traditions
in sports, the emotional center-ice handshake between the
victor and the vanquished. *(Colleen Coyne Collection)*

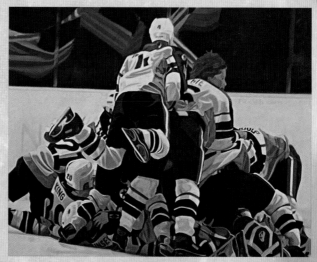

The 'dog pile' celebration seconds after the horn sounded
to end Team victory over Canada in the first-ever women's
Olympic ice hockey tournament. The painting, from a photo,
hangs in the home of winning goaltender Sarah Tueting –
who is at the bottom of that pile. *(Sarah Tueting Collection)*

The Team USA goaltenders' union celebrates with a bottle of bubbly, from left: Mike Richter of the New York Rangers, Sara DeCosta and Sarah Tueting, and John Vanbiesbrouck of the Florida Panthers. *(The Sarah Tueting Collection)*

Team USA captain Cammi Granato and Colleen Coyne flash golden smiles to match their new jewelry. *(Colleen Coyne Collection)*

Beaming captain Cammi Granato and alternate captain Karyn Bye, owners of countless silver medals, finally flaunt some gold of their own. *(The Associated Press)*

From left, Angela Ruggiero, Sue Merz, Alana Blahoski and Shelley Looney, sporting leis in Hawaii, a 10-day celebration following their victory in Japan. *(Colleen Coyne Collection)*

PART THREE

ALL THAT GLITTERS

Beyond Crime
and Punishment

"Mistakes were made. Others were blamed... I may as well cut my losses and make a hasty exit while I still had enough self-esteem to walk upright. Crawling was so demoralizing."

—Darynda Jones, author

Two nights after winning gold, several of the Team USA women joined men's team captain Chris Chelios and teammate Gary Suter for dinner that lasted into the wee hours of the morning. They were still celebrating at the restaurant when some members of Team USA's men's team were humiliating themselves, embarrassing their country and insulting their host nation by vandalizing their Athletes Village rooms in a drunken disturbance. For Chelios and Suter, the party with the gold-medalists was the perfect alibi. For the women, however, the party was pretty much over. With three days remaining until the Closing Ceremonies, this was the last time the women's hockey team players would be permitted out past midnight, thanks to a preposterous decision to punish the women with a silly curfew while the men were sprinting toward the exits.

Until then, the 1998 Olympic Winter Games had been an historic, relatively successful experiment for international hockey on both the men's and women's sides. In retrospect, however, from USA Hockey's standpoint, it was a case of two monumental extremes: surprising gold for the women, but abject failure for the men, pre-tournament favorites who failed to even advance to the medal round, then wrecked the place on the way out.

Sayonara Nagano.

Throughout the Games, the Athletes Village had become a mutual admiration society – for both the men and the women of Team USA and Canada. Shelley Looney recalled how excited she got as she and teammate Chris Bailey were walking around the Village and strolled past Steve Yzerman. The captain of her hometown Detroit Red Wings, Yzerman was someone Looney had idolized since she was a young girl.

"Let's go," Bailey said, tugging Looney's arm and pulling her toward Yzerman. "You're going to meet him right now." And they did. Didn't matter in the slightest that Yzerman was there competing with Team Canada. His Red Wings, Looney's team, were enjoying a dynastic run in the NHL; in about four months they would win their second straight Stanley Cup. But what impressed Looney even more was a few days later when she found Yzerman behind her in line at the Village cafeteria, often described as a mall food court about the size of a Costco store.

"Hi Shelley," Yzerman said.

For a moment, she was dumbstruck. *"Are you kidding me? Steve Yzerman remembers my name?"* she thought to herself. It got better. During the course of their short conversation, Yzerman whispered: "Don't tell anybody, but I'm rooting for you guys."

"I was so surprised," Looney said. "But when I thought about it, I figured it had something to do with his daughters. They had dual citizenship, of course, but they were raised as Americans, in the Detroit area. Maybe they were rooting for us, too."

The women continued to encounter their heroes like Wayne Gretzky, Brendan Shanahan and Jaromir Jagr at a social hangout sponsored by Nike. "We were enamored," Looney recalled. "We looked up to those guys growing up."

The respect and admiration flowed both ways. The Team Canada men were conspicuous by their presence in large numbers at their women's team games. They dressed fashionably in garb provided by Roots – the beginning of the style revolution for Canada's Olympians. Red and white jackets over black pants trimmed with red-and-white piping, topped off by a unique red cap designed by Roots.

The American men were less noticeable at games involving their women's team. Though they were present in smaller numbers, those who showed up were into it every bit as much as their Canadian counterparts.

"The girls were really fun to watch, and they were really good," said Mike Modano, a Detroit area native and center for the Dallas Stars. "And you could tell what a great rivalry it was between Canada and the U.S. It reminded me of some of those series we had against Colorado and Detroit about that time. Just great hockey. . . and prison rules."

John Vanbiesbrouck, a Team USA goaltender in Nagano and vice president of USA Hockey as the 25th anniversary of the 1998 Games approached, also tried to see as many games as he could. But logistically it wasn't easy getting around to the major venues – or getting tickets. Also, GM Lou Lamoriello kept a tight rein on his players throughout the tournament, at least until its shocking conclusion.

"I can only speak for myself, but there was a ton of interest – serious interest on the guys' side," Vanbiesbrouck said. "I was really excited for our women's team. I remember Pat Lafontaine and I left a team meal kind of early. We told Lou we had to go watch the game. He gave us permission. It was the gold-medal game, and tickets were so hard to get. My wife was there, and we had to sit in separate corners of the arena."

They were privileged to witness something unforgettable.

"A great moment, for sure," Vanbiesbrouck said of the upset victory over Team Canada. "I've loved that moment ever since."

While the Team USA women were the toast of the town in both the

United States and Japan, the American men suffered a 4-1 loss to the Czechs in the quarterfinals. A co-favorite with Canada to win the gold medal, the Americans finished an embarrassing sixth. About 10 hours later, all hell broke loose.

Three apartments in the Athletes Village complex shared by American players were trashed in a late-night, alcohol-fueled frat-boy fracas. Ten chairs were broken and three fire extinguishers were emptied. Six of the chairs and a fire extinguisher were thrown from a fifth-floor room to a courtyard, according to *The Associated Press*. Damage was estimated at $3,000. No injuries were reported, although some teammates worried that goaltender Mike Richter might need medical attention after he inhaled contents of a fire extinguisher emptied on him as he slept.

"It's a very unfortunate incident," then USA Hockey Executive Director Dave Ogrean said. "They embarrassed our host country and they brought disrespect to our sport."

Both USA Hockey and the NHL promised restitution and a thorough investigation.[13] Then players, management and the NHL Players Association quickly circled the wagons to protect the guilty. To this day the perpetrators have not been named publicly, though much speculation has centered around a small contingent of players with ties

---

13 NHL Commissioner Gary Bettman held an impromptu news conference in Nagano a day after his league's players had trashed their Olympic Village dorm rooms and dishonored the Nagano Games. He vowed to serve justice to the guilty parties. He had the perfect man for the job: NHL Director of Security Dennis Cunningham, a professional with impeccable credentials. A graduate of the FBI's National Academy and a 25-year veteran of the New York City Police Department, Cunningham spent his last two years at the NYPD heading up Internal Affairs. There is little doubt among League staffers that Cunningham learned exactly who was responsible for the broken furniture and abuse of the fire extinguishers on that infamous night, but his findings never surfaced. The NHL realized that busting the guilty parties would damage its relationships with the Players Association, its member clubs and its star players. So the ripples from Bettman's angry words in Nagano eventually settled. No action taken, no punishments handed out – the disgrace compounded.

to the Boston area. Team USA General Manager Lou Lamoriello was incensed, saying those responsible "should be ashamed of themselves." U.S. Olympic officials were equally infuriated by the lack of judgment displayed by highly paid professionals competing in a country where good manners are a fundamental principle of society and vandalism is rare.

Late nights had become the norm for several players on the U.S. men's team, as they were spotted frequently in local bars until the early morning hours on several occasions. Team USA coach Ron Wilson defended his decision against imposing a curfew on his players.

"They're men," Wilson said. "I'm not going to throw a curfew at these guys. They're the best athletes we have, they know how to take care of themselves." Curiously, those same men adhere to strict curfews set by their coaches during the NHL season.

It was beyond shocking – the dismal performance on the ice as well as the juvenile behavior away from the rink. The U.S. squad was laden with talent. Six of its members were 50-goal scorers in the world's best professional hockey league. Just 18 months earlier, Team USA men had won the World Cup in impressive fashion, defeating Canada in a best-of-three finale. Now this, the worst performance ever by an American Olympic hockey team. Certainly it called into question the decision by the National Hockey League to allow its players to compete on this world stage.

Naturally, the men couldn't get out of Nagano fast enough. It was the women's team that had so much to celebrate and be proud of that wound up paying the price. While the men were all scurrying home, leaving on the first flights they could book, the women found themselves being treated like high-schoolers attending the junior prom.

"Once that happened with the men, we were told we had a curfew at midnight every night until we left," Shelley Looney said. "We were the story, and they [the USOC and USA Hockey] didn't want to have any more incidents."

The crime and punishment of the USA Hockey's two squads had devolved into a theater of the absurd, another farcical chapter in the sporting battle of the sexes. The millionaire NHL-ers got out of Dodge while the women, all amateurs forced to actually work for a living to support their passion for hockey, wound up being punished.

In the end, however, what hurt and angered the American women wasn't so much the curfew that limited their merriment following their golden performance; it was how some of the men dismissed the entire Olympic experience as something beneath them.

"This was the biggest waste of time ever," Team USA forward Keith Tkachuk said after his team was eliminated. The women were not amused.

"When they were saying things like, 'Thank God it's over. Now we can go back to playing real hockey,' that really angered us," said Lisa Brown-Miller. "We were like, 'This is it for us. This is all we have, and we're all in, heart and soul.' And those guys just didn't seem to care."

Clearly one team was there to play hockey, the other to enjoy saki. And in the final hours of the Nagano Games, USA Hockey was juggling two enormous headlines – one by the men that had disgraced the country, and the other by the women who brought immense pride and joy. So for a few days at the end of the Games, USA Hockey turned out the lights. The party was over – even for a group of women who had so much to celebrate.

The Ben Smith
Paradox

"As he was valiant, I honor him. But as he was ambitious, I slew him."

—Brutus from Julius Caesar

If Ben Smith's performance in Nagano were graded, he would receive an A-plus without dispute—near perfection in every way, shape and form. If, however, he were graded on all three of his Olympic head coaching stints, the results would be decidedly mixed—his career punctuated by a precipitous slide down the podium: from gold to silver to bronze.

Over the entire Nagano gold-medal experience, Smith was universally appreciated, some might even say loved, by his 1998 team. His refusal to play favorites as well as his deadpan humor, punctuated by inane quips that left his players simultaneously grinning and shaking their heads in confusion, were the endearing trademarks that complemented Smith's historic success. Dethroning Canada in the sport's Olympic debut—upsetting hockey's natural order on the world's biggest stage—catapulted Smith into both the IIHF and the U.S. Hockey Halls of Fame, the latter in both the team and individual categories.

His decision-making in the two years leading up to and through Nagano achieved the Midas rating: everything he touched turned to gold. Whether it was instantaneous, in-game adjustments, or excruciating cuts that ended careers, every time Smith threw the dice, they paid off handsomely.

1. Mike Boyle: Cashing in a favor and bringing his players to the world-class strength trainer immediately gave Team USA a rare edge over its rivals. Canada had no official strength trainer from 1996-98.

2. Bob Webster: The equipment manager who was so much more. The affable "Webbie" was Smith's only non-negotiable demand in his contract talks with USA Hockey. Webster made every player feel like a first-class hockey citizen, claiming the premier locker room for his women even in Canadian rinks, tailoring their equipment to their exact specs, and making himself available for custom skate sharpening 24-7. Webster was also the catalyst for the eleventh-hour move to get team psychologist Peter Haberl to Nagano.

3. Peter Haberl: Smith sought out Haberl in 1996, bringing the young doctoral student on board – originally without pay. Haberl's contributions were undeniable, especially his preponderance of aid in the unfounded controversy involving Sandra Whyte.

4. The Burlington Lockout: Insisting that his team stand in the hallway after its brutal collapse to Canada on national television, locked out of its own dressing room while surrounded by Canadian victory cries, was sheer brilliance by Smith. None of the American players ever forgot it, and it was cited as the primary inspiration for

Team USA's comeback in the St. Valentine's Day Massacre of Canada during the Olympic round-robin.

5. The Controversial Cuts: It is impossible to imagine how much pressure was on Ben Smith to keep Stephanie O'Sullivan, a fellow Bostonian and a top-six forward who was averaging a point-per-game on the pre-Olympic tour. Defender Kelly O'Leary was only months removed from the IIHF World Championship All-Star team at the time of her cut. Erin Whitten was widely described at the beginning of the pre-Olympic tour as the best women's goalie in the world. Nevertheless, Smith made those tough cuts, and all three of their replacements–Sue Merz, Gretchen Ulion and Sarah Tueting–were major contributors in the gold-medal game. Smith was a perfect three-for-three in these high-stakes gambles.

6. Swapping out Whyte for Ruggiero on the Power Play: Because of the selfless nature of the 1998 team, Smith's special-teams adjustment caused nary a ripple in the room, but its effects on ice were indisputable. Whyte generated two power-play goals from the point in the gold-medal game, perfectly executed primary assists. Smith had the ideal chess piece in position to checkmate Canada.

7. The Round-Robin Timeout: The most influential timeout in hockey history. After Smith spoke to his troops about "doughnuts," and a "hill of beans," Team USA went out and scored six unanswered goals. The momentum didn't stop there. Including the goals from the gold-medal game, the Americans outscored Canada 9-1 after Smith's timeout. Midas, indeed.

8. The Gold-Medal Game Starter: Fifty-fifty decisions can be the toughest of all. What was there to choose from between the two Sara(h)s in goal? Neither choice could be questioned, at least not until the game was won or lost. Smith waited until the final practice, made no special announcement, and chose the winning Sarah, who surprised even herself with her other-worldly performance. Meanwhile, the other Sara cheered her heart out for her rival and close friend.

Throughout the entire Nagano experience, Smith rolled a perfect eight-for-eight. Had his experiment in coaching women ended there, he would have exited the sport from the summit of Mt. Olympus. But there was a gold medal to defend—on home soil no less—so Smith soldiered on without hesitation. In 2002, on the cusp of sports immortality, Smith saw his once hot dice suddenly turn stone cold. He would eventually make Olympic history once again, only this time from the opposite end of the podium.

From the first moment in the runup to Salt Lake City, the 2002 Winter Games were an entirely different animal than Nagano, both for Smith and his charges. The players were no longer nameless entities, desperate athletes willing to work two jobs to chase their five-ring dreams. Some were now celebrities, many having appeared on late-night network talk shows and immortalized on the cover of Wheaties cereal boxes.

Smith parlayed his own elevated status within the corridors of power in Colorado Springs, convincing USA Hockey to house and train his athletes not for just the Olympic year, but for the 2000-01 season as well. This placed a significant burden on America's best and brightest, women chasing degrees at the nation's premier universities. They were now being asked to spend two seasons sequestered in Lake Placid, a fun winter sports getaway, but a cultural gulag to this group of renaissance women. Putting their lives on hold for a stipend of $1,000 per month was a big ask.

Cammi Granato, Smith's trusted leader and the sport's premier captain in 1998, soon found herself at odds with the entire power structure of her national governing body, including Smith. It all began on Day One of their gold-medal defense.

Inspired by her sisters on USA's national soccer team, Granato arrived at training camp in the late summer of 2000 with an official letter, a legal document seeking improved working conditions and increased financial compensation for her team. She expected to be treated with the respect due an elite athlete. She could not have been more mistaken. She was left feeling like a shamed child.

"I felt like a kid that had done something very bad," wrote Granato in a piece for ESPN. "I had an associate coach look me in the eye [years later] and tell me that our actions cost our team the gold medal in the 2002 Olympics."

Thus began the us-vs.-them mentality that colored the next two years. In spite of the simmering feud between management and labor, Team USA strung together a staggering run of 13 consecutive wins against Canada leading up to the Salt Lake City Games. But there was no joy on Team USA, goodwill having been replaced by the hat trick of team decay: enmity, distrust and jealousy.

One of the major reasons for Team USA's undefeated record vs. Canada was the sensational play of gold-medal netminder Sarah Tueting.

Her deteriorating personal relationship with Smith personified the new world order within the team. Loathing had replaced what had once been adoration.

"I loved Ben," said Tueting about her Stage I relationship with Smith, the gold-medal collaboration stage. She will never forget the letter she penned to her coach after winning it all in 1998. "True leaders see the diamond in the rough. Apply pressure and believe. I grew into what you believed," Tueting recalled two decades later. "It was this whole love letter. Basically it was like, 'I am *so* grateful, I am *so* happy, thank you so much for believing in me.' And I really felt that about Ben at the time. For the '98 Olympics he saw the best in everybody. He pulled us into that future."

Then Tueting segued into a description of their Stage II relationship, the one that sputtered and collapsed in Salt Lake. She spewed R-rated language, verbiage similar to what Smith later used to describe Tueting. She prefers not to dwell on how their relationship took a turn for the worse. "Don't even get me started," she said. "It was like a total switch. But in '98, I thought he was the cat's meow, a fantastic coach that really believed in people, and very fair. I thought he was great."

That trust and understanding vanished during the next quadrennial. The loyal goalie was now filled with contempt for her coach. From Smith's point of view, his players had changed after winning the gold. Leading up to Nagano, his team believed in the creed, "Let's do whatever we can to win this thing." Smith is convinced that their unshakable altruism had faded away. "I think it morphed into something different."

Veterans from the 1998 team concur. "Our team played selfless hockey from the get-go, we supported each other," said Lisa Brown-Miller, who worked for NBC's broadcast team in Salt Lake City. "Then you saw a difference in 2002, it was a very different dynamic. 'Let *me* get the limelight.'"

"We couldn't come together as a team like we were in '98," said Shelley

Looney, who was on that troubled 2002 squad. "Everybody wanted to be in the spotlight. We didn't get along."

Prior to the 2002 gold medal game, Team USA was not tested on Salt Lake City ice, dismissing pretenders like Finland, Sweden and Russia without breaking a sweat. Outsiders had little idea what kind of turmoil roiled within the Americans' dressing room. Media, fans and sponsors all presumed that Team USA was destined to win its second straight gold medal. But there were clues to the contrary.

Days before the gold medal game, Karyn Bye admitted that a virus was running through the team. That statement could have been interpreted literally or figuratively. Indeed there was a virus, a team sick of being holed up for nearly two years under the heavy thumb of Ben Smith.

Throughout the Salt Lake City Games, Smith would always joke with the media corps whenever he was asked who would start in goal for the gold-medal game. He answered without hesitation. "Sara(h)," he'd say with a chuckle, letting the writers and broadcasters figure it out for themselves. In reality, there was little chance Smith was going to start the woman with whom he had traded barbs for the past year. Tueting, the goalie whose excellence had penetrated the skulls of Canada's best shooters for the previous six months, spent the gold-medal game stapled to the bench, even after Canada sprinted out to a 3-1 lead.

The 3-2 final score was not indicative of Canada's dominance. In the post-game news conference, Smith clung to the theory that his team's 13-0 pre-season record against Canada was a hockey feat equaled only by the dynastic Soviet Red Army. That story fell on deaf ears. NBC talent and production were busy speculating whether this would be Smith's farewell: Would the dedicated boatsman literally sail away from hockey from his home port in Gloucester, Massachusetts?

No he would not. Smith surprised many when he returned for a final gold rush in Torino in 2006. His first piece of business was a shocker: cutting captain Cammi Granato. This singular act was cited as the primary reason Team USA failed to even reach the gold-medal game. Like his hero, the NFL's ruthless Super Bowl champion coach Bill Belichick, Smith was determined to replace his veterans before they passed their prime, regardless of status and achievement.

The leadership void doomed Team USA in 2006 from the start. New captain Krissy Wendell was an exquisite talent, but the weight of the "C" on her sweater was too much to bear. In the medal-round semifinals, Sweden's Maria Rooth erased Team USA's 2-0 lead with a pair of goals, and then buried the Yanks with the shootout winner. Swedish goaltender Kim Martin was equally heroic, turning aside 37 of 39 American shots.

Both Rooth and Martin, as well as two other members of Team Sweden, had been recruited to University of Minnesota-Duluth by Smith's 1998 rival Shannon Miller, who coached them all to NCAA titles. Prior to the 2006 Games, Miller asserts that she prepared Team Sweden by supplying her former players with notes on breakouts and special teams.

She will never forget how proud she was while watching her former college players propel Sweden to the women's version of the Miracle on Ice. "Those were my girls, and they were using my systems," said Miller, whose phone rang in Duluth while Team Sweden was still celebrating in front of her on live television. It was Maria Rooth's mom Gudrun, calling from the raucous Palisport Olympico in Torino.

"She was crying and screaming," Miller recalled. "She kept saying, 'Thank you, thank you so much! Look what you've done!'"

Sweden's historic upset of Smith's last women's team—the only American squad to fail to reach the Olympic gold-medal game—had Miller's fingerprints all over it, yet there is no trace of gloating in the memory of her rival's demise. "I just remember being proud that everyone involved in women's hockey was being lifted up by what happened," said Miller. "It wasn't just Team USA and Canada going for the gold again. That was so important for the growth of our game."

Smith made a point of praising Sweden's Martin in his somber post-game. "Obviously their goaltender played very well."

There is no shortage of irony in the fact that Miller's proteges victimized her coaching antagonist, the man who would never utter Miller's name in public. The two coaches, Smith and Miller, will forever be linked in Olympic hockey history, for better and for worse.

History will be kind to Smith, as it should. Both his greatest victory (1998 gold) and his bitterest defeat (2006 bronze) ultimately lifted women's hockey to new heights, as did the arms race he created with rival Canada. His decade of dedication to the fledgling Olympic sport gave it both credibility and gravitas. Smith's multiple Hall-of-Fame inductions will preserve his legacy, and in this assessment, represent his final grade.

Beheaded

"This is the end of the line... you're number's up"

—Ben Smith

August 2005, Lake Placid. Cammi Granato is flying, feeling better on the ice than she had in ages. She's in perhaps the best physical condition of her life after training hard all summer with National Hockey League players after a serious knee injury threatened to derail her career. Even better, she's on top of her game mentally, knowing this would be her final season with Team USA – hopefully ending with another gold medal at the 2006 Winter Games in Torino. She knows it. Her family knows it. They're all prepared.

As good as Granato is feeling, however, she can't shake this notion that something isn't quite right. She's sensing some uneasiness among some of her teammates, but that isn't so unusual at a tryout camp with roster adjustments looming. She's hearing some wild rumors, which also isn't so unusual as the stress levels increased. She quickly dismisses them. But the coaching staff is acting strangely as well.

Something isn't right, she tells to herself. *It's just strange, weird.*

She tries to shake that off too, until one of the coaches skates up to her and asks, right out of the blue, "Have you talked to Coach yet?"

"No, why?"

"Oh, just curious. No big deal. It's all good." And he skates away before she can say another word.

Well why wouldn't it be good? What's going on?

As she's leaving the ice, team leader Gavin Regan approaches.

"Coach wants to see you in his office," Regan says.

"Sure, OK, what's up?"

"No idea. He just said he needs to talk to you."

Granato showers and dresses quickly, that feeling that something just isn't right gnawing away at her. She ascends the stairs two at a time and knocks on a door.

Ben Smith is sitting behind his desk. In a chair nearby is one of his assistants, Mike Gilligan.

"Hey Coach, you wanted to see me?" she asks, flashing a quick, tentative smile.

Smith waves her in, motioning toward an empty chair. Cammi Granato, national team member for 15 years and captain for most of them, takes a seat and waits.

Defending Olympic gold in 2002 on U.S. soil proved to be an unpredictable and rocky road for the Americans. Canada avenged its soul-crushing defeat in Nagano by winning the next three IIHF World Championships. Then the Americans reeled off an incredible 13 straight wins over Team Canada in the runup to the Salt Lake City Games.

"We were like a machine," Granato recalled. "We were trained well, and we were undefeated going into the tournament. We beat Canada every game leading up to the Olympics. The strength of our on-ice product was so good that we could kind of ignore all the off-ice stuff that was there."

To be sure, there was a lot of off-ice stuff. It began in 2000, when

Granato and her teammates, borrowing a page from the Team USA women's national soccer team, had the audacity to ask for some of the same rights USA Hockey was bestowing on its men's team – everything from equal pay to similar marketing efforts down to access to tickets for family members at certain events. Nothing more than the men were getting, they asked only for equal treatment.

"And it really blew up in our faces," Granato said. "They [at USA Hockey] did not take it well. Ben did not take it well. Peter Haberl literally looked in my face and said, 'This is going to cost you guys the gold medal.' That was our team psychologist. Straight to my face. I mean, it was bad.

"That was before social media. Nobody took our side. Nobody understood us. There was a definite split. Relationships were severed. [Smith] couldn't understand it. He was like a different person after that. Everything turned. There was more distance. It was like we went against him, when we were really just fighting for our rights – and we had never known how to fight for those rights prior to that."

Granato and her gold-medal teammates had talked with some of their counterparts on the women's national soccer team. "We just realized that we were allowed to ask for those things, too," she said. "But we were kind of out there, isolated. It was USA Hockey against us. And it was tough."

That issue festered during the team's two full seasons in Lake Placid prior to the Olympics – an ill-fated decision by Smith to centralize his team in the small upstate New York village. His goal: to build a hockey superpower. It accomplished quite the opposite.

"That was a lot for everybody," Granato said. "You've got to picture our life there: No internet, eating cafeteria food every day, no one around. There were days when we'd go on the ice twice a day then do bike sprints. No freedom. No balance at all."

Granato echoed Soviet-era national team players who felt imprisoned in their majestic hockey camp, known as *Archangelskoe*, a gilded cage located on one of Moscow's outer rings where they would spend eleven months a year, with little opportunity to visit their families. There was nothing else to do but train, eat and sleep under the watchful eye of their iron-fisted coach and warden, Viktor Tikhonov.

Like the former Soviets, Granato and her teammates felt like hostages in their own camp, sensing that Smith isolated them as a group to keep them out of trouble. It was the same way he would have handled his college men's teams to keep his players from carousing around the college nightlife.

"He was worried we'd be out drinking," Granato said. "We kept saying, 'This isn't the men's game. Girls aren't like that. Our bodies can't handle it.' We needed more trust, and it wasn't there."

Smith, meantime, felt he was building a superteam, even suggesting publicly that he had assembled the most dominant squad since the Soviets brought their national team to Lake Placid. But that team didn't win either.

In the absence of faith and leadership from the coaching staff, team unity—the hallmark of the 1998 team—began to erode. Winning a gold medal, it turns out, has far-reaching implications. Suddenly, the klieg lights go on and everyone is paying attention, especially the media. For some players, there were lucrative endorsement opportunities. For others, not so much. Then another team comes together four years later, some older players replaced by more youthful legs.

"We had some really, really good young players coming in, and that was really hard for some of our veterans," Granato said. "They did not take to that very well, these new players stepping in and playing on the top line, the top six. That was different for all of us.

"In 1998, everybody was a rookie. Everybody embraced their roles. We really worked hard on that team aspect. We lived and breathed it together, and all of us felt the same level of excitement. We gave up our style for the benefit of the team. We had all these unity symbols, bracelets and necklaces. We all bought into the role."

Four years later, the chemistry was potentially volatile. "This time around, there wasn't that buy-in to the roles," Granato said. "We were missing that leadership from the coaching staff. They were angry at us."

There's more. America was at war as it prepared to host those Salt Lake City Games – and it hit too close to home for Team USA's women. Granato and her teammates recall vividly a joyful Kathleen Kauth running and leaping into her father's arms when she learned she had survived the pre-Olympic cut. Shortly after that, Don Kauth, a bank analyst who worked on the 85th floor of the World Trade Center, was killed when the South Tower was struck by a plane piloted by terrorist hijackers on September 11.[14]

"Now we're dealing with Kath's loss, which was devastating, and with war happening on our own territory," Granato said. "When the Olympics happened, we would stay up at night talking about Osama bin Laden, watching our flag burning on the TV news. That was our prep going into the games. And when you're in your own country and everyone has you a shoo-in to win the Games and all this other stuff is happening. . . It's a lot of pressure."

But on the ice they were still so good, rolling through four preliminary opponents in Salt Lake by a combined score of 31-1 – even with the flu plaguing their roster – heading into another gold-medal showdown with Canada. Little wonder that they felt they were strong enough to overcome anything.

"I think we had this false sense, like, 'Oh, we're good. We might not get along as well, but we're so good on the ice,'" Granato said. "Then we get to the final game and we didn't play our best hockey until the last six minutes. By the time we finally started to play, it was too late."

Unlike Nagano, the gold-medal game in Salt Lake City was hardly a showcase for women's hockey – unless you like special-teams play. And

14 Kauth wouldn't make her Olympic debut until 2006.

players do not.

Officials called 19 minor penalties in that game – 13 on Team Canada, including an astounding eight straight in the middle of the game. "Absolutely atrocious," Canadian star Hayley Wickenheiser said. And she was right. Even the Americans didn't like it.

At one point, Granato approached the referee and pleaded with her: "Please, just let us play." Both teams were competing with the malevolent edge that typified their games. Many of the calls were for roughing, body-checking and high-sticking.

"It completely takes you out of rhythm. It takes your whole bench out of rhythm and it changes the course of the game because there's no flow," Granato said. "You're not letting the teams decide [the outcome]; you're letting the power plays decide."

Both Team USA goals were scored with the man-advantage – the first by Katie King that tied the game at 1-1 early in the second period, and the second in the furious closing minutes of the game by Karyn Bye, a slapshot that pulled the Americans to within a goal. But in the end, their failure to score with the extra skater cost them the gold medal.

For that they blame their coach. In the four years that followed their gold-medal performance in Nagano, Smith became more and more imperial over his team. The off-ice stuff – like keeping them in Lake Placid – was demeaning enough. But they found his on-ice tactics to be stifling, bordering on nonsensical.

"He took more control of us as the years went by," said one player, who spoke on the condition of anonymity. "It was very controlled. Too controlled. Before, we had a lot more freedom to be creative."

In Salt Lake City, however, Smith had commanded his power play units to begin their attack from the same spot on the ice. "All those power plays starting in the same place," another player said. "We got stuck, and we never adjusted. That hurt us. We had plenty of chances to win."

In times of adversity, Granato noted, teams must rely on their unity – their willingness to sacrifice for one another. But it wasn't there with that Salt Lake City team.

"We just couldn't fall back on it," she said. "We played our worst hockey of the entire year in that game. It was a devastating way to go. As a leader, I've looked back on it over and over thinking, 'I should have done this. I should have done that.' You just wish you did more to get us closer to where we were in '98 as a group."

Canada won, 3-2. And then it got ugly.

Not content to just shake hands and skate off with the gold medal, the Canadians went public with the outrageous – and later to be revealed as unfounded – rumor that Team USA had been disrespecting Canada's flag.

"The Americans had our flag on their floor in the dressing room, and now I want to know if they want us to sign it," Wickenheiser told Canadian television immediately after the game.

Granato and her teammates were infuriated.

"I know for a fact that it just didn't happen. As a captain, I can say it *never* would have happened," she said. "You have a code of conduct that you live by as a person, but it's also about the Olympic code. It's all about respect in those games. That's what you notice when you're there. It's all about fair play.

"And also, our country was at war. *Our* flag was being burned over in the Middle East. And we're accused of stepping on their flag? It doesn't get worse than that. But it became folklore. It became truth in Canada. I still, to this day after living here [in Vancouver] for 20 years, get asked about it.

"We were talking with some of their players afterward and we said, 'Do you guys realize what you're doing here? You've just created an international incident.' As if we weren't feeling bad enough. We had just been kicked and beaten, and we were devastated. And now our character is being questioned. That was really hard."

For Team USA, it was a painful lesson about how story can become truth. It might not be real – and in this case there wasn't a crumb of evidence to support a rumor the Canadians had concocted to inspire themselves in that one game – but it has become ingrained in Canadian history to the point that few in that country believe otherwise.

"You couldn't convince the Canadian side – or even some of our American reporters," Granato said. "It just made me look at media in a different way. I lived through something that became a truth, but it wasn't."

Now she and her team would have to wait four more years, Torino in 2006, to try to set it straight.

The silence didn't last long. The guillotine fell swiftly, just seconds after Cammi Granato took a seat in her coach's office that August 24, 2005, the final day of tryouts in Lake Placid for the team that would represent the United States in Italy six months later.

Ben Smith's eyes met hers and he spoke: "This is the end of the line, Cammi. Your number's up. We're cutting you."

His words left her momentarily speechless. Not in her wildest imagination did she see this coming, did she feel she deserved this. Hadn't she done enough for the program to be able to leave on her own terms? Finally, she managed to speak.

"What are you talking about?"

"You're cut. We just wanted to let you know tonight because we're moving the team out tomorrow," Smith said.

"I'm just floored. I didn't really have the sensibility to fight for my case," she said. The first thing she did after leaving Smith's office was head to her room and call her brother, Tony. "They just cut me," she told him, still in a state of shock.

Moments later, assistant Mike Gilligan knocked on her dorm-room door, intending to explain further the decision to let her go.

"Well, you know. . ."

"You can't tell me I'm not one of the top 12 forwards on this team," she said, cutting him off in mid-sentence.

"Yeah, we know you can still give some offense and, blah, blah, blah," Granato said, recreating their conversation. Again, she cut him off as he spoke.

"Get out of this room. Just get out of here," she said, spitting out her words with no small dose of rage. She packed quickly and left, unable to put the training center in her rearview mirror fast enough – still trying to make sense of it all.

Granato felt like she was in the best shape physically and mentally in her 15th season with the national team at age 34. She also felt confident in her own self-awareness – that *she* would know when her time as a player was ending. And just in case she didn't, she was certain that her support group, including family, friends and high-level hockey people, would intervene with honest assessments. In other words, they would tell her when the time came. And she was good with that.

But this made no sense. Especially after the previous fall, barely nine months earlier, when her physical conditioning was among the best on the team. The testing proved that. Then she got hurt and tried to play through it on a torn knee ligament. The result was something quite less than a Granato-like performance in the World Championships in April – even though the Americans finally found a way to beat Canada on that stage.

Always thoughtful and deliberate in the way she responds to interviewers' questions, Granato paused and chose her words more carefully before trying to explain her understanding of what had transpired on that fateful cut day.

"I probably should have communicated a little clearer how bad my knee was [in April] because it affected my skating," she said. "And I probably should have communicated to him how good I felt, how great of physical shape I was in for this camp. I regret not telling him to test me on the ice right then. He hadn't seen me all summer. I really wish I would have said something."

Then again, she added, based on those weird vibes she was feeling throughout the tryout camp, maybe it wouldn't have mattered because it seemed as though Smith had his mind made up before the first day of tryouts. That's the kind of move that Bill Belichick, the NFL mastermind Smith publicly praised and admired, was famous for – dumping a player before he was physically unable to compete at the NFL level.

"I think he just looked at the number [34] and thought I was too old," she said. "He was always talking about guys in the NHL who were still playing when he thought they were done.

"Or he just wanted me out of there, maybe thought I was around too much. I have no idea, really, but I think it was about control. He wanted more and more. He wanted it so bad. The whole thing was just so weird. That was a very tumultuous year for those players."

The news of Smith's apparent "power-grab" didn't sit well with some of Granato's former teammates.

"Disgusting," is how Sue Merz described Smith's decision for ESPN interviewer John Buccigross.

"He attacked Cammi. He beheaded [the] captain," said Sarah Tueting, who had her own ugly battles with Smith in 2002 before retiring. "That was absurd. She was the heart and soul of the team."

"Cammi Granato *is* USA Hockey," longtime teammate Angela Ruggiero told Phil Hersh of the Chicago Tribune. "She's the glue to the team," said another gold-medal teammate, Chris Bailey.

The shock of Granato's dismissal made headlines around the hockey world.

"Her teammates were crushed when she didn't make their team," Shannon Miller, then a championship coach at the University of Minnesota-Duluth, told the *Edmonton Journal*. "There have been lots of great women playing the game, but ones like her are few and far between. I have a great deal of respect for her. She's been the best role model for their program – and she'll probably be the best role model they ever have."

Granato wasn't alone on that brutal cut day in Lake Placid. Another prominent veteran, Shelly Looney, who scored Team USA's golden goal in Nagano, was also dismissed from the program. To suggest that the American side could have used those two for their stabilizing veteran presence as well as their offensive production in Torino would be an understatement.

Team USA had little problem in its first two games, beating overmatched Switzerland and Germany by a combined score of 11-0. But the Americans ran into some issues in their next two matches. Though they managed to get past pesky Finland, 7-3, their offense dried up against the Swedes. Backstopped by goaltender Kim Martin, who played the game of her life, Sweden shocked the United States in the biggest upset to date in women's hockey with a shootout victory.

Canada had little difficulty with Sweden in the gold-medal match, winning 4-1. Team USA regrouped and beat Finland, 4-0, to settle for the bronze. Typically teams celebrate a victory that earned them the bronze medal. But American defender Angela Ruggiero described it a bit differently: "Rock bottom."

Granato watched the tournament from an NBC studio in Torino, working as an analyst. She took no satisfaction in watching her teammates fail to advance to the gold-medal game, but neither did she pull any punches when asked about a path forward for a program she helped put on the map.

"I feel for the girls," Granato said. "They didn't make it to where they should have. I know what it takes to train for this and I know this isn't what they wanted. I can't sit here in the studio and say I could have helped them. That wouldn't be fair. But do I wish I was there? Yes. I should be there. I always felt I belonged on this team."

She also predicted "change for the better," hinting at the obvious: Smith had reached his end with Team USA as well.

"That's USA Hockey's job now," Granato concluded. "They have to figure out why this team has gone from gold to silver to bronze. The U.S. women's hockey has been going backwards and needs to have checks and balances. You can't just give one person the run of the show."

Granato's last act as captain, it turns out, was memorable. After scoring a goal and three assists in the 2005 World Championships, she held the IIHF World Championship trophy over her head for the first time. After eight straight losses at the Worlds, Team USA had finally beaten Canada in that event.

Since being cut from the women's national team, she has worn many hats – and one of them was her hockey helmet. She played two seasons of professional hockey with the Vancouver Griffins of the National Women's Hockey League [2001-03]. Granato helped launch a brand of gender-specific hockey gear called BelaHockey. She married former NHL star Ray Ferraro in 2004 and the couple had two sons, Riley, born in 2006, and Reese, born in 2009. She is stepmother to Ferraro's two sons from a previous marriage, Matt and Landon.

She served as a rink-side reporter for NBC's NHL coverage and as a color commentator for the network's coverage of the 2006 and 2010 Winter Olympics. This was not her first stint in broadcasting. Shortly after winning gold in 1998, she worked as the color commentator for Los Angeles Kings radio broadcasts.

A year prior, Granato politely declined an invitation to attend an NHL development camp from New York Islanders General Manager Mike Milbury, a testament to her prowess on the ice. "I don't think either of us had the illusion she'd be on the power play, but I thought it was a good chance for her to gauge where she was," Milbury told *Sports Illustrated*. He was one of the first to realize that Granato was becoming the entire sport's grand ambassador. "It's incredible what she's meant to hockey. She's given it a profile in this country, more than good men players have been able to do."

More recently, Granato hosted the "On the Bus With Cammi & AJ" podcast with former teammate A.J. Mleczko. And in February 2022 she published her first book, *I Can Play Too.*

"I've been wanting to do something like this since the boys were little," she said. "Our nightly ritual was reading at bedtime. Their shelves were full of books. Mostly sports books, and I noticed there wasn't a lot of female representation in that space. So I wrote about a little girl playing hockey."

If it sounds familiar, well, it should.

"The message is for anyone who felt they were passionate about something but didn't feel like they fit because they looked different or felt different," Granato said. "I want kids to know that they should be able to pursue what they love to do and not to worry about what others say or think"

In other words, it's for all the little girls who want to throw on some shoulder pads and play tackle football with the boys on the playground – or anything else some people might say little girls shouldn't do. Wasn't that the same battle she was fighting nearly 40 years earlier?

"Aren't we past *I Can Play Too*?" she asks. "Then I realized we're not. We're still fighting for space in sport – and in anything, really."

Progress for girls and women and sports has been slow and often frustrating. "Look at the women's soccer team that just won a 20-year fight [for equality]," Granato said during wide-ranging interviews in early 2022.

"The lawyers got involved, and that was way back then, and they just got it done. That's incredible. It shows you how slow the growth has been. But at the same time, there has been growth."

Granato is immensely proud of the battle won by Team USA's women in 2017 when they threatened to boycott the World Championships. USA Hockey eventually caved to the women's demands.

"A very, very big win, and that should never be discounted," she said. "The courage it took those girls, and how they managed to get unity from everybody below them when USA Hockey threatened to bring in other players. That was incredible. But there's still a lot of work to be done."

And she's doing her part, advocating even as she continues to break new ground – or rather shatter more glass ceilings – in a sport she has never left. In September 2019, Granato became the first woman pro scout in the NHL when she was hired by the expansion Seattle Kraken. In February 2022, about the time her book was being released, Granato joined the Vancouver Canucks as just the third female assistant general manager in NHL history. And she is leading other women into front offices around the league.

"Cammi Granato has been instrumental in my career," said Meghan Duggan, a decorated leader in her own right as she captained Team USA to the Olympic gold in SouthKorea in 2018. She retired on that high note, and in 2019 was named director of player development for the New Jersey Devils. Although she never played with Granato, she still feels indebted. "Her leadership is just incredible. And in the last 6-7-8 years, she was someone I leaned on for advice – even when my playing career was over. She's just. . . one of the greatest of all time. She really is."

The smart money is on Granato becoming the NHL's first general manager one day, which should surprise no one when it happens.

For much of her career, Cammi Granato was the face of women's hockey. Now, her star ever rising, she is the face of women in hockey.

Life at the Bottom
of a Box

"If I have learned anything in this long life of mine, it is this: In love we find out who we want to be; in war we find out who we are."

—Kristin Hannah, author

Digging through a box of old pictures and timeless memories, Sarah Tueting finds a copy of an email she received in the Surf Shack in Nagano,one that nearly a quarter century later still brings tears to her eyes.

It's from a little girl whose mother let her play hooky so she could watch Team USA play in the Olympics. "My mom let me get up early and miss school," the girl wrote, "and now she said I could get hockey skates!"

Tueting digs a little deeper and finds another letter, written by Ginny, her grandmother's best friend. Ginny had lost her son to cancer 50 years before. He was an athlete, though after his death Ginny stopped reading the sports pages. But watching Tueting play in Nagano inspired her to write.

"Because of your Grandma, and we are Gold Star wives together, I watched the Olympics and it gave me a piece of my son back after 50 years," Ginny wrote in the most emotional thank-you note Tueting has ever received. Even as she shares this story, she is fighting back tears, insisting she is not worthy.

There's more. A little deeper in the box, she uncovers more photos taken by her grandmother. Turns out Grandma was watching TV and she saw her granddaughter during an appearance in Minneapolis. Grandma was so proud, she put on a little jacket, with "Tueting 29" on it, and sat there by herself taking photos of the TV with her granddaughter filling the screen. Just because she was so happy and proud.

Tueting's box was filled with memories like that, things she had tucked away and turned her back on long ago. And when she decided to share some of it with Jenny, one of her closest and oldest friends, well, Jenny was beyond angry.

"Are you kidding me? You were in *Rolling Stone*?" she screamed. "Why am I just seeing this now?"

A rather complex question for a woman whose entire life has been a complex question. And the answer began to unravel only after her phone rang. A couple of guys were writing a book about her team's historic gold medal victory over Canada at the Winter Games in Nagano, and asked if she would she be willing to consent to an interview.

That's when Sarah Tueting, who as a little girl took her first set of goalie pads to bed with her, decided to open that box of a life set aside. And suddenly, so much that she had hidden away all those years – including some of the best parts of herself, it turns out – came flooding back as a highlight reel in her mind's eye.

In the immediate aftermath of winning gold in Nagano, she had found herself experiencing things she never could have imagined. "I was like a kid in a candy store. What? I'm going to the Grammy's? Being on Letterman? Taking a private plane with Newt Gingrich?" she said, rattling off some of those improbable moments. "And then this idea of all these kids looking up to you. That was so humbling."

As an introvert, she explained, it was all a bit much. Surreal. Difficult to negotiate.

"On the one hand, you have had your dream come true. To have put in all that effort, and to have a little bit of fame. . . But all that is secondary to the fact that you've just realized that dream at the age of 21. It was an amazing high, but also – given my spirituality and my inborn interest in these things – I was like, 'Oh shit. Now what? This isn't going to bring me lasting happiness."

While Tueting continued to compete on the U.S. Women's National Team, making the 2002 Olympic team as well, she began slowly closing the door to that part of her life – and slamming it shut when the Salt Lake City Games ended badly for her personally in a split with both her coach and her teammates. She decided then that there was more to her life than hockey, like art, music, writing, philosophy, motherhood and life coach.

"I really disassociated myself entirely from my hockey identity," she said. "I just didn't want to be known as a hockey player."

Decades later, when she opened that box stashed under her bed, part of her came pouring out. One of the good parts she had long forgotten. "Now to bring that back and to integrate it, especially through my kids, it does bring confidence," she said. "And it brings out a certain part of me that has come out in this phone call, that I haven't felt in a long time: 'Don't fuck with me.' Especially if you put my back up against the wall."

Part of that lost confidence stemmed from a bad marriage, Tueting acknowledged. "And then there was that part that was dormant and reignited, that when the shit hits the fan you want me in your corner. You want me holding the ropes. You want me in the tank with you. And that will always be with me, that kind of confidence."

Rather suddenly, and to her apparent joy, Sarah Tueting at age 45 had tapped into that reservoir of strength that oozed out of her about the time she reached legal drinking age. It also got her thinking of how we strive to express our best selves through sport – and what sport can do for us in those uncommonly rare moments when we find what athletes tend to describe as "the zone." Or perhaps when that zone finds us.

"That whole spiritual aspect of what happens when your mind is so quiet, when you are a clear expression of force," Tueting explained. "Artists feel that. Musicians feel that. And athletes, like Michael Jordan and the shrug."

Growing up in suburban Chicago, Tueting played close attention to Jordan when he was leading the NBA's Bulls to perennial championships in the 1990s. And she remembers his iconic reaction to making six three-point baskets in the second half of a game in the Finals. After his last one, he turned toward Magic Johnson, another NBA all-time great who was broadcasting that game, and simply shrugged. It was if Jordan was saying he couldn't begin to explain it either; he just could do no wrong at a point in the contest when his team needed him most.

Tueting experienced her moment, too, that golden toe save in the closing minutes of the victory over Canada in Nagano. As she tried to explain it for the umpteenth time in her life since then, you could almost feel her shrug.

"How do we empty enough to let something else play through us? When we're in total alignment with the puck," she asked, the life coach in her beginning to assert itself. "I couldn't possibly miss because I wasn't there. I was in harmony with life, I was in harmony with the game. How do you then replicate that within life itself? Not to decide this is the goal I want and go after it, but instead, empty so completely that I come in harmony with life?

"I surrender to life. I surrender to the game, I surrender to the flow of the puck. That's when magic happens. . . We're just the expression of force expressing itself in one pure form – and that's our purpose in life, to just get out of the way."

It may not have been exactly magic, but something fairly remarkable happened when Tueting showed her friend Jenny another memento from Nagano. It is a painting from a photograph commissioned by her father of the dog-pile in the seconds after Team USA captured gold. Sarah is at the bottom, unseen, all of her teammates on top of her.

"This belongs in your house!" Jenny said. And who was Tueting to argue, especially after thinking it all through? It was a touchstone of one of the most memorable times of her life. While it may not define her, it certainly reminds her of the person she once was – another part of her that should make her proud.

"That's it. That's the value of the Olympics to me," she said, again trying to describe her performance in Nagano. "All of that training led to that one nugget, the taste of emptiness, the taste of void, the taste of not being present, the human not being present, so sports can express and experience through you.

"If all of that led to one moment, then that's worth all the training in the world."

It's also worth keeping that box around – and sifting through it now and then.

The Power of Losing

By Keith Gave

When she was racking up victories and national championships at the University of Minnesota-Duluth, Shannon Miller had a chance encounter with legendary University of Michigan men's hockey coach Red Berenson.

"His team must have been playing our UMD men's team," Miller said. "He was just stepping off the elevator when I saw him. Now I just love the Red Baron, and I say, 'Hey Red, I just wanted to say hi. I'm Shannon Miller.'"

Berenson smiled and responded: "I know who you are. You're the one who wins all the time."

The comment rendered Miller almost speechless. *Red Berenson knows my name!* she thought. Miller quickly recovered. She could tell Berenson was in a hurry.

"Hey coach, do you think you'll ever have a women's hockey program at Michigan" she asked.

"Not as long as I'm around," Berenson said. And he walked away.

After 33 seasons during which his Wolverines won 848 games and two national championships, Gordon Arthur "Red" Berenson retired from coaching in 2017. The University of Michigan, one of the wealthiest athletic programs in the nation, 30 miles from a place that boastfully calls itself "Hockeytown," in a state with seven NCAA Division I men's hockey programs, two Canadian Hockey League major junior teams, some of the oldest and most successful youth hockey programs in the world, still had no NCAA women's team.

Neither did Michigan State, nor Northern Michigan, Michigan Tech, Western Michigan, Ferris State or Lake Superior State. In 2022!

In a word, that is disgraceful.

There were two native Michiganders on Team USA's 1998 gold-medal team: Lisa Brown-Miller, the most senior player on the roster, and Shelley Looney, the Canada killer who scored the golden goal. Both are career coaches. Brown-Miller served as head coach at Princeton University from 1991-96, winning an ECAC championship and earning Coach-of-the-Year honors before resigning to train for the Olympics.[15] In 2022, she was in her third season as coach of Aquinas College in Grand Rapids, Michigan, competing as a club sport. Looney was in her third season at Lindenwood University, rebuilding the program in St. Charles, Missouri.

No disrespect intended, because both women are doing splendid work at their respective colleges, but Brown-Miller and Looney should be using their Olympic gold-medal credentials to recruit and develop hockey players in Division I programs closer to home, at the University of Michigan, or Michigan State, or any of the other five programs in Michigan that offer ice hockey as a scholarship sport on the men's side.

Meantime, all the boasting about gender equity is at best insincere and vain. At worst, it's disingenuous and shameful. And frankly, it's no surprise that rumors of "a culture of sexism" in the hockey department in Ann Arbor made headlines in 2022.

---

15 Too many men on the ice? On her return home to Michigan from Nagano, Brown-Miller learned she was pregnant. In 2021, her son Alex had just graduated from the Air Force Academy and was training for the service's Special Tactics Squadron – similar to the Navy Seal program. "It's not easy,'" Brown-Miller said, "and sometimes I have to remind him: 'Remember, you have some Olympic Gold Medal blood in you.' And every now and then, he'll confess: 'Mom, I do tell myself that sometimes.'"

In the heart of my sports-writing career – way back when newspapers were relevant – I had the honor of chronicling the exploits of a Detroit Red Wings team with a roomful of magnificent hockey players, including many Olympians. About 15 years after the Miracle on Ice, I approached Mike Ramsey in the back of the room. When I think about it now, it seems cruel, but at the same time I was sincerely curious regarding his take on one of sports' greatest moments.

Ramsey was 19 years old after completing his freshman season at the University of Minnesota, and there he was in Lake Placid, wearing the colors of his country, fending off a furious onslaught by one of the greatest hockey clubs ever assembled – the mighty Soviet Union's national team – when broadcaster Al Michaels was screaming those iconic words: "Do you believe in Miracles?"

As Ramsey was trying to describe what it was like for him at those final, frenetic seconds, he kept stealing glances to his left. At the stall next to his, Viacheslav (Slava) Fetisov, one of the sport's all-time great defensemen, looked like he was about to explode, his face getting redder and redder. And he was muttering obscenities in two languages under his breath.

Fetisov was a young member on that Soviet team that somehow, inexplicably, lost to a bunch of no-name college kids – the one team their Communist leaders back home said they had to beat. To America's Cold War adversary, it was a matter of national honor and pride. The Soviets, who had dominated international hockey since Russians began playing the sport seriously in the mid-1950s under the tutelage of Anatoly Tarasov, left Lake Placid with the silver medal. They returned home in shame.

"(Expletive) lucky," Fetisov kept whispering privately, among some other choice phrases. "We play them a hundred times again, we beat them a hundred times."

As a matter of fact, Ramsey had no argument with that. It was a miracle to him, too. And he was there, right in the middle of it all. But with the benefit of hindsight, all things considered, perhaps it wasn't such a horrendous moment after all.

"We know now that Soviet hockey can take credit for the remarkable growth and popularity of hockey in the United States," Fetisov said 40 years later when he was a member of Russia's Parliament. "You're welcome, America."

For many years after Team USA's upset of Canada at the inaugural women's Olympic ice hockey tournament in Nagano, some members on the wrong side of that outcome tended to downplay their silver medals. Rather, they were prone to say, "We lost the gold." Because their mindset going into the Games was that winning anything but gold was unimaginable.

Then it happened. And the repercussions on the other side of their border were stunning. Suddenly, young girls in record numbers were trading in their figure skates for hockey skates. The numbers of girls competing in youth leagues in America skyrocketed. In 1990, when some members of that 1998 team were young girls beginning their hockey careers playing with and against boys because that was their only opportunity to play, there were fewer than 7,000 registered female ice hockey players in the United States, according to USA Hockey. By the time the American women won their second Olympic gold in 2018, there were nearly 80,000 females registered to play hockey in the United States – including the 23 women who struck gold in PyeongChang.

Until she was seven years old, Kendall Coyne didn't know another girl who played hockey. But in the summer of 1998, when she attended

Cammi Granato's hockey camp in suburban Chicago, she met 100 other girls who shared her passion for the sport. Coyne, later Coyne Schofield, recalled for an interviewer how excited she was to go back to school that fall and tell all her doubting friends that "girls really do play hockey! That moment at camp fueled me to do something that would change my life forever – play in college, represent Team USA and play in the Olympics."

Further west in North Dakota, the Lamoureaux twins, Jocelyne and Monique, were similarly inspired. They were eight years old when the American women won in Nagano. It ignited their dream that materialized in essays they wrote for school about playing in the Olympics one day.

"Without that gold medal, without that team, there is no way women's hockey would be where it is today," Jocelyne Lamoureux-Davidson said.

Twenty years later, Monique Lamoureaux-Morando scored a goal that would force overtime in the gold-medal game with Canada. And Jocelyne scored the decisive goal in a shootout that gave the Americans their second Olympic gold medal.

The 1998 team wound up on the cover of a Wheaties box, and various team members made appearances on many of the national TV talk shows, including Leno, Letterman, Today, Good Morning America, Regis and Kathie Lee. Most of them attended school assemblies, their shimmering gold medals inspiringboth girls and boys.

American colleges and universities took note – everywhere, it seemed, except in Michigan. In 1998, there were just 14 Division I teams, and the University of Minnesota was the only one west of New York State. Most of them were in New England. The women's game was still three years away from its first sanctioned NCAA championship tournament.

By the 2019-20 season, there were 41 teams eligible for the NCAA women's hockey championships. One of them was the University of Minnesota-Duluth, where Canada's Olympic coach Shannon Miller exiled herself after the Nagano Games. She started a program from scratch, and she wasn't the only Canadian to take advantage of the growth of the sport in the United States.

American college and university athletic programs are celebrated for developing elite athletes who often graduate – degree or not – into the professional ranks of their sport. So it is in women's hockey. In 1998, only four women on Team Canada's roster had experience with a U.S. college hockey program. In 2018, 21 of Canada's 23 players had competed for an American college or university. In 2022, only one of 23 women on Canada's Olympic roster didn't spend some formative time playing college hockey in the United States.

For the Canadian women, losing the gold-medal game in Nagano was beyond devastating. "I just remember feeling as if we'd let people down, that we'd let our country down," Jayna Hefford told my friend, Eric Duhatschek of *The Athletic*, in an interview prior to her induction into the Hockey Hall of Fame in 2018. "I remember in the dressing room afterward, everyone was so unhappy and one of our trainers was trying to get the girls to take a picture with their medals on. She said, 'I know you don't want this now, but trust me, someday you're going to look back and you're going to want this picture.'"

Hefford remembers some talk about trying to see a silver lining in the loss (no pun intended), to appreciate the value of having the Americans win that first Olympic gold.

"People said it was probably the best thing that could happen for women's hockey," Hefford said, "because it helped grow the sport in the U.S.

"Well, as a player on the losing team, that's the last thing you're worried about. But looking back, it was probably true. It helped grow the game, and it certainly did a lot for women's hockey in the U.S."

So to Jayna Hefford, Hayley Wickenheiser and all their heroic and heartbroken sisters on Team Canada who lost the gold but *won* the silver medal, rise up together and say it loudly. You've certainly earned the right:

You're welcome, America.

The Best Rivalry in Sports

By Tim Rappleye

During the 1995-96 season, Karyn Bye was a live broadcast stage manager, helping the Olympic Regional Development Authority (ORDA) produce men's college hockey out of Lake Placid and surrounding North Country. As producer, I was the beneficiary of the hustle, smarts and sense of urgency from the athlete known as K.L. There were plenty of examples of Karyn saving the day on live TV, whether it was guiding Harvard hero Ethan Philpott directly across the ice to arrive just in time for his interview, or using her strong hands to halt a fan about to cross in front of broadcast talent during on-camera segments.

After working her first couple of events, she had pretty much figured out how live TV works in the field, becoming a star in her own right. Several times our acclaimed director Bruce Treut would take delight in K.L.'s derring-do behind the scenes, especially her shortcut across the ice during the ECAC Championships.

I knew she was a hockey player; having produced the 1994 Women's World Championships, I watched her play through a truck full of monitors. In all honesty, I hadn't been terribly impressed with Team USA. They surrendered without much of a fight in the gold-medal game against Canada. But I loved Karyn's work as a stage manager, moonlighting for ORDA while she worked out at the U.S. Olympic Training Center.

One Saturday in the winter of 1996, Karyn and the ORDA

cable-pullers, audio assistants and electrical technicians all trucked up to Ithaca for a Cornell men's game. During the production meal hour, most of us grabbed lunch in the Lynah Rink press room above the ice. I shared a sandwich with my graphics coordinator Tim Panek, a hockey lifer from Buffalo. We noticed a handful of players involved in a vigorous game of shinny. Panek and I assessed the action critically: the skaters had jump, there was lots of elite edgework, and some of them could absolutely blast the puck. One of the players looked familiar, so we zoomed in, trying to get an ID. Finally we figured out that the player in sweatpants was one of our own—*Karyn!*

A few minutes later Bye joined us at the table. It turned out she was drilling with Cornell coach and former national team stalwart Julie Anderberhan, the future wife of Ben Smith. It was Karyn who had been firing pucks with the velocity of an elite college player, regardless of gender. Panek and I gave Bye the most awkward compliment imaginable, "Hey K.L., we thought you were a guy." She just smiled and shrugged. "Thanks guys."

In 1996, women's hockey in the United States was a well-kept secret. The Cornell's women's program was still a year away from becoming a varsity sport. Two years earlier, Bye and Cammi Granato were forced to become expats to keep their Olympic dream alive, playing as graduate students at Concordia University in Montreal. The IIHF would only sink the necessary funds to stage a women's World Championship every other year, starting in 1990. And the only reason women's hockey pricked the consciousness of the United States was when it was named an Olympic medal sport. Granato was the only recognizable name to America's sporting public, and that was because her brother Tony was an NHL star. Seeing Bye and Anderberhan fly around that afternoon, pounding pucks off the Lynah Rink pipes and dasherboards, was a revelation: these women could really play.

Thanks to her energy and attitude, there was undeniable star quality to Karyn, but in the hierarchy of sports television, she was more grinder than prima donna. On the weekend of the 1996 ECAC Men's Championship broadcasts, the women's national team had just arrived in Lake Placid to begin training for a Four Nations tournament. Our production team scheduled a live interview with Cammi Granato to air during the first intermission of the ECAC title game. In one of her last gigs, Bye was stage-managing the studio, making sure her teammate Cammi was comfortable under the hot lights. There was absolutely no tension between the star and the subordinate.

A minute into the interview, director Treut rolled a highlight of a Team USA goal from the 1994 World Championship game, one of the few video clips we could find to support our intermission segment. After the highlight ran its course, Treut cut back to the live studio shot, where his cameraman had instinctively zoomed out, revealing both Cammi and Karyn. The two athletes both beamed wide grins when they looked up from the monitor. They had clearly enjoyed the highlight, Karyn most of all, because it was a replay of her scoring dash against Canada from the 1994 gold-medal game. The stage manager had blossomed into a hockey star on live TV.

After the ECAC men's season, I followed Karyn and her mates along their Olympic quest. Although the 1997 Women's World Championships were obscure in the U.S., they were a very big deal in Canada, a blue-chip property for the television executives at TSN in Toronto. Personally, I had moved on to a staff job at NHL Productions, and was able to convince our operations managers to record the USA-Canada gold-medal game, figuring we might be able to use some highlights on our weekly show "NHL Cool Shots."

I knew a couple of the Team USA players in addition to Karyn, and thus had a rooting interest. Having covered plenty of Olympics and World Juniors, I figured a Canada-USA game would make great theater. Unfortunately, as all American hockey fans know, TSN is prohibited from being aired in the United States, no matter how many tiers of cable you pay for. So I drove the 30 miles to the NHL's New Jersey studios on a Sunday evening, happy to stand in front of a monitor in a cavernous hall filled with videotape recorders. I'm pretty sure that the maintenance guy on duty that night and I were the only people in America who saw this event on live television. I would periodically wave him over to see the action unfold.

Every couple of decades a live sporting event makes history. I wasn't around for Johnny Unitas beating the Giants in sudden death in 1958 to bring the NFL into the modern TV age, but I was a rabid Red Sox fan in 1975. I saw how Game Six of the World Series between the Sox and the Cincinnati Reds ushered in a new standard for drama in TV sports. I read later how the Reds' Pete Rose asked Boston's Carlton Fisk if he, too, realized what an historic night they were experiencing.

None of the dozen women I would later interview from the 1997 World Championship ever had the luxury of being able to step back and process the magnificent moments transpiring in Kitchener. But everyone not in uniform realized history was being made that night, from Don Cherry, to IIHF president René Fasel, to the millions of viewers throughout Canada. Prime Time. Sunday Night. A women's hockey Super Bowl, only better.

There was a wildly controversial goal that gave Canada the lead in the second period, a lead that held up until Stephanie O'Sullivan, Boston's most popular female hockey player, tied the game. I grabbed the guy carrying all those skinny screwdrivers and hurriedly briefed him about the O'Sullivan family saga. It was about that time when Sunday in the Jersey videotape arcade became a slew of manic swings, a series of "and thens..."

And then Canada grabbed the lead in the third, pandemonium erupting in Kitchener. Depression darkened the NHL's videotape hall.

And then Brown University star Katie King had her Carlton Fisk moment, arms flailing, legs pumping down to her tiptoes, the Americans tying a game we thought was destined for the toilet. My new best friend in the Dickies pants now got it; he was watching a live game for the ages. We were two men sweating out a sporting contest of Homeric proportions, a contest played by women.

And then it roared into overtime.

And then Canada drew two American penalties to claim a five-on-three skater advantage.

And then. . . a shot rang through the building.

The frenetic action came to a screeching halt, a merciful reprieve to all except the Team USA forward lying motionless on the ice.

America's Shelley Looney had sacrificed her face to block a ferocious scoring bid by Team Canada. TSN's videotape unit rolled three fright-film replays of Looney paying the gruesome price, while the Team USA trainers dealt with the carnage in real time. They essentially scraped Looney off the ice before guiding her to the bench. This was the moment when all of Canada fell in love: with Looney's courage, with Team USA's fighting spirit, and most importantly, with this ungodly rivalry playing out in front of everyone that mattered. Add a couple of mooks in New Jersey to that list.

And then Canada finally converted the winning goal off a goal-mouth scramble.

And then TSN did what it does best, beaming cascading images of Canada's victory-fueled insanity, one atop the other.

Numb, my new bestie and I stared in disbelief at all the red-clad maniacs waving fingers to signal Number 1, crushed by Hayley Wickenheiser double-pumping both arms in her sprint to center ice, disgusted by

Shannon "Darth Vader" Miller punching the sky. It was as beautiful as it was awful. Team USA had played the glorious but bloodied Hector to Canada's Achilles.

It was all over but the agony shot, the image of the emotionally crushed, tear-streaked warrior in defeat. Of course it was Karyn, my production winger from Lake Placid, my favorite ally in a live truck, the stoic K.L. Bye. I could feel my sentiments twist and then snap as the TSN cameraman zoomed in on my pal, who was biting her glove to keep from collapsing into a puddle of tears.

I drove home across the Hudson River later that night, trying to process the enormity of the sporting event I had just witnessed, something unknown to the Big Apple glowing five miles to the south. Would this Johnny Unitas moment remain a secret to America's sporting world? My brain was bursting with story lines and intense imagery: Shelley Looney's shattered cheekbone, my rugged stage manager embodying *The Who's* classic-rock refrain: "naked, stoned and stabbed." I had just seen the birth of a sports rivalry that transcended all others, and it was staged by women. Was this my secret to carry until Nagano? My head was ready to explode when it touched the pillow at midnight.

Six hours later, I heard the paperboy bounce Monday's *New York Times* off the front door of the family condo. Still buzzing from the sports opera I had lived through the night before, I unfolded America's newspaper of record. On the front page—not the sports page—was a photo of Team USA women, and the ensuing story that commenced their countdown to Nagano. I sipped my coffee and exhaled, drinking in the new world order: Canada-USA women's hockey, the best rivalry in sports.

A Golden Legacy

"I think this gold medal means almost as much for women as 1980 meant for the men."

—George Crowe, Dartmouth women's coach

Contrary to popular belief, the concept of girls actually playing hockey didn't suddenly materialize during the prelude to the 1998 Olympic Winter Games. It just seemed that way to most Americans, awakened to the sport after they noticed their team flaunting gold medals on the cover of their box of breakfast cereal.

Breakfast of champions, eh?

In fact, the first-ever women's ice hockey game was played in Canada, naturally, in 1891 – more than 130 years ago. And professional women's hockey began to emerge in that country as early as the 1920s. But even in Canada, opportunities for girls in minor hockey were limited, at best.

In the United States, those prospects were virtually non-existent. Young girls who were serious about skating typically wore leotards and toe-picked figure skates, not hockey skates. They chose to work on their forward swizzles and backward wiggles, not stick-handling a puck around cones wearing shin guards and shoulder pads. And for those few who actually wanted to test their skills in competitive ice hockey, it would have to be with and against boys. So it was for generations of American girls whose participation numbers didn't start moving the needle until the late 1970s.

By 1990, there were about 6,000 girls registered to play in the United States, many of them inspired—just like boys their age—by the 1980 Miracle On Ice. Those girls were all-too-willing to spend their allowances on Canadian-made hockey sticks and tape. Their parents, willing or not, would spend much more of their disposable income outfitting their daughters with pricey skates and other protective gear – and even pricier ice time for practices and games. Only to hear others say things like, "Oh, isn't that cute. She wants to be a hockey player! Don't worry, she'll grow out of it someday."

But *she* didn't. When someday came, she had navigated puberty, changing into her equipment in cars, hallways or broom closets – and captaining her boys' team because she was its best player.

When someday came, she was wearing the colors of her nation, skating in the World Championships against other nations and getting pummeled—like all the other teams—by their neighbor to the north. For another generation, Canada remained the world's lone superpower in women's hockey.

When someday came, she was competing in that first Olympic women's ice hockey tournament in Nagano, Japan.

And someday, when she skated away with the gold medal after a monumental upset of Canada, those little girls who wouldn't quit – Chris Bailey, Laurie Baker, Alana Blahoski, Lisa Brown-Miller, Karyn Bye, Colleen Coyne, Sara DeCosta, Tricia Dunn, Cammi Granato, Katie King, Shelley Looney, Sue Merz, A.J. Mleczko, Tara Mounsey, Vicki Movsession, Angela Ruggiero, Jenny Schmidgall, Sarah Tueting, Gretchen Ulion and Sandra Whyte – had turned girls' hockey into a thing.

Their sport went viral. The growth was exponential. By the time Team USA managed to beat Canada for Olympic gold again in 2018, 83,000

American girls were lacing up their skates, many of them inspired by that 1998 team. "Girls now have us. They can dream of becoming us," said Team USA forward Lisa Brown-Miller. "I didn't have that when I was young."

Thanks in no small part to the prescience of former USA Hockey executive director Dave Ogrean, college hockey has become the supreme finishing school for elite teenage women. One of his first pieces of business after arriving in Colorado Springs in 1994 was the creation and implementation of the two most visible institutions in NCAA women's hockey: the national championships and the Patty Kazmaier Award for player of the year. It was intended to dovetail with the anticipated buzz from women's participation in the Nagano Games. Bullseye.

When Team USA was awarded gold medals in 1998, there were just 10 NCAA varsity women's teams. By the early 2020s, there were 80. Rosters were flooded with women from both Canada and the United States, Olympic dreamers who were riding the crest of the Title IX wave. Today, American college hockey develops virtually every women's national team member on both sides of the border, and dozens more from Europe. Playing for the three Midwest superpowers—Wisconsin, Minnesota and Duluth—is "The Show" in women's hockey in terms of facilities, trainers and coaching. Along with the boys National Team Development Program, the explosive growth of women's hockey is Ogrean's enduring legacy.

But until 2017, coeds with Olympic dreams skated face-first into Plexiglass upon graduation. America's national governing body had no inclination to accommodate Olympic women candidates with anything like the compensation, marketing and development that they heaped on the men.

There was a professional hockey option, but it was rarely stable, a revolving carousel of dueling leagues, that until 2022, paid women two decimal points less than their male counterparts, with no health insurance. Twenty years after Shelley Looney and Chris Bailey were working second jobs and pooling tips to make rent, most Team USA World Championship heroines were once again flirting with poverty to keep their five-ring dreams alive during non-Olympic years. The need for radical change in working conditions grew rapidly after Nagano, and years of pent-up frustration toppled over onto the unsuspecting masters of American hockey's governing body in 2017.

With no small influence from their soccer sisters on the U. S. national squad, Team USA hockey women banded together to stage a wildcat strike on the eve of the 2017 IIHF World Championships. This threat of a boycott was an overt act of aggression, an affront to the patriarchal bosses of amateur hockey in the United States. It jeopardized not only relationships, but playing careers and reputations. This was no gambit for players with weak stomachs.

"We are asking for a living wage and for USA Hockey to fully support its programs for women and girls and stop treating us like an afterthought," said national team captain Meghan Duggan. That statement was issued barely two weeks prior to the 2017 World Championships, an international pre-Olympic event being staged at the USA Hockey Arena in suburban Detroit. "We have represented our country with dignity and deserve to be treated with fairness and respect."

From that point forward it was Game On, a worker vs. management showdown in the neighborhood of some of America's historic labor wars of the 20th century. USA Hockey executives resorted to time-tested management tactics: mischaracterizing the player demands, setting false deadlines, and the ultimate strike-breaker: hiring scab labor.

It was a two-week war, with both time and circumstances favoring the women. As hosts of the IIHF World Championships, USA Hockey desperately needed to field a team. This left them two options: accommodate the players' demands, which required a major paradigm shift, or simply find 20 new players to replace them. To the competitive men who ran USA Hockey, it would be the latter; in their minds, they would fight and they would win. That's how it had always been. National team members were demanding something USA Hockey had never before considered: compensating players during non-Olympic years. In their minds, that was a deal-breaker.

"USA Hockey's role is not to employ athletes and we will not do so," said a defiant Jim Smith, then president of USA Hockey.

Their stance of letting the female athletes fend for themselves was unshakeable, but there were two serious problems with that position: 1) USA Hockey spent upwards of $3.5 million annually to develop teenage boys at their National Team Development Program; and 2) thanks to adroit messaging by the women's team and their lawyers, a groundswell of support drowned out whatever message the suits were emitting from Colorado Springs.

"Being a world-class athlete should not be a part-time job," Billie Jean King, the Susan B. Anthony of sports gender equity, said via Twitter. The battle lines of this 21st Century David vs. Goliath showdown were officially drawn over the issue that has plagued women players and management since the inaugural Olympic tournament—how to support the players. The roles of the two combatants were readily defined in overly simplistic terms: a national governing body on the wrong side of history vs. a band of defiantly courageous women. The insurgents were well-organized and armed with a 21st century slingshot known as social media. Goliath took a loud and heavy fall.

All four major sports unions in the United States voiced support for the feline underdogs, as did Mike Eruzione, U.S. Senator Amy Klobuchar of Minnesota and 20 of her chambermates. Social media, the weapon sorely lacking from Cammi Granato's arsenal in her attempt to organize in 2000, turned the tide for Team USA in 2017. The hashtag #BeBoldForChange was the prevailing message on tens of thousands of tweets and Instagrams supporting the players' cause.

Major news outlets like the *Washington Post, New York Times* and even *The Guardian* from the United Kingdom leapt into the fray, giving the vociferous women ample space to air their grievances. USA Hockey responded with terse position statements from Smith, Ogrean and corporate flak Dave Fischer. Sports media behemoth ESPN eviscerated USA Hockey management, as columnist Johnette Howard battered the cabal from Colorado Springs with her inside sources and relentless reporting. Not only did this story of labor strife resonate across the Atlantic, but more important was the fusion bubbling from its core: Detroit, with its long and truculent labor history.

"Team USA's timing for the wildcat strike was impeccable, and so was its sense of geography," said co-author and former newspaperman Keith Gave, a reporter for the *Detroit Free Press* from 1985-98. "The cradle of unionism, home to some of the most powerful labor organizations in the world, like the United Auto Workers, the Teamsters and major elements of the AFL-CIO – in a place called 'Hockeytown.' The walkout was big news in the Detroit media, and Team USA's women found solidarity among the rank and file, especially its fans demanding to see them compete in the World Championships in suburban Plymouth."

That rank and file included an over-50 women's team that threatened to picket USA Hockey Arena. *Michigan Public Radio* fanned the flames with Team USA interviews on its drive-time show "Stateside." The striking athletes were serenaded with local support in the Motor City to go along with all the national media coverage.

It was not the war of words that brought USA Hockey to its knees, however; it was the battle for the hearts and minds of the potential substitute players. And thanks to the tireless canvassing of captain Meghan Duggan, Hilary Knight, and the Lamoureux twins, hockey's sisterhood went undefeated. Not a single player approached by USA Hockey succumbed to the allure of representing their country on the global stage. And they solicited them all: former national team players, college freshmen, and – in management's last desperate gasp – lowly beer leaguers. There would be no scabs. Not if it meant violating the now-sacred cause of gender equity. ESPN quoted a source within the USA Hockey bunkers as saying their staff "underestimated," the will of these determined women. "They didn't think [they] had the guts to do it."

The suits were dead wrong. Less than three days prior to the start of the 2017 World Championships, USA Hockey capitulated to the formidable will and tactics of the Team USA women. They granted the players everything they sought: four-year contacts starting at $70,000 annually; maternity compensation; flight upgrades to business class; a bump in per diem; and even a committee to promote and market women's hockey. The lawyers from Ballard Spahr, the same firm that represented Team USA soccer interests since 2000, guided the hockey women to a resounding victory.

USA Hockey president Smith spun the result as "coming together and compromising." The rest of the world labeled it more accurately—"a rout." Capping their landmark victory at the bargaining table, Team USA took to the ice and won the 2017 World Championship gold medal, beating Canada twice to consolidate its bountiful fortnight. "It's the most meaningful thing I've ever been a part of," said Knight, who scored the golden goal in overtime.

For Cammi Granato, the labor victory for Team USA in 2017 was cathartic. "I'm so unbelievably proud of this team, how the players so strongly and boldly stood up for what they believed," Granato wrote in a story for ESPN. "I know how hard it is to do that... stick your neck out like they have."

She recalled being denigrated after her initial attempt to negotiate with USA Hockey back in 2000. "We were made to feel like we were lucky to have a program at all," Granato said. Seeing the next generation finish the job—one that she paid such a steep price to attempt—filled her with admiration. "This group is unbreakable."

Executive director Dave Ogrean spoke words of reconciliation at the conclusion of the tempestuous strike in March of 2017. "I'm very relieved and I'm very positive about the outcome." Yet there was inevitable backlash from such a sweeping victory by the players.

Shortly after the contract was finalized, NBC's *Olympic Channel* hired one of the biggest names in sports television, Ross Greenburg, to produce an up-close-and-personal documentary centered on the Team USA women. The results were disastrous. "The production was in place, we started shooting, and were basically shut down by USA Hockey," said Greenburg, still miffed years later. "The U.S. women's team was very happy to see us covering them from the inside, but because of the tension, USA Hockey shut us down. They treated our production team very badly, unprofessionally. It was not a pleasant experience."

Clearly, the spirit of the new contract's emphasis on enhancing the team's marketing had been quashed. The establishment was convinced that the terms of the new contract stretched the boundaries of reason and common sense, and some members of the 1998 team agree with that assessment. Laurie Baker is now an assistant athletic director at Concord Academy in Massachusetts. She deals with balancing athletic budgets on a daily basis, and she's not convinced that Team USA women generate the kind of revenue necessary to justify the big benefits to players, unlike their soccer sisters.

"Women's soccer had their push, they would fill the stands, they had sponsors," said Baker. "They could say, 'We're better than the men.' Women's hockey isn't there yet. It's definitely not. What's the money being generated? Are people going to the games? Where's the back piece? If there's no money, there's no money to be given. It's not equitable."

Former IIHF president Dr. René Fasel echoes Baker's opinion. Despite his deep appreciation for women's hockey, he knows first-hand how difficult it is for the sport to break even, let alone turn a profit.

"Every year we spent three to four million Swiss francs on the Women's World Championships," said Fasel. "Unfortunately we do not get enough sponsors or TV money for the women's games. We invest a lot, and we try to do it because they deserve it, but still, we need more sponsors and more financial support for sure."

The viability of women's hockey is a tender subject, and there are members of the '98 team who share Baker's opinion, but will only speak off-the-record, words not uttered publicly for fear of being ostracized. Siding with management to compensate women less than men in any endeavor is potentially volatile. Ask the male tennis pros who are castigated for saying women should not receive equal prize money at major tournaments. No one likes being labeled as being on the wrong side of gender politics.

So the women of USA Hockey now find themselves teetering on a fulcrum between two extremes: robust compensation on one side; toiling with financial hardship on the other. This scenario of balancing between what is fair and what is extreme is comparable to the labor deals negotiated by well-represented pros in all the major league sports, deals that result in labor battles at the conclusion of nearly every collective bargaining agreement.

The simpler days of women blindly trusting USA Hockey's ruling patriarchy died in the last century. No one wants to return to the era of star players with no health coverage waiting tables before driving to practice in uninsured cars. It remains to be seen if the popularity of women's hockey will grow to justify their new compensation. Recent stars Knight and Kendall Coyne Schofield were doing everything in their power to expand the reach and appeal of women's hockey.

The counterpoint to Fasel and Baker is that women's hockey is a ratings heavyweight in the Olympics, starting in Nagano in 1998. Even Fasel admitted, "I think the audience ratings was bigger for the women's game than the men's USA games. It was a big surprise."

The women's hockey ratings bonanza was no anomaly, at least at the Winter Games. The 2022 Canada-USA gold-medal game in Beijing, buttressed by robust promotion on NBC, drew far larger ratings than any NHL regular-season games. The fact that interest in women's hockey goes into a four-year hibernation after each Olympic spectacle is one that torments the participants.

Less than 24 hours after the painful loss to Canada in the Beijing Games, Coyne Schofield, Team USA's captain, choked back tears – not from the heartbreak of failing to win gold but for her passion to fight for more opportunities and equity for the women dedicating themselves to the sport.

"We need to continue to push for visibility," she said. "We need to continue to fight for women's hockey because [the status quo] is not good enough. It can't end after the Olympic Games."

As if on cue, a white knight in the form of entrepreneurial billionaire John Boynton thrust women's professional hockey into the limelight in late January 2022. As the part-owner of three teams in the newly renamed women's Premier Hockey Federation (PHF), and chairman of the league's board of governors, Boynton was the driving force behind a $25 million injection into the six-team league. This financial windfall more than doubled the salary cap for the league's teams and allowed for health insurance for PHF players, a rare luxury. Boynton admits the timing of that announcement was no coincidence: the Canada-USA Olympic rivalry was a prominent storyline at the 2022 Beijing Games, and he struck while the iron was hot. A month after Canada defeated the United States for the women's hockey gold medal, the PHF championship game was aired live on ESPN 2, with Discover as the presenting sponsor. All the developments had a too-good-to-be-true feel to them, and with good reason.

Boynton appeared on the sports industry podcast "Sporticast" to pump his product—professional women's hockey bolstered by Olympic heroes who define the sport. The business plan he described had a major flaw, however. There were no robust revenue streams. Unlike minor league baseball, women's pro hockey has no reliable attendance base, and its arenas are all rented. Broadcast revenues are negligible, and despite catchy merchandise, it's hard to project sustainability without additional major sponsors.

Having a professional hockey league propped up by wealthy industrialists sounds very much like Russia's Kontinental Hockey League (KHL), which appears to be no coincidence. Since 2000, Boynton, who is fluent in Russian, made his fortune in Moscow with Yandex, Russia's largest internet company. In the early 2020s, Boynton was Chairman of the Board of Yandex, a company in the crosshairs of EU sanctions. He had a chummy relationship with President Vladimir Putin, the dictator whom Boynton comically defended as a talented hockey player. Cronyism between Putin and professional hockey owners is straight out of the KHL/oligarch playbook, and may prove to be fool's gold for female professionals in North America, regardless of how close Boynton feels to several former national team members, fellow Harvard alums Angela Ruggiero and Julie Chu in particular.

Following the 2022 Games, it was up to a new generation of stars to help fill seats and inspire consistent viewership, to prove to skeptics like Baker and Fasel that a women's professional hockey league is a solid investment. Counting on the NHL to rescue women's hockey by aligning with the PHF–something Boynton alluded to in the "Sporticast" podcast–was unlikely at least until the league becomes profitable. Colleen Coyne, defenseman on the 1998 gold medalists and current president of PHF champion Boston Pride, has firsthand experience trying to integrate with the NHL.

"What kind of support are we getting from the NHL? None," said Coyne. "We'll get a little help from the Bruins if we want to promote something. It's like looking for investors on "Shark Tank." If you don't have a record of growing, of being successful, it's going to be impossible. My thing is, let's get this to a point where we're not knocking on the NHL's doors, they're knocking on ours. As an optimist, I'm willing to just wait for the right time. In the end, we may not need them."

The solution for a solvent women's professional league is the timeless but challenging entertainment formula: TV viewers and fans in the seats. That is no easy feat in today's crowded sports marketplace.

In addition to Coyne, several other Team USA alums are making their mark in professional hockey, like Duggan, who captained the 2018 gold-medal team. After retiring, she got married and was then hired by the New Jersey Devils as manager of player development. "People are starting to recognize women as elite athletes and as elite contributors to our sport – and that is something that started with that '98 team," Duggan said. "Women bring different backgrounds and perspectives, and organizations in hockey are starting to move the needle a little bit when it comes to being more diverse. I'd love for it to get to the point one day when we don't have to call it women's hockey or men's hockey.

"It's exciting to see and be a part of leading the charge and expanding gender in hockey operations, but I also look forward to the day when we don't even have to discuss gender. For now, it's very important that hockey is diversifying in small ways. I just look forward to a day when there are a lot more women in roles like mine."

Meanwhile, the 1998 old guard continues to shatter glass ceilings and carry women's hockey to new heights in its own way: Granato is on the fast track of NHL management; A.J. Mleczko approaches the pinnacle of network sports broadcasting;[16] and Angela Ruggiero spent eight years as a member of the IOC's athletes' commission. In one of her final acts as a member of the IOC, Ruggiero placed Olympic gold medals around the necks of the victorious Americans in 2018. Having won the inaugural gold in 1998, she has experienced the residue of the late Art Berglund's mantra: *Gold medals change lives.*

"That gold medal really put us on a platform," said Ruggerio. "It showed the whole international community that women's hockey was out there, and that it was impressive. And winning helped put us on the map, a landmark occasion for the sport. It changed the game, it changed the sport, it opened many doors – but they haven't fully opened yet."

At the grass-roots level, however, the nation's response to Team USA's 1998 upset over Canada has been prolific. "It was an inflection point for us," said Coyne. "That performance in Nagano brought a tremendous amount of parents coming out of the woodwork who had never really considered their daughters playing hockey. Until then, it was always someone else's little girl playing hockey with the boys.

"But seeing us all together on that Olympic stage, I think it opened a lot of minds that may have been similar to my mom's, when she would say, 'I'm not sure this game is so great for my daughter.' I think it might have calmed some people's nerves and gave the idea of girls playing hockey some validity."

That was certainly true in the nation's hockey hotbeds of Massachusetts,

---

16 Since retiring as a player Mleczko has become a fixture on NBC's Olympic coverage of women's hockey. She is also a mainstay on the iPhone group chats held by the 1998 gold medalists. Sometimes those roles merge. Such was the case in PyeongChang in 2018 when the group chat was going full-force during the women's gold-medal match. A.J. managed to contribute texts regularly during the intermissions, which thoroughly impressed her teammates. They decided to exploit the opportunity. "We were prodding her," said Laurie Baker, who asked A.J. to use one of coach Ben Smith's favorite words on the air. Early in the third period, Mleczko delivered, using the designated word "flabbergasted," which left all her mates in stitches.

Minnesota and Wisconsin, where participation numbers among girls exploded. "I love it, just absolutely love it," said Wisconsin native Karyn Bye, who as a youngster had to modify her name to K.L. on travel-team rosters to camouflage her gender. "I love being able to see all these girls going to the rink and playing on the U-8, U-10 and U-12 teams, and the different high school girls' teams.

"And look at all the colleges! Back when I went to college, the University of Wisconsin and Minnesota were just club teams. And now look; they fight to see who's going to win the NCAA championship almost every year. There are just so many opportunities for girls and women to continue to play. And to think back and know I played a role in that. Not just me, but our whole '98 team. I mean, I remember talking to people after the Olympics and they would say, 'I didn't even know women's ice hockey existed until the Olympics.' So to be part of that is pretty special."

"Special" is a go-to cliché in hockey, used in place of dozens of superlatives. But when trying to characterize the ambition, determination and landmark accomplishments of the 1998 gold-medal women, special – bordering on miraculous – might be the perfect description.

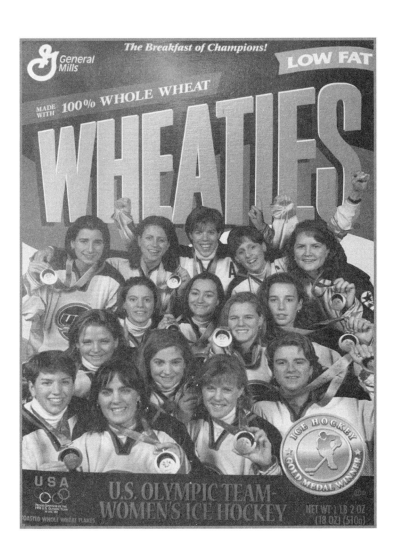

Acknowledgements

All those to whom we owe a tremendous debt of gratitude in the writing of this book would fill to overflowing the Big Hat Arena in Nagano, Japan.

And the first among those we thank are the 20 women sitting on the bench for the home team, the ones who allowed our daughters to dream real dreams when they skated off with Olympic gold at those 1998 Winter Games. But we owe a special thanks to several of those women who were so generous with their time, and their patience, during extended interviews, some involving numerous phone calls, Zoom and FaceTime meetings. We are forever indebted to Cammi Granato, the gracious captain who trusted us enough with this story to lend her endorsement and spread the word among her teammates. Many answered our call, including Karyn Bye, Lisa Brown-Miller, Colleen Coyne, Sara DeCosta, Jenny Potter, Shelley Looney, A.J. Mleczko, Angela Ruggiero, Sarah Tueting and Sandra Whyte. Several were kind enough to dig into their personal archives and share some priceless photos, including Bye, Tueting and Coyne.

The coaches from that inaugural Olympic showdown between Team USA and Canada, Ben Smith and Shannon Miller, respectively, were especially generous with their time in several interviews over many hours. Team USA assistant coach Tom Mutch and three other team staffers, psychologist Peter Haberl, equipment manager Bob Webster, and strength trainer Mike Boyle offered critical detail to this story. Mutch earned the lion's share of Hart Trophy (MVP) points for his willingness to break through all the inevitable logistical logjams we encountered during our writing and research. Any time one of the women needed a nudge, Webbie cashed in a favor and we were good to go.

This book may never have materialized were it not for a chance encounter with John Vanbiesbrouck at the annual Prospects Tournament in Traverse City, Michigan, sponsored by the Detroit Red Wings. We were hawking earlier projects when Vanbiesbrouck stopped by to suggest an idea for our next book with a single word: Nagano. A member of Team USA's men's team in Japan, the first to allow NHL players to compete, Vanbiesbrouck was at the Traverse City event in his role as executive vice president of USA Hockey. He's also a founding member of the women's hockey fan club since witnessing that improbable 1998 gold-medal victory over Team Canada in person. This would be a worthy project, he suggested, not only for the remarkable story of that team and how it managed to upset the dominant Canadians, but also for the way many of these women – on both sides of this incomparable rivalry – continue to shatter glass ceilings in a variety of professions and endeavors.

Thank you to Lee Johnson, the Hobey Baker of women's hockey, and her Massport Jets colleagues Bobby Travaglino and Joyce Inserra for sharing their story, and photos, of the women on whose shoulders those '98 gold medalists stand. We are similarly grateful for other pioneers of the sport, players like Cindy Curley, Erin Whitten, Kelly Dyer, coaches Laura Halldorson and Bob Ewell, as well as John Emmons Sr. and John Emmons Jr., who spent significant portions of their careers promoting women's hockey while developing opportunities for girls to enjoy the game. And we thank many of those who came later, inspired by that '98 team, among them Kendall Coyne Schofield, Brianna Decker and Hilary Knight, for her courage to take pen to paper and write the foreword to this book.

Depthless gratitude goes to the three couples, married with children, produced by this rivalry because, in the end, love conquers all, eh? Thank you for taking some time to speak with us and share your remarkable stories, Jayna Hefford and Kathleen Kauth, Gillian Apps and Meghan Duggan, and Caroline Ouellette and Julie Chu. You gave us far more than we deserved to expect when we set out on this project. You give us hope.

Thanks, too, to Dave Ogrean, Katie Million and Dave Fischer of USA Hockey, and to Dominick Saillant and Jason LaRose of Hockey Canada for providing photos and important game details. To Amy MacKay for her brilliant editing, copy editing and proofreading. To designer Tara Carlin, for her work on the cover of the book. And to John Starr and his staff at the Kalkaska Kaliseum, home to one of the most renowned women's programs in the Midwest – and the perfect meet-up spot halfway between our homes in Traverse City and Houghton Lake. A special thanks to Charles Blundon, who donated a spare laptop to help with secondary printing chores.

To our wives, Amy and Jo Ann, for everything and more; it will be nice to spend some time together again. And finally, to Anne and Doug Stanton, founders of the distinguished National Writers Series for their match made on stage at the Traverse City Opera House – putting a couple of hockey guys together to talk about another book. Three years later, this: A Miracle of Their Own.

A miracle indeed.

Index